Findings of Research

in Miscue Analysis:

Classroom Implications

P. David Allen
1931-1976

This book is dedicated
to the memory of Dave Allen,
who believed
in children and songs,
laughter and God.

Dorothy J. Watson, coeditor
and the miscue research group

Findings of Research in Miscue Analysis:

Classroom Implications

Edited by P. David Allen
University of Missouri-Kansas City
and Dorothy J. Watson
University of Houston-Victoria Campus

 Clearinghouse on Reading and Communication Skills
National Institute of Education

 National Council of Teachers of English

Credits

NCTE EDITORIAL BOARD: Charles R. Cooper, Evelyn M. Copeland, Bernice E. Cullinan, Donald C. Stewart, Frank Zidonis, Robert F. Hogan, *ex officio*, Paul O'Dea, *ex officio*
Staff Editor: Diane Allen. Book Design: Rob Carter

ISBN: 0-8141-1733-3
NCTE Stock Number: 17333

Published October 1976
ERIC Clearinghouse on Reading and Communication Skills
National Council of Teachers of English
1111 Kenyon Road, Urbana, Illinois 61801
Printed in the United States of America

The material in this publication was prepared pursuant to a contract with the National Institute of Education, U.S. Department of Health, Education, and Welfare. Contractors undertaking such projects under government sponsorship are encouraged to express freely their judgment in professional and technical matters. Prior to publication, the manuscript was submitted to the National Council of Teachers of English for critical review and determination of professional competence. This publication has met such standards. Points of view or opinions, however, do not necessarily represent the official views or opinions of either the National Council of Teachers of English or the National Institute of Education.

Library of Congress Cataloging in Publication Data
Main entry under title:

Findings of research in miscue analysis.

    Includes bibliographies.
    1. Miscue analysis—Addresses, essays, lectures.
I. Allen, Paul David, 1931-1976. II. Watson, Dorothy Jo, 1930-   III. Eric Clearinghouse on Reading and Communication Skills. IV. National Institute of Education. V. National Council of Teachers of English.
LB1050.33.F56   370.15'2   76-45092
ISBN 0-8141-1733-3

Contents

Foreword

The National Institute of Education (NIE), recognizing the gap between educational research and classroom teaching, has charged ERIC (Educational Resources Information Center) to go beyond its initial function of gathering, evaluating, indexing, and disseminating information to a significant new service: information transformation and synthesis.

The ERIC system has already made available—through the ERIC Document Reproduction Service—much informative data, including all federally funded research reports since 1956. However, if the findings of specific educational research are to be intelligible to teachers and applicable to teaching, considerable bodies of data must be re-evaluated, focused, translated, and molded into an essentially different context. Rather than resting at the point of making research reports readily accessible, NIE has now directed the separate ERIC Clearinghouses to commission from recognized authorities information analysis papers in specific areas.

Each of these documents focuses on a concrete educational need. The paper attempts a comprehensive treatment and qualitative assessment of the published and unpublished material trends, teaching materials, the judgments of recognized experts in the field, reports and findings from various national committees and commissions. The author tries to answer the question, "Where are we?"; sometimes finds order in apparently disparate approaches; often points in new directions. The knowledge contained in an information analysis paper is a necessary foundation for reviewing existing curricula, planning new beginnings, and aiding the teacher in *now* situations.

Findings of Research in Miscue Analysis: Classroom Implications offers new and influential information for classroom teachers and those interested in further research into the complex mental processes involved in reading.

Bernard O'Donnell, Director, ERIC/RCS

Symbols, Abbreviations, and Other Marks Used in Miscue Research

ER	Expected response
OR	Observed response
brothers bothers	Longhand superscriptions denote substitution miscues—oral observed responses that differ from expected responses to printed text.
∧	Insertion miscue (word not in printed text, added by oral reader). Example: Mr. Barnaby was a very *business* ∧ busy man.
(word)	Circled word or words; circled period or other punctuation indicates omission miscue—word in printed text, omitted in oral reading.
st -	In substitution miscues, partial word plus hyphen stands for partial word substituted in oral reading for text word.
Billy cried	Reversal miscue of words in text by oral reader
<u>Then he</u>	In passages recording miscues, underlines denote regressions—portions the reader repeats in oral reading. (Regression codings follow.)
©⌐	Miscue corrected through regression. Example: © *the* Then he . . .
ⓤⓒ⌐	Miscue with unsuccessful attempt at correction through regression. Example: ⓤⓒ *all* *Ted* Tell me what you see . . .
Ⓐ⌐	Reader anticipates difficulty with a subsequent word. Example: Ⓐ I see the toy *airplane* for me.
Ⓐⓒ⌐	Reader abandons correct form. Reader replaces an initially correct response with an incorrect one.

(RS) ⌐_____ Running start regression. Reader regresses not to change the part repeated but to attack material coming up next in

the text. Example: When his father saw⌐the fawn, he said, "What a beauty!"

ⓓwith Circled letter *d* preceding a miscue superscription denotes a variation in sound, vocabulary, or grammar resulting from a dialect difference between the author and the reader.

∮ Nonword miscue. The reader either produces a nonword orally in place of a text word or supplies a phonemic dialect variation.

Examples: I sat in a large $larther leather chair.

What his mother $cawed called him depended on what he did last.

+ Oral reader sounds out the word in segments. Example: I guess they do have a sooth+thing soothing sound.

Stories used by the miscue research group in their studies of children's oral reading included the following: "Poison," by Roald Dahl, which appears in *Adventures in English Literature, Grade 12,* edited by Mary R. Bowman et al. (New York: Harcourt Brace Jovanovich, Inc., 1968); "Sheep Dog," by James C. Stovall, which appears in *Widening Views, Book VIII,* by William D. Sheldon and Robert A. McCracken (Boston: Allyn & Bacon, Inc., 1966); and "Generation Gap," by Roger Rappaport, which appeared in *Look* magazine January 13, 1970.

This volume has been made possible through the cooperation of the Center for Expansion of Language and Thinking (CELT) and its members who provided technical, editorial, and financial assistance.

The Center for Expansion of Language and Thinking, a nonprofit educational collective based in Tucson, Arizona, exists primarily to further research and innovation in education by supporting research in language and thinking. CELT members are educators interested in improving the quality of teaching and learning. This volume is dedicated to these fine professionals.

The Editors

Introduction

The Miscue Research Studies

P. David Allen
As chairperson of the Division of Elementary Education at the University of Missouri-Kansas City, P. David Allen taught undergraduate and graduate courses in reading and language arts.

In the period 1965 through 1974, researchers at Wayne State University made intensive studies of children's miscues in oral reading. Their research led to fresh insights into the complex mental process that constitutes reading. This volume brings together for the first time the concepts and assumptions underlying that research, the basic research design, the complex nature and function of the Goodman Taxonomy of Oral Reading Miscues, the findings of the research, and finally its implications for reading instruction.

This research summary differs from other such summaries in the field of reading. Individual studies are not presented in depth, nor is the volume laden with large quantities of figures and tables. The purpose of this summary is to clarify for the reader what oral reading miscue research is about.

Each of the contributors was involved directly with the research. Ten doctoral dissertations are represented here as well as four federally funded projects. Other contributors were involved in areas where insights from the research, as well as from miscue analysis, have been applied to other projects.

Fourteen doctoral studies resulted from oral reading miscue analysis at Wayne State alone. Researchers from all over the United States and Canada are now using the Goodman Taxonomy in various ways, and a direct application of the research can be found in the Reading Miscue Inventory developed by Yetta Goodman and Carol Burke (1972. See reference list following this article). Widespread use of the Oral Miscue Concept suggests that there is a general understanding and acceptance of oral reading miscue analysis and its subsequent implications for further reading research and reading instruction. This is not necessarily the case. Comments this writer has heard, as well as references in the literature, indicate that many

3

people in the field of reading are only vaguely aware of what this research is about. Many people think this research is related to a false concept, the "linguistic reading approach," which was prevalent in the sixties. Others assume that it is concerned with dialect study. Since these and other misconceptions exist, it is advantageous at this point to look back to the days when oral reading miscue analysis began to take on form and substance.

The late 1950s and early 1960s were trying times for reading people. Criticism was rampant from all sides. Sputnik set off reper-cussions that affected the total educational system. Mathematics and science underwent radical curricular changes, and reading instruction did not escape unscathed. Rudolph Flesch's book, *Why Johnny Can't Read,* also contributed to the controversy. Perhaps the prime factor in this ferment was concern over the ever-increasing number of urban children who were not learning to read. During this period, terms such as *culturally disadvantaged* and *culturally deprived* appeared in the literature as well as theories which advanced the notion of language deprivation (Deutsch, 1963). Large sums of federal monies were spent on enrichment and remedial programs. In 1965, the National Council of Teachers of English appointed a task force with the charge to "gather information about the hundreds of independent and uncoordinated programs in language and reading for the disadvantaged that had sprung up in every part of the country" (R. Corbin and M. Crosby, 1965, p.v.). Apparent to members of the task force as they traveled around the country were the almost frantic efforts of educators looking for new and dynamic solutions to their problems. Some educators turned for help to other disciplines, including linguistics.

Exactly how linguists became involved with reading educators is probably a moot point. One effect of Flesch's book was that it inadvertently focused attention on the work of Leonard Bloomfield. Flesch mistakely referred to Bloomfield's method as a phonic approach (Flesch, pp. 100-08). Bloomfield's materials used a phoneme-grapheme correspondence approach. The materials ultimately appeared in a book entitled *Let's Read, A Linguistic Approach,* edited by Clarence Barnhart (Bloomfield and Barnhart, 1962). In 1963 Barnhart edited and published an expanded version of the original materials in a primer series called the *Let's Read Series* (Bloomfield and Barnhart, 1963). Other linguistic series employing similar phoneme-grapheme correspondence approaches appeared in rapid succession. The "linguistic approach" was born.

This was not the only area in which linguists were involved. It was no accident that they were represented on the abovementioned NCTE task force. Many educators were concerned about the possibility that dialect differences might profoundly affect instruction in reading and the language arts. Consequently, some linguists including William Labov, Raven McDavid, and Roger Shuy became involved in meetings and conferences several years prior to 1965. For example, an important conference occurred in Bloomington, Indiana in 1964. The proceedings of this conference were edited by Shuy (1965) and illustrate the influence that linguists interested in dialect differences, as well as other aspects of the nature of language, had on educators during that period.

The range of topics discussed at the conference indicates that linguistic involvement was not limited to the issues of linguistic readers and language diversity. During this period there was ferment about the nature of English grammar. The concept of descriptive or structural grammar certainly was not revolutionary at that time, considering the earlier important works of Sapir (1921) and Bloomfield (1933) as well as Fries' definitive *The Structure of English* (1952). The impact of structural linguistics on English instruction began to be felt. The influence of descriptive or structural linguistics on the curriculum is illustrated by the writings of Paul Roberts. In 1954 he published a college text, *Understanding Grammar*, which used a prescriptive or traditional approach to the teaching of English grammar. In 1956 his *Patterns of English* appeared for high school use. This text was based on a structural grammar approach, as was his programmed text, *Understanding English*, which was designed for college use. Later publications indicate a further change in Roberts' thinking.

The descriptive linguists were challenged. In 1957 a small book by Noam Chomsky entitled *Syntactic Structures* was published. *Syntactic Structures* introduced a new theory of grammar which came to be known as "transformational-generative" or simply "transformational grammar." This development contributed to a lively interchange between Chomsky and the descriptive linguists, not to mention a few traditionalists. A typical interchange was held at the University of Texas in 1958, as part of a series, with working papers presented by J. H. Sledd, Ralph B. Long, Henry Lee Smith, Jr., and Noam Chomsky. The proceedings were published in 1962 (Third Texas Conference).

These developments in the area of grammar profoundly influenced the way in which we viewed language and how to study it. This influence is discussed in an important article by G. A. Miller (1962) in which he raises some important questions concerning the study of language and psychology's role in such a study. These questions were raised just a few years after the appearance of B. F. Skinner's *Verbal Behavior* (1957) and Chomsky's review of Skinner's work (1959). Interest in the work of Vygotsky (1962), Piaget (1926, 1954), J. McV. Hunt (1961) was renewed, as well as in modern Soviet research, as represented by Luria and Yudovich (1959). All of this led to a clearer line of demarcation between two distinct views of psychology— behaviorist as opposed to cognitive. Developments added new dimensions to that growing area of interest, psycholinguistics, which had, prior to this time, a limited focus on phonological matters (Saporta, 1961).

A parallel, related development took place in the areas of language acquisition and language development. An examination of writing and research, 1955-65, reveals the significance of this period in terms of findings about language acquisition. We must begin with Jakobson and Halle's *Fundamentals of Language* (1956), Roger Brown's early contributions (1957, 1958), and proceed through the long list of researchers including Berko (1958), Ervin (1961), Bever (1961), Weir (1962), Mehler (1963), Braine (1963), Menyuk (1963), Slobin (1963), Brown and Bellugi (1964) and Cazden (1965), concluding with summaries of Bellugi and Brown in their monograph, *The Acquisition of Syntax* (1964) and Smith and Miller's *The Genesis of Language* (1966). The second decade, 1965-75, was equally as productive in the field.

Important advances were also made in the study of the language development of school-age children. Strickland (1962), Loban (1963), Ruddell (1965) and Hunt (1965) made significant contributions to this area, and their research had important implications for further research as well as for the development of better reading materials for elementary school children.

Finally, interesting research was conducted in the area of oral reading. The works of Kolers (1969, 1970), Weber (1967, 1968), and Clay (1967) had important implications for the study of the reading process.

Imagine the stimulating environment of the early sixties for those involved in the study of language and reading. Consider the limited scope of linguistics concerned only with the "linguistically labeled" materials or dialect study. Fortunately a broader viewpoint prevailed and brought scholars of diverse interests and concerns together on numerous occasions. Leaf through the various proceedings of the Project Literacy Conferences held at Cornell in 1964-65 to find this richness of diversity. This sharing on the part of people representing the various disciplines profoundly affected research in reading. The oral reading miscue research is one outgrowth of this interchange.

The Wayne State Oral Reading Miscue Studies are descriptive studies which attempt to analyze the observed oral reading responses of readers within a psycholinguistic framework. The instrument used to provide the analysis is The Goodman Taxonomy of Reading Miscues, which evolved concurrently with the studies. It should be pointed out that each study and each contributor added to the Taxonomy, and as it now stands it represents the combined efforts of the research team.

The studies discussed here were conducted in the period between 1965 and 1974. Common to all studies are the following features:
1.   The miscues of children reading orally from an unfamiliar text were analyzed. A miscue is defined as the deviation between the oral response of the reader and the expected response of the text. One basic assumption of the studies is that every response which the reader makes is cued in some way by the reading situation and these responses will vary qualitatively.
2.   A limited number of subjects were studied by each researcher. These are depth studies, analyzing hundreds of miscues. The fifteen subjects of the writer's study made 1,521 miscues. In turn, this yielded over 42,000 units of raw data for computer analysis. Page's three subjects generated 32,000 units of data. Approximately fifteen hours were required for each subject by the researchers to complete the procedure of taxonomic analysis.
3.   While each study may have a particular point of interest, all studies contain the basic psycholinguistic descriptions of the miscues generated in the studies.

The organization of this volume is as follows: Carolyn Burke completes this Introduction with a discussion of the theoretical base for the research. The second section discusses in detail the major categories of the Taxonomy. The third deals with what was learned from the research concerning the reading process, as well as implications for instruction, materials, and special areas concerned with reading. The appendices contain the latest Goodman Taxonomy of Reading Miscues, a brief description of the oral reading miscue studies discussed throughout the volume, and finally a bibliography of related writings. All of the examples used throughout the text are taken from the research.

One final point should be made with regard to this book. It was necessary for the editors to decide whether to strive for evenness of style among the many contributors or to let each writer's style and personality remain intact. We chose the latter alternative for two reasons. First of all, the contributors are above all colleagues and friends—unique individuals representing a variety of backgrounds, experiences, and points of view. Second, an approach recognizing individuality is entirely consistent with our view of language, thought, and education in general.

References

Bellugi, U., & Brown, R. (Eds.) The acquisition of language. *Monograph for the Society for Research in Child Development,* 1964, **29** (1).

Berko, J. The child's learning of English morphology. *Word,* 1958, **14**, 150-177.

Bever, T. G. Pre-linguistic behavior. Unpublished honors thesis, Department of Linguistics, Harvard University, 1961.

Bloomfield, L. *Language.* New York: Henry Holt, 1933.

Bloomfield, L., & Barnhart, C. *Let's read: A linguistic approach.* Detroit: Wayne State University Press, 1962.

Bloomfield, L., & Barnhart, C. *Let's read series.* Bronxville, N.Y.: C.L. Barnhart, 1963.

Braine, M.D.S. The ontogeny of English phrase structure: The first phase. *Language,* 1963, **39**, 1-13.

Brown, R. Linguistic determinism and the part of speech. *Journal of Abnormal Social Psychology,* 1957, **55**, 1-5.

Brown, R. *Words and things.* Glencoe, Ill.: Free Press, 1958.

Brown, R., & Bellugi, U. Three processes in the child's acquisition of syntax. *Harvard Educational Review,* 1964, **34**, 133-151.

Cazden, C. Environmental assistance to the child's acquisition of grammar. Unpublished doctoral dissertation, Harvard University, 1965.

Chomsky, N. *Syntactic structures.* The Hague: Mouton, 1957.

Chomsky, N. Review of "Verbal behavior" by B.F. Skinner. *Language,* 1959, **35**, 26-58.

Clay, M. The reading behavior of five-year-old children: A research project. *New Zealand Journal of Educational Studies,* 1967, **2** (1).

Corbin, R., & Crosby, M. (Eds.) *Language programs for the disadvantaged.* Urbana, Ill.: National Council of Teachers of English, 1965.

Deutsch, M. The disadvantaged child and the learning process. In A.H. Passow (Ed.), *Education in depressed areas.* New York: Bureau of Publications,

Teachers College, Columbia University, 1963.

Ervin, S. Changes with age in the verbal determinants of word-association. *American Journal of Psychology*, 1961, **74**, 361-372.

Flesch, R. *Why Johnny can't read*. New York: Harper & Row, 1955.

Fries, C. *The structure of English*. New York: Harcourt, Brace & World, 1952.

Goodman, Y. and Burke, C. *Reading miscue inventory: Procedure for diagnosis and evaluation*. New York: Macmillan, 1972.

Hunt, J. *Intelligence and experience*. New York: Ronald Press, 1961.

Hunt, K. W. *Grammatical structures written at three grade levels*, NCTE Research Report No. 3. Champaign, Ill.: NCTE, 1965.

Jakobson, R., & Halle, M. *Fundamentals of language*. The Hague: Mouton, 1956.

Kolers, P. Reading is only incidentally visual. In K.S. Goodman, & J.T. Fleming (Eds.) *Psycholinguistics and the teaching of reading*. Newark, Del.: International Reading Association, 1969.

Kolers, P. Three stages of reading. In H. Levin, & J. Williams (Eds.) *Basic studies on reading*. New York: Basic Books, 1970.

Levin, H. & Williams, J. (Eds.) *Basic studies on reading*. New York: Basic Books, 1970.

Loban, W. *The language of elementary school children: A study of the use and control of language and the relations among speaking, reading, writing, and listening*, NCTE Research Report No. 1. Urbana, Ill.: NCTE, 1963.

Luria, A.R., & Yudovich, Ia. *Speech and the development of mental processes in the child*. London: Staples Press, 1959.

Mehler, J. Some effects of grammatical transformations on the recall of English sentences. *Journal of Verbal Learning and Verbal Behavior*, 1963, **2**, 346-351.

Menyuk, P. A preliminary evaluation of grammatical capacity in children. *Journal of Verbal Learning and Verbal Behavior*, 1963, **2**, 429-439.

Miller, A.A. Some psychological studies of grammar. *American Journal of Psychology*, 1962, **17**, 748-762.

Piaget, J. *The language and thought of the child*. New York: Harcourt, Brace, 1926.

Piaget, J. *The construction of reality in the child*. New York: Basic Books, 1954.

Roberts, P. *Understanding grammar*. New York: Harper & Row, 1954.

Roberts, P. *Patterns of English*. New York: Harcourt, Brace & World, 1956.

Roberts, P. *Understanding English*. New York: Harper & Row, 1958.

Ruddell, R.B. The effect of the similarity of oral and written patterns of language structure on reading comprehension. *Elementary English*, 1965, **55**, 403-410.

Sapir, E. *Language: An introduction to the study of speech*. New York: Harcourt, Brace & World, 1921.

Saporta, S. (Ed.) *Psycholinguistics: A book of readings*. New York: Holt, Rinehart & Winston, 1961.

Shuy, R.W. (Ed.) *Social dialects and language learning.* Proceedings of the Bloomington, Indiana conference, 1964. Urbana, Ill.: NCTE, 1965.

Skinner, B.F. *Verbal behavior.* New York: Appleton-Century-Crofts, 1957.

Slobin, D.I. Grammatical transformations in childhood and adulthood. Unpublished doctoral dissertation, Harvard University, 1963.

Smith, F., & Miller, G.A. (Eds.) *The genesis of language.* Cambridge, Mass.: MIT Press, 1966.

Strickland, R.G. The language of elementary school children: Its relationship to the language of reading textbooks and the quality of reading of selected children. *Bulletin of the School of Education,* Indiana University, July 1962, **38**.

Third Texas conference on problems of linguistic analysis in English. Austin: University of Texas, 1962.

Vygotsky, L.S. *Thought and language.* Cambridge, Mass.: MIT Press, 1962.

Weber, R. A linguistic analysis of first-grade reading errors. Unpublished research report, Cornell University, 1967.

Weber, R. The study of oral reading errors: A survey of the literature. *Reading Research Quarterly,* Fall 1968, **4** (1).

Weir, R. *Language in the crib.* The Hague: Mouton, 1962.

Reading Miscue Research: A Theoretical Position

Carolyn L. Burke

An associate professor of education at Indiana University, Carolyn L. Burke is chairperson of the Graduate Reading Program on the Bloomington campus and coauthor of *Reading Miscue Inventory— Procedure for Diagnosis and Evaluation.*

This chapter is intended to serve a purpose like that of the rough carpenter, who sets up the structure of a house and then lets others do the finishing work. Structure is the initial critical issue that must be examined when one is dealing with theoretically based studies such as reading miscue research.

Theoretically grounded research starts with the presuppositions of the investigator. All researchers have initial perspectives on the problems they study. The notion of the neutral, unprejudiced, and calculating scientist who withholds judgment is truly a sterile and nonproductive view.

Prejudgments are initial attempts to organize surface-level chaos. The investigator sorts any available information, however minimal or chaotic, into alternate logical patterns. The preferred pattern becomes the investigator's research design. The intent of the research is to test the usefulness of that preferred pattern. Each piece of data collected either supports the initial structure or causes the researcher to re-model. Reading miscue research, like all theoretically based studies, has not emerged without structure; it has not grown like Topsy.

Research Imperatives and Reading

School children have been making reading errors, and school people have been concerned with eradicating these errors for as long as any of us can remember. It is probably safe to say that, in our society, reading facility is the most significant single accomplishment on which other accomplishments are based.

There is a strong cultural imperative relating to the necessity of becoming a reader. Because of its social significance, reading has never suffered from a lack of concern on the part of educators, or from a lack of study on the part of researchers. In fact, there is a very real danger that when we begin to make renewed research efforts, we will retrace the steps of others, running around the same track again and again.

If we are going to make new inroads into investigating reading and into developing instructional procedures, we must examine what appears to be a very familiar situation from what we hope will be a new perspective.

The very familiarity of the situation sometimes misleads or stops researchers before they do needed in-depth probing. Reading miscue research has gained its perspective by focusing on the psycho-linguistic nature of the reading process. And that is what this collection of studies is about.

Language, Thought and the Miscue Research

Miscue researchers view reading as a very special manifestation of the language process. That is, reading is an instance of language, and a model of reading can be developed which will handle every piece of reading behavior and be compatible with a more global model of the language process.

We also believe that thought and language comprise two distinct but definitely interrelated processes and that each of these processes can be modeled or represented by a structural design. Any specific piece of overt behavior must either be fitted into these designs or become the cause for adjustments to the models. One's perspective on this inter-relationship influences the kinds of questions one asks about reading. The following three questions can act to document this influence.

Question 1: *If it is indicated that initial speech efforts develop from indivisible wholes toward specialized and interchangeable structures, can a counterpart be found in the initial reading process?* We are familiar with the talk of young children and with their use of what appears to be isolated words representing whole thoughts and whole sentences. No mother has trouble when her child says, "water." If she finds him standing at the sink, she knows that her youngster means "Get me a drink of water," while she assumes a very different meaning if the comment is made while approaching a decorative fountain in a garden. Children's speech starts with this telescoping of whole thoughts; it is later, as they gain facility with oral language, that they are able to isolate and manipulate the linguistic features that are involved and to say, "I want a drink of water," or "Look at the spray of water." If this is true in speech, and if we view reading as an expression of the language process, we should be able to find some parallel in the initial reading process.

Question 2: *If an individual can process from three to seven discrete bits of data within a specified number of seconds, what limits are placed on the reader by the very nature of the thought process?* Here we must look into the kind of research that deals with the psychology of learning and developmental psychology. Much has been done recently to determine what controls the speed and quantity of material individuals can handle. Whatever these limitations are, they have to be imposed on the reading process also. Because reading is a thought-related process, it conforms to the limitations of thought development and processing.

Question 3: *If the oral language structure of children is in the process of developing, what related developmental changes can we expect in their reading?* If psychologists tell us that school-aged children, particularly those entering primary grades, are still develop-ing in the way they handle and process information, then we must assume that there is a carry-over into the language process. There will be developmental differences in the way these young children can process reading information.

These questions and others have central significance in miscue research. In our attempts to answer them we will draw the connection between theory and behavior and between thought and language.

The Limits of Observable Behavior

Instances of overt behavior, viewed in isolation from surrounding and impinging elements of the environment, have no intrinsic value. Consider a driver whose car hits the vehicle ahead. A few years ago the common result of such an accident would have been the awarding of a traffic violation along with the full responsibility and blame for the occurrence. The decision was based on one piece of visible evidence— one car hit the other. Today the police are interested in the whole context of the accident. Did the driver fail to keep his eyes on the road? Did the steering mechanism malfunction, or the brakes fail? Was his vision obscured? Did a pedestrian or another vehicle swerve into his path? Was he traveling too fast for the road conditions? Did the driver ahead make a sudden stop? This long list of questions is representative of those asked by the police, and it is not uncommon for both drivers to find themselves ticketed for two or more violations which the law feels were contributing factors to the accident. This switch in police policy reflects two changes in attitude: first, responsibility cannot be delegated solely on the basis of an observable act, and second, an individual behavior or decision can seldom be singled out as the cause of an accident. In fact, a growing realization of the complex relationship between any single action and the context in which it occurs is one of the arguments now being used to support no-fault auto insurance.

Both of these positions—the limits of information obtainable from isolated overt behaviors and the interrelationship of factors leading to observable occurrences—have relevance for reading research efforts. Consider a child who reads the word *can* in place of *could*. On the basis of this isolated behavior, it can be noted that the initial letters and initial sounds are the only elements that the two words have in common, and to conclude that the reader arrived at this substitution by making minimal use of phonic word attack skills. Other possible contributing factors become evident when the substitution is examined within the context of the material.

"You ~~could~~ *can* get a sponsor."
Mr. Barnaby was impressed. "Humm," he said, "you have an idea of value." He walked around the office, thinking. "Yes. We *could* have a contest and pick a baby out of all the babies in town."

1) Within the sentence, the two items *can* and *could* perform the same grammatical function. 2) The meaning of the sentence is fully acceptable and has been changed only minimally in relationship to the tentativeness of the act. No matter how you choose to read the sentence, in terms of the paragraph which follows it, you've done very little to alter the meaning of the text. 3) Just two lines further on, the reader successfully read *could* when it occurred in the sentence, *We could have a contest and pick a baby out of all the babies in town.*

Within the same story this reader substituted the nonword *philollosiphical* for the expected response *philosophical.* The quality of this unexpected response is very different from that of the first one discussed: *"Philollosiphical,"* *I shouted.* It can be noted that: (1) there is a high degree of phonemic and graphemic similarity between the nonword and *philosophical*—much higher than between *can* and *could;* (2) the use of a nonword causes a loss of meaning; (3) the retention of the derivational ending indicates a retention of the grammatical function; and (4) when we look at the item in terms of the sentence in which it occurred, we become aware that the structure provided no semantic context cues.

The two substitutions, *can* for *could* and *philollosiphical* for *philosophical,* point up the fact that an individual reader will use varying strategies in approaching text and that this variation can be related to changing text circumstances. As we note and collect varying instances of reader's strategies and categorize them with regard to the circumstances in which they occur, we can not only begin to document the importance of maintaining the relationship between instances of observable behavior and the whole situational context, but we can also begin to map the interdependence of the systems of the reading process. The relationships we find are going to have reference only within that process.

Reading as a Process
A process has to be an active ongoing interdependence of systems. It is not represented by any one of the systems that compose it, and it is something more than a collection of items. A very simplistic comparison can be drawn between the making of a sandwich and a cake. The sandwich is a collection of items: bread, butter, meat. They are brought together so that each item retains its own identity and its own distinctive features. These items are, in fact, recognizable in the sandwich as separate entities. On the other hand, a cake is a compound

of items: flour, salt, butter, eggs, sugar, milk and baking powder. These items are mixed and exposed to heat so that the product acquires properties of taste, texture and volume that aren't directly related to any of the ingredients that go into the cake. All the ingredients are needed for a good cake, and all the systems must be present and functioning if the process is to operate.

Distinctions can be made between systems which aren't functioning fully and systems which are not functioning at all. A running automobile engine represents a second example of a process. The engine combines an electrical, a combustion, and an exhaust system. It can continue to run when one or more of the systems is only partially functioning. There can be a missing cylinder or a dead cell in the battery and the process will continue, but the process stops when any one of the systems breaks down entirely. With a cracked cylinder head or a dead battery the engine will no longer run. We can talk about a process operating as long as all of the relevant systems are in some way functioning. We can no longer talk about process when we isolate a system from it.

Reading stops when any one of its three necessary systems— graphophonemic, syntactic, and semantic—is segregated from the process. For example, naming words from a list is not reading, even though it utilizes one of the reading strategies. Words in a list lend themselves only to direct recognition and recall or to graphophonemic application. There is no environment to give list words either a grammatical function or a meaning. Consider the word *can* in the following list.

    use
    can
    work
    result
    carrots
    stop

Is it a verb marker *(I can work as hard as he can)* or a noun *(buy one can of vegetables)* or a verb *(Can the tomatoes first, they're the ripest)*? Whatever alternative passes through the mind of the reader is based solely upon a context the reader imposes. Neither recognition of a list item or a lack of it has any direct bearing on how that item will be treated in context.

In one study, fourth-grade children were able to read correctly, within the context of a story, two-thirds of the items they had missed on a word list (K. Goodman, 1965). In a second study, primary-aged children read a story in which they encountered *circus* eight times—four times as an adjective (*circus bear*) and four times as a noun (*The circus is...*). They were much more successful in handling *circus* as a noun than they were when it appeared as an adjective (Y. Goodman, 1971).

When used in isolation, the graphophonemic system takes on a different character, a different stress. Items misread on a word list tend to have very high graphic (look alike) and phonemic (sound alike) relationships to the expected response—a much stronger relationship than is found when substitutions occur in the reading of continuous text. The number of nonwords produced in handling the list will also be much greater than that produced in continuous text.

Reading tests frequently establish minimal reading situations which greatly impair the operation of one or more of the language systems. One common procedure is to introduce a sentence or short paragraph with one underlined word in it followed by several items, one of which is supposed to be a synonym for the underlined word.

> It was the largest *vessel* he had ever seen.
>   a bottle   a garment   a hallway

None of the reading systems are tested, only direct recall. The reader either instinctively and instantly recognizes one possible definition or takes an arbitrary guess of the *eenie, meenie, miney, moe* variety. It's perfectly possible for a reader to be able to orally produce the expected sentence to mean, *It was the largest ship he had ever seen,* and then be confronted with the three choices. In such a case readers can actually leave the situation questioning their own knowledge. They might no longer be sure that oceangoing ships are vessels.

Such test items are in syntactic context. No reader would question that the item is a noun. That cue comes both from the structure in the sentence and from the fact that the choices are: *a* bottle, *a* garment, and *a* hallway (each key word being marked by a determiner). But, there is no reading strategy that can be applied in determining the answer to the question. The effective use of semantic strategies will not allow the reader to learn this meaning of *vessel* as an act of reading. It might be just as well, if you want to find out whether the student knows that a vessel can be a bottle, simply to ask the question. The task called for by the test is not a reading task. A good reader can get this item wrong through lack of background knowledge.

When an individual system is isolated from the reading process its functions are either distorted or destroyed. To be measured and examined, the language systems must be kept within the context of the ongoing reading process.

Author-Reader Relationships

Reading involves an interaction between the language process of the reader and the language process of the author. Readers examine a piece of text on the basis of the control they have of language. They have available to them the context and the organization of their own language systems. Authors write their texts on the basis of their control of language and have available to them the content and organization of their language systems. Inevitably there are points at which the systems of the author and the reader don't match. When this mismatch is represented in the author's text, it becomes possible that the reader will be unable to handle the unfamiliar structure. For example, an author might possess knowledge of one or more foreign languages. Think of all the German and French expressions sprinkled into popular novels and movies and how many of these are passed over by readers/ listeners who do not know these languages.

A similar situation arose for a number of the children in the miscue research. They were given a text to read that had the name *Sven* in it. The children had two main responses to this foreign item. One group stressed the graphophonemic system and produced the word *seven*. These readers inserted the necessary vowel sound to separate what was, for them, the impossible phoneme combination represented by *Sv* and produced the nearest-sounding English item. They made this item conform to the letter/sound relationships of English.

A second group of children was much more immediately attuned to the grammatical and semantic constraints in which this word appeared and they were aware that the word had to represent a man's name. They chose to substitute the name *Steve*—a choice which made use of all three of the language systems.

The possibility of a mismatch between author and reader is not built only on the intrusion of foreign language influence. The whole concept of dialect is built around the small but regular variations in the structures used by speakers of the same language. In each of the following examples the meaning of the sentence is retained while the reader alters the structure toward that of his or her language.

headlights
I switched off the headlamps of the car.

minute
Stop. Wait a moment, Timber.

no
I don't have any pennies.

Freddie told how he (had) fix(ed) the clock.

phones   *be*
... the two telephones in(to) which he(d) been talking.

In yet other instances a structurally ambiguous text will cause
readers to produce predictable alternate variations. Read the following
piece of poetry by Dylan Thomas.

> The small, furred friars squeal in the dowse of day
> In the thistle aisles, the vaulting does roister,
> The horned bucks climb quick in the wood at love.

How did you read the word d-o-e-s which occurs on the second line?
As a verb do? As a plural noun doe? When enough readers are sampled,
both alternatives occur. Did you fail to see the possible alternatives for
the word until they were pointed out to you? There is nothing glaring
about such an occurrence, nothing that causes you as reader to focus on
your particular choice. In this situation there is nothing we can do to
resolve which would be the right word. Dylan Thomas was probably
not interested in telling and might not have remembered later—if he
knew at the time he wrote it. We have to live with the mystery.

Because there are points at which the author's and the reader's
language systems do not match, even the most proficient and experienced readers will encounter structures and meanings with which
they are unfamiliar or which they do not anticipate.

Reading and Exactness

Reading, even for the most proficient reader, is not an exact process.
The operations of the thought process, as well as those of the language
process, insure the occurrence of some variation. The speed at which
proficient readers have been timed far outstrips the measured capacity
of the brain and the nervous system to handle discrete bits of information. We have to conclude that reading cannot be an exact processing
of every available graphic bit that is on the page. This simple fact has
led researchers such as Frank Smith (1970) to theorize mathematically

that readers must, of necessity, be able to handle word and phrase level segments of language as single units of information. We're forced to the conclusion that proficient readers sample and predict from the printed page. The cloze procedure illustrates this theory.

Fill in the missing items in the following structures.

You can't teach an old dog new _____.
MacArthur was one old _____ who didn't fade away.
This act could have the gravest _____.

The last item requires more thought than the first two because there are simply more possibilities. The first sentence happens to be a phrase with which we're familiar. In the second sentence we remembered, "Old soldiers never die, they just fade away." Then we processed the information in relationship to the fact that MacArthur was an old soldier, so that we came to the situation with some background of information and we related that information to the structure provided. In the last instance there were several suitable alternatives which fit within the grammatical structure—*consequences, results, effect.* However, regardless of the specific item selected by any individual reader, the chosen words will most likely be synonyms. The cloze procedure operates because reading employs sampling and guessing procedures based upon a person's experiential background and intuitive use of language structures.

Examining the Reading Process

So far, we have attempted to build two major propositions. First, that a process will operate only when all of its systems are functioning; second, that reading as a process will always involve some variations from the printed text. Given these two propositions, we can now consider the relative significance of reading variations.

When things go as planned, it is very difficult to note the functioning of the involved factors. Can we assume that a driver was careful because his trip didn't end in an accident? In fact, the happy ending to the trip might be attributed to light traffic, fair weather, good roads, and other drivers staying out of his way. We can't, on the basis of expectation alone, build a foundation for understanding how a system is operating or what the scope of a process is. When a reader produces exactly what is expected, we have no way of knowing what systems or strategies are being employed. When a reader produces the expected responses, we do not know what words she recognizes by sight or for which ones she applies available reading strategies. All we know is that the reader produced what we expected to hear.

When things don't go as planned, we are provided with a window into the functioning of the reading process. We can ask which language cues were available to be applied in this circumstance, and which cues were actually used by the reader. We assume that the driver applies the same general driving strategies on the accident-free days as on the day of an accident. We assume that the reader applies the same general strategies to text in the instances in which expected responses are produced as in the production of unexpected responses. Unexpected responses to print—*reading miscues*—become the focus of our attention. If we collect and categorize reading miscues, we will be able to outline the reading process and to evaluate the effectiveness of individual readers.

Miscue Research Procedures

In collecting miscues we are under several restrictions. We want miscues to reflect the strategies a reader employs when faced with unfamiliar material. We want the situation to be one in which the reader is reading for meaning and must rely only upon his or her own resources in handling the material.

To this end, the students in reading miscue research studies are given stories which they have never before seen, and are asked for an uninterrupted oral reading. They are told they will receive no help during the reading and that they must handle all unknown words or troublesome structures without aid. The students are also aware, prior to their reading, that they will be asked to retell the story in their own words upon completion of the task.

Reading is a fleeting experience, yet miscues must be preserved in the context of their original environment. To this end, we audio- or videotape each of the reading and retelling sessions and develop a worksheet of the text marked with the reader's miscues.

My Brother Is a Genius

```
                    brothers                it's a
0101          "If it bothers you to think of it as baby sitting," my father said,

              they                                  Ⓐ
0102         "then don't think of it as baby sitting. Think of it as homework. Part

                            e –
0103          of your ⟨education⟩ You just happen to do your studying in the room
```

0104   where your baby brother is sleeping, that's all." He helped my mother

0105   with her coat, and then they were gone.

0201   So education it was! I opened the dictionary and picked out a

0202   word that sounded good. "Philosophical!" I yelled. Might as well

0203   study word meanings first. "Philosophical: showing calmness and

0204   courage in the face of ill fortune." I mean I really yelled it. I guess a

0205   fellow has to work off steam once in a while.

In categorizing the miscues we are under several restraints. We must attempt to determine, for each miscue, all of the possible contributing factors without arbitrarily assigning any one causal relationship. Our measures must reflect the operations and interactions of the three language systems. At the same time we have to develop measures which have internal consistency and the breadth to handle all possible occurrences. We must know that we can deal with all of the variations that occur between the least proficient beginning reader and the most sophisticated adult reader. And finally, we must have an organization that will allow us to manipulate large quantities of data, knowing that individuals during the reading session can produce anywhere from thirty to three hundred miscues.

To this end, the Goodman Taxonomy of Reading Miscues has been developed. (See Appendix A.) The Taxonomy consists of approximately nineteen questions, with each question involving from four to twelve possible responses.

Sets of questions from the Taxonomy attempt to tap the specific operations of an individual system. For example, several questions from the Taxonomy pertain to the syntactic structure of language:

Taxonomy Questions

18
What is the grammatical function of the text word involved in the miscue?
19
What is the grammatical function of the miscue?

12, 13, 14, 15, 16
Which of the various syntactic levels—word, phrase, or clause—
are involved as a result of the miscue?
6
What is the syntactic acceptability of the sentence when it is read
with the miscue in it?
8
How great a syntactic change has the text structure undergone?

Still other sets of questions tap the graphophonemic system (3, 4, 5, 11) and the semantic system (1, 7, 10, 17).

Each miscue is examined in terms of all nineteen of the Taxonomy questions, so that we can make statements about: (1) an individual miscue's relationship to the text, (2) a miscue's relationship to other miscues that are made, (3) the varying influence of the language systems on the miscues, and (4) the degree to which the reading process is disrupted.*

The operation of the reading/writing process can be viewed as three-dimensional—with the graphic material and the processes of the language being intersected by the reader/author. The individual questions of the Taxonomy always represent at least a two-dimensional perspective. One of the participants—reader or author—is set against one of the systems. The third dimension is added when comparisons are made and relationships drawn between the Taxonomy questions.

The analysis is an in-depth probe which attempts to explore and to measure the quality of the variations which can occur during reading. To provide such information, the coding of the individual questions of the Taxonomy is statistically interrelated. For example:

1.   The miscues made by each reader are calculated to determine the number of miscues occurring per hundred words. The miscues per hundred words can then be compared against such figures as the percentages of miscues that the reader corrects or that are syntactically and semantically acceptable. In this way we begin to develop the relationship between the qualitative and quanitative aspects of miscue occurrences.

2.   The same process operates in terms of grammatical functions. Once we've decided the grammatical function of the miscues, we can get

---

*At this writing, the basic Taxonomy has gone through more than ten modifications. Also, for the purposes of any one study, individual categories have been modified, inserted, or deleted.

some notion of the reader's tendency to retain the grammatical function of the text, i.e., to substitute a verb for a verb, a noun for a noun, etc. We can develop that information for the individual reader, and for groups as a whole, and begin to look at one reader's retention of grammatical function, in relation to what the "average" looks like for other readers of the same age and proficiency.

The coding of one reader's miscues will produce a profile of the reading strategies employed. The coding of an age or developmental group will begin to delineate a developmental pattern in relationship to the individual variations that exist within a group. The coding of differing groups will begin to delineate the parameters of the reading process. It is our ability to apply the consistent format of the Taxonomy of Reading Miscues to the miscues of all readers—regardless of age and/or proficiency—which allows for the comparison of such findings. Aside from the findings we are producing as a research team, the Taxonomy itself was one of the first significant products.

References

Goodman, K.S. A linguistic study of cues and miscues in reading. *Elementary English*, 1965, **42**, 639-643.

Goodman, Y.M. *Longitudinal study of children's oral reading behavior.* (USOE Project No. 9-E-062, Grant No. OEG-5-9-325062-0046) Washington, D.C., United States Department of Health, Education, and Welfare, September, 1971.

Smith, F. *Understanding reading.* New York: Holt, Rinehart & Winston, 1970.

The Taxonomy

The emergence and expansion of reading miscue research has been accompanied by the development of the instrument used in categorizing the miscues. The Goodman Taxonomy of Reading Miscues provides the researcher with a means of investigating miscues in light of all parts of the language system—graphophonic, syntactic and semantic. And within each of the three substructures the Taxonomy investigates various dimensions of that individual structure.

The questions in the Taxonomy are designed to describe each miscue in linguistic detail and finally to determine to what degree it affects the reading process.

The Goodman Taxonomy can be used to code and analyze in depth the miscues of the beginning reader as well as the experienced, the inept reader as well as the proficient, and readers from diverse linguistic backgrounds.

The developing nature of the Goodman Taxonomy is significant. It has been altered and adapted in order to fulfill the needs of specific research problems. Subsequent changes and redefinitions by future researchers into the process of reading are expected.

The purpose of this section is to acquaint the reader with each major category of the Taxonomy. Each portion deals not only with specific classifications and coding procedures but also with the background and assumptions underlying each category. In some instances, categories dealing with similar aspects of the research, i.e., semantic acceptability and semantic change, are grouped together for discussion.

It is suggested that the reader refer to the Taxonomy in Appendix A while reading this section, in order to get a more complete understanding of the research instrument used in the oral reading miscue studies.

Correction

Helen A. Martellock
The principal of Field Elementary School, Detroit, Helen A. Martellock
has done research on the oral and written language of middle school
children.

Background and Assumptions
Correction is that category in the Goodman Taxonomy of miscues
which is used to determine what a reader does with a miscue in oral
reading. When readers correct, they are indicating they recognize that
they have made a miscue and that they have the necessary competencies and strategies to correct the miscue.

Correction attempts by a reader indicate that reading is a process
of scanning and guessing. As the reader processes the material, he or
she is required to anticipate what will come next. Often when the guess
does not produce a meaningful utterance, the reader finds a need to
correct. This is also true when the reader's guess produces an utterance
which does not fit syntactically with the material being read.

Correction is a natural part of the reading process and is indicative
of the strengths the reader has. Correction attempts indicate that the
reader has command of the basic structures of his language. They also
indicate that the reader is getting meaning from print. When the reading
attempt fails to produce meaning for the reader, he goes back or
regresses, and corrects for meaning.

The Taxonomy
Correction attempts are coded as follows in the Taxonomy.

0   No correction is attempted.
1   The miscue is corrected.
2   An original correct response is abandoned in favor of an
    incorrect one.
9   An unsuccessful attempt is made at correcting the miscue.

When this information is coded for each miscue, it is then possible
to compare the data with the information gathered from other levels of

analysis in the Taxonomy and draw appropriate conclusions and inferences with regard to a number of variables. Such an analysis permits answers to questions such as the following:

1.   Is correction related to syntactic acceptability? If so, to what degree?

2.   Is correction related to semantic acceptability? If so, to what degree?

3.   Do miscues caused by dialect divergence between the reader and the author result in correction attempts?

4.   What types of miscues more frequently produce correction attempts?

5.   Is correction related to reading material selection?

When correction phenomena are studied in relation to the other categories of the Taxonomy it is possible to gather much information about the strengths of an individual reader.

It is also possible to make inferences about reading instruction for a group, based on analysis of the reading behavior of a defined population.

With this kind of information, it is possible to devise instructional strategies which will strengthen the reading behavior of individuals, to provide insights into general reading instruction and to set up guidelines for the production and selection of reading materials and programs.

Dialect

Louise J. Jensen
An associate professor of English at California State University, Chico, Louise J. Jensen is director of the Learning Resources and Tutorial Center on that campus and teaches undergraduate and graduate courses in linguistics and applied linguistics.

Prologue

When talking with a group of people recently I happened to mention that I had read *The French Lieutenant's Woman*. I pronounced "lieutenant" as /leftenant/. My friends had a laugh at my Canadian dialect and informed me that the pronunciation of *lieutenant* is

/lutenant/. No matter how the word is pronounced we had all read the same book and derived meaning from it. The interesting fact in this case is that John Knowles, the author of *The French Lieutenant's Woman* is British and his pronunciation of *lieutenant* corresponds with mine. I am coming closer to an "accurate" rendition of his text in terms of pronunciation than most American readers are. I am sure you would rather believe, and rightly so, that the pronunciation which is natural to your spoken language is the one that will carry the most meaning for you.

A similar phenomenon occurs with Anthony Burgess' *A Clockwork Orange*. In one place he says *the sun shone brightly*. Again this is a British author. His pronunciation of *shone* has what is sometimes called a short *o* or /ɔ/ in phonemic transcription. You probably read it as *shone* with a long *o* or /o/. How much meaning did you lose by saying shōne instead of shŏne? What if you had said shŏne? You probably would have lost meaning.

Background and Assumptions

Written language does not correspond to anyone's dialect. Spoken language and written language are different in many ways. The closer readers can come to their own spoken language in their reading the more likely they are to derive meaning from what they read.

Dialects differ from one another in at least three systems: the phonological, grammatical and lexical or vocabulary systems.

1.   Phonological. This is the pronunciation system, sometimes called "accent." The examples given above, *shone* and *lieutenant*, are examples of phonological differences.

2.   Grammatical. Grammatical differences include inflectional endings, sentence structure, etc. Some examples are the past tense of *dive*, is it *dived* or *dove*? In some dialects it is quite regular to count one crayon, two crayon, three crayon.

3.   Lexical. This involves our vocabulary choices; Headlights vs. headlamps, pop vs. soda, etc.

In the early stages of the research the three kinds of dialect differences were coded. It soon became apparent, however, that the phonological differences were not important to reading with meaning. In fact, the more natural the pronunciation, the more likely the children would understand what they read. Consequently, phonological differences are no longer coded in the main research. There are still some substudies where pronunciation is looked at in detail, but for reading in general it seems a rather insignificant factor.

Grammatical differences are coded. Even this practice is being questioned.

The Taxonomy

What happens when we code a dialect miscue? Phonological differences are marked but are not coded. With the other miscues we work across the taxonomy categories and ask questions such as, "Is this a grammatical sentence *within the reader's dialect?*" By *grammatical* we are not talking in some prescriptive sense but rather, "Is this a possible structure within the speaker's dialect?" *He ain't got no money*, then, would be grammatical in the dialect of one who could and would say that sentence.

We also ask, "Does this sentence have meaning *within the dialect of the speaker?*" *Our teacher say if you know how to think*, etc. How much is the meaning changed for the reader by the miscue?

Lexical dialect differences occur less frequently in reading and are examined in terms of grammar and meaning. One familiar example from the research: *He swung the car around so the headlamps would not shine in the window.* Most readers read this as *He swung the car around so the headlights would not shine in the window.* Again the substitution does not change meaning; the reader has simply switched to an alternate surface structure.

In examining data such as this in terms of meaning change, it becomes obvious that the dialect "problem" is not the problem we once believed it to be. When the teacher is aware that a translation to the dialect of the reader is an indication of a proficient processing of meaning, he or she will be better able to facilitate the reading of children with varied dialects.

Graphic and Phonemic Proximity

Anne Gilleland Harris
At Southern Illinois University, Edwardsville, Anne Gilleland Harris has taught graduate and undergraduate courses in the teaching of reading. In 1975, she worked with a group of students in SIU's new Teacher Corps Program.

Background and Assumptions

The graphic and phonemic proximity categories measure the degree of similarity between what a reader actually says and the text words. Text and actual responses are compared in terms of word configuration and sound similarity.

It is useful to consider the two categories together for several reasons:

1.   There is a relationship between the important sounds in English and the limited number of symbols used to represent them; however, the relationship is not a simple one-to-one matching process. Rather, graphic and phonemic cue systems represent two sides of the same coin. The phonemes of oral language combine to form units of meaning; these sound symbols are combined, in turn, to convey the thoughts and ideas of a speaker. Likewise, the graphic symbols of written language are combined to convey the ideas of an author. Both graphic and phonemic cues, then, exist at the surface level and fulfill similar purposes in their respective mediums.

2.   Beginning readers come to the reading task as competent language users. One of their tasks is to discover the relationships between the graphic cue system and their own highly developed phonemic system.

3.   Teaching techniques which stress phonics, structural analysis and word attack skills attempt to match graphic cues with sound cues.

At the same time it is equally important to examine graphic and sound proximities separately. This is so for the following reasons:

1.   Obvious relationships between sound symbols and printed symbols are tenuous at best.

2.   Graphic display begins the oral reading process while the oral response represents a tentative sort of conclusion. Between the initial sampling of graphic cues and the tentative conclusion—or oral response —a number of factors can intervene and influence the oral response.

3.   Teachers' manuals do not usually recognize the highly developed and complex phonemic system possessed by readers. In fact, teachers' manuals and other instructional materials encourage teachers to teach children "their sounds." The Goodman Taxonomy separates the phonemic category from the graphic category to discover how the two systems are actually used by readers.

The Taxonomy

The Goodman Taxonomy, then, uses two separate but comparable categories to study the graphic and sound proximities of miscues. The phonemic proximity category and the graphic proximity category are arranged as follows:

Phonemic Proximity	Graphic Proximity

Little or No Proximity

0	no similarity	0	no similarity
1	some common sounds	1	some common letters
2	single key sound in common	2	single key letter in common
3	end portions in common	3	end portions are similar

Moderate Proximity

4	beginning portion in common	4	beginning portions are similar
5	common beginning and middle portions	5	beginning and middle portions are similar
6	common beginning and end portions	6	beginning and end portions are similar

High Proximity

7	beginning, middle and end portions are similar	7	beginning, middle and end portions are similar or, there is a reversal of three or more letters
8	differ by a single vowel or consonant or vowel cluster or, there is a morpho-phonemic difference or, there is an intonational shift	8	single grapheme difference or, a reversal of two letters
9	homophones	9	homographs

Each category includes a scale which runs from a low of zero or no similarity to a high of nine or total matching. Research done by Hanna, Hanna, Hodges and Rudorf contributed to the determination of levels within each category. That is, the categories are research-based and are as comparable at each level as present knowledge permits.

Since the graphic and phonemic scales are separate, comparisons of a miscue's graphic and phonemic proximities to text words are possible. For example, a reader who substitutes *Sally* for *her* has made a substitution that is zero on both the graphic and phonemic scales. If the name *Clardo* is substituted for *Claribel*, the substitution is of moderate proximity in both the phonemic and graphic categories. Homophones (e.g., *dear* for *deer*) and homographs (e.g., *read* /rid/ and *read* /rEd/) are exact matches in the phonemic and graphic categories respectively. The graphic and sound proximities of miscues sometimes differ from each other as the following examples illustrate:

Text Word	Oral Reading	Sound Similarity	Graphic Similarity
said	and	low	moderate
apartment	anpartment	high	high
imperil	imperial	high	high
one	member	low	low

In addition to the zero-to-nine progression of each scale, there is a blank category. The phonemic and graphic proximities of some miscues cannot be measured. Only word-for-word substitution miscues are accommodated by the two categories. Omissions of words, insertions of words, and phrase and clause level substitutions cannot be accommodated by the two categories. Examples of such miscues are the following:

Blank Category

Text: "Here take one," said the man.
Reader: "Here one," said the man.
Text: He knew Tom would be back soon.
Reader: He knew $\overset{that}{\wedge}$ Tom would be back soon.
Text: suck the venom out
Reader: suck out the venom
Text: all of them
Reader: all the men

The zero category and the comparability of the two scales permit analyses of the relative strengths of the sound and graphic cueing systems. The mean graphic proximity level can be computed and compared with the mean phonemic proximity level.

Syntactic Acceptability, Syntactic Change, and Transformations

Catherine Buck Montoro
A doctoral student in the School of Education, University of California at Los Angeles, Catherine Buck Montoro has taught English as a second language to both children and adults.

Background and Assumption

An important assumption behind the Taxonomy is that any sentence may be examined from two points of view: we may examine both its syntactic organization and its semantic organization, both its grammar and its meaning. The syntactic and semantic components of a language are virtually inseparable, and they are dependent upon each other in the most profound ways. The Goodman Taxonomy does, in fact, accommodate to this reality in several of its categories. However, when we consider the acceptability of a sentence and whatever changes the reader may have made, it is most useful to make an arbitrary separation of sentence grammar from sentence meaning. Syntax and semantics are examined separately because readers can and do produce very grammatical nonsense. For example:

> $ *burros*   *shagging* $ *downness*
>   Two burros, their long grey ears sagging in drowsiness, stood in the midst of the sheep.

We know it is also possible for a reader to alter the grammar of a sentence considerably, without damaging semantic acceptability. For example:

>   *frightened deer ran*
>   He was surprised that the little fawn didn't run away.
>   *left*   *herd wandering*
>   He lifted his head wearily and talked to his dog, as all herders do.

It is for this reason that acceptability and change are two separate categories in the Taxonomy. Each category includes a scale of values which enables us to determine just how acceptable and how greatly changed the reader's sentence is.

The Taxonomy

Having made these generalizations, let's turn exclusively to the acceptability category for a moment. Recall that the grammaticality of any sentence is determined with reference to the reader's own dialect. Recall also that the reader has available the option to correct his miscues or to press on. Given this option, then, the entirety of the sentence which the reader has produced must be read, with all of his uncorrected miscues intact. It has been stated that the previous two sentences are fully acceptable grammatically, but now imagine that the first sentence had been read like this, as it was, in fact, by one reader.

He was surprised that the little fawn didn't run away.
he   frightened deer ran

The sentence is no longer fully acceptable, because the miscue *he* has rendered it ungrammatical. In fact, according to the Taxonomy, both miscues must be coded as only partially acceptable: The miscue *he* forms an acceptable grammatical structure with the prior portion of the text, and the miscues *frightened deer ran* with that part of the text which follows.

Having briefly established both complete and partial acceptability, let's examine these sentences.

His eyes caught sight of a red jacket.

They packed Mother Whitemoon's baskets carefully.
be careful

It is here that we reach the bottom of our acceptability scale, for the miscues are acceptable neither with the prior nor the following portions of the text. Our reader has, from one point of view, destroyed the syntax of the text.

Before the extent to which these readers have altered the structure of the sentence is determined, it is necessary to examine the changes from a qualitative, rather than any quantitative, point of view. By qualitative, we mean, What kind of syntactic change—if any—has the reader's miscue produced? The question *What kind of change?* is dealt with in the category called transformations.

Many miscues produced by readers do not necessarily cause any fundamental change in the grammatical structure of the sentence.

infection
Her eyes became soft with pride and affection.

Happily, he ran.

Other miscues affect syntax more deeply.

She put on a bright cotton dress.

She often heard coyotes singing a protest from distant ridges.

The readers who produced the two miscues in the first pair of sentences made surface structure changes only, but the readers who produced the miscues in the second pair of sentences moved through different deep structures to generate something new. It is only these deeper level changes which shall be called transformations.

Since the Goodman model of reading is based firmly upon the notion that a reader reaches down into this deeper level of structure in order to extract meaning from what she reads, this distinction between the deep and surface structure changes is a particularly significant one. Not all transformational grammarians would agree with the undeniably arbitrary nature of this distinction in some cases—that is, which miscues actually do cause a true transformation and which do not. But then, not all transformational grammarians concern themselves with either the purpose or the application of reading miscue research, with real children reading real language.

If the transformation category enables the researcher to answer the question, "What kind of change has occurred?" then there must be other alternative responses available in addition to the two just mentioned. Deep and surface structure changes are not the only possibilities. A third is that the reader deviated from the text because the author had produced a structure which was either unusual or impossible within the reader's dialect.

Then he noticed that this one's leg was broken.

These miscues represent just such a dialectal adjustment on the part of the reader. The deep structure of the author's sentence and the deep structure of the reader's sentence are the same, but the two surface structures are generated by two different sets of rules.

A fourth possible response to the question, "What kind of change?" is that the reader failed to reach the deep structure of the text and also failed to produce one of his own.

His eyes caught sight of a red jacket.

This miscue has destroyed the author's syntax and shows no evidence of moving toward anything that could possibly be called grammatical.

Up to this point the following questions have been asked: (1) Is the reader's miscue grammatically acceptable? completely? only partially?

or not at all? and (2) Does the reader's miscue cause a transformation, that is, is the reader moving through the same deep structure, or through one different from the author's?

A third question must be asked: Just how much has the reader altered the text? Since this category—syntactic change—analyzes the structure which the reader has created, it is logical that this category should be used only when the reader has in fact generated an acceptable sentence. Stated more explicitly, syntactic change is coded only when the reader's miscue has produced a grammatical sentence.

Because of the generative, creative quality of language, the reader is capable of altering the text in an infinite number of ways. Because of these infinite possibilities, a much longer scale of values is needed in the syntactic change category than in the acceptability category. There are nine possibilities in the syntactic change category. Rather than illustrate all nine categories, we consider four miscues which illustrate very different degrees of syntactic change.

> *Sparkle*
> When Spiro Agnew fires his speechwriter...

It should be noted that no grammatical change has occurred. This would be coded as a 9.

> *wants*
> He wanted to go back to school.

There is a change in person, tense or number of the observed response, so this miscue would be coded as a 7.

> He had a (horse-drawn) carriage.

There is a major change within the structure of the phrase, in this case, the deletion of an embedded clause *that was drawn by a horse*. This would be coded as a 5.

> *a bite?*
> (Where did) it bite you?

The syntax of the observed response and the expected response are unrelated. The miscue is coded as a 0.

In summary, three questions regarding a miscue and syntax are asked. (1) For syntactic acceptability: Is the sentence still grammatical? (2) For transformations: What kind of change has occurred? (3) For syntactic change: To what extent has the reader's miscue altered the syntax of the text?

Semantic Acceptability and Semantic Change

William D. Page
The director of the Experienced Teacher Reading Programs at the
University of Chicago, William D. Page is an assistant professor in the
Department of Education. He teaches graduate courses in reading,
language arts, research and philosophy of education.

Background and Assumptions

In linguistics, semantics is the study of meaning. In miscue research,
reading is viewed as a process which includes attempts to reconstruct
the author's meanings (K. Goodman, 1970). The study of meaning in
reading has not been popular lately. Emphasis has been on code
cracking and phonics. Perhaps this lack of emphasis on meaning
reflects the disfavor with meaning that is exhibited by psychology (I. A.
Richards, 1974, p. 108). Can we tolerate teaching children to play a game
that looks like reading while ignoring concern for whether those
children understand the messages of print? Quine's caustic comment on
linguists applies to reading researchers as well. "Pending a satisfactory
explanation of the notion of meaning, linguists in semantic fields are in
the situation of not knowing what they are talking about" (W. Quine,
1964, p. 21). Though miscue researchers have never set out to solve the
perplexing problems of defining meaning, the characteristics of the
miscue research process and the idea that the purpose of reading is to
reconstruct the author's ideas make it necessary to approach the
difficult terrain of meaning. Meaning, in the context of miscue analysis,
is treated as analogy, or the relationship between a reader's idea and
what the idea represents.

A meaning or analogy may be the relationship between an idea
and an object, or an idea and another idea. An idea may refer to a group
of objects, or a group of ideas, or any combination of ideas. An idea
represents things other than itself by analogy (S. Langer, 1953, p. 30).

Meaning in language is often treated as a lexical function, the
association of a word or sign with a "referent" (C. Ogden and I.
Richards, p. 11). As Peirce put it, "A sign, or *representamen*, is
something which stands to somebody for something in some respect or
capacity" (C. S. Peirce, 1897, p. 99). We often think of a dictionary or
lexicon as the one place we can find out what a word means. What we
ignore when we do this is the fact that a word is a sign in language and

gains meaning from its use in context "... the meaning of any sign consists in its relationship to other signs... " (I.A. Richards, 1974, p. 108). As an example, the word *dog* usually refers to a canine animal, but if I say, "My car is a *dog*," you don't expect it to bark. Similarly, *dogging* it, a hot *dog*, *dog* tired, *dogged* persistence, a fire*dog*, do not have living, barking, canine referents.

Reading involves contextual meaning and lexical meaning. Contextual meaning is a function of both grammatical and semantic interrelationships in language. The redundant information of language produces a web of semantic interdependencies. A speaker of English can identify inconsistencies in the web, and miscue research capitalizes on this facility. The decision process in miscue analysis is called coding because the information is coded for computer keypunching as the decision is made. Numerals from the Goodman Taxonomy of Oral Reading Miscues represent the decisions (K. Goodman, *Theoretically Based Studies of Patterns of Miscues ... , 1973).*

The Taxonomy: Semantic Acceptability

In coding Semantic Acceptability, the entire sentence is used with all the uncorrected miscues. This permits the observer to deal with the reader's responses as a whole, enabling the analysis to get at how the reader is processing information in relation to meaning. It is possible to determine how the reader's specific miscue fits with the reader's total response. The observer's knowledge of language is used to discern the semantic acceptability of the miscue. By dealing with the entire, uncorrected sentence, fragmentation of the reader's response is avoided. Fragmenting the reader's response would require guessing at what's going on in the reader's mind. Miscue research restricts itself to observable performance in the coding process, fully recognizing that there are important sources of variability within the observation process itself.

The taxonomy of Semantic Acceptability (Table 1) includes five miscue classifications. Each classification represents specific, identifiable semantic characteristics of the miscue being considered. The observer examines the miscue and assigns a numeral to it. If the miscue is totally unacceptable semantically, that is, if it appears to have no semantic relationship to the context, it is coded with the numeral 0. A miscue that semantically fits the portion of the sentence preceding, but is incongruous with what follows is coded with the numeral 1. The numeral 2 is used to represent a miscue that does not fit the prior portion of the sentence, but is semantically acceptable with the remainder of the sentence. If a miscue is semantically coherent with the total sentence, but incongruous with the passage, a 3 is assigned. The numeral 4 is reserved for the miscue that is semantically acceptable with the total passage.

Table 1*

0	Totally Unacceptable
1	Acceptable with Prior Portion of Sentence
2	Acceptable with Following Portion of Sentence
3	Acceptable within Total Sentence
4	Acceptable within Total Passage

In coding Semantic Acceptability, another conditional requirement of the miscue is observed. Semantic Acceptability is never scored higher or more acceptable than Syntactic Acceptability (K. Goodman, 1969, p. 27) which uses the same numeral and classification system. This requires that Syntactic Acceptability be coded before attempting to code Semantic Acceptability.

The reasoning behind this syntactic condition is based on the idea that although syntactic structures can be studied independently of semantic context as it occurs in language, the reverse is not fully feasible. The study of meaning in language can not be carried on with oral reading miscues independent of syntax without an enormous degree of speculation. Miscue research is restricted to performance that can be judged by an observer who speaks and reads the language without undue speculation.

As a result, no attempt is made to code a miscue *more* semantically acceptable than it is syntactically acceptable. Miscue studies treat meaning as a function of language use. If a miscue is not syntactically acceptable, it is assumed that it is generally unproductive to try to guess at what the reader's meanings might be. Thus a decision about the feasible limits of exploration of miscues was made in terms of how useful the results would be.

The major question to be answered in coding Semantic Acceptability concerns how well the miscue fits the context semantically. This is a question of coherence in language which a speaker of the language, English in this case, has little difficulty deciding. The miscue is treated as it occurs in language and its meaning is treated as part of a full

---

*See Section 7, Semantic Acceptability, in Appendix A.

grammatical structure. The grammatical structure used to make the judgment is the reader's response with all its uncorrected miscues considered intact.

The Taxonomy: Semantic Change

The category called Semantic Proximity (K. Goodman, 1969, p. 25) deals with the degree of change or the semantic distance between the observed response and the expected response. Just as coding Semantic Acceptability required that the miscue fit specific syntactic conditions in the category of Syntactic Acceptability, Semantic Proximity has specific precoding conditions.

The miscue must be semantically acceptable with the total sentence or within the total passage. The miscue is coded with either a 3 or 4 in Semantic Acceptability (see Table 1). Miscues coded 0, 1, or 2 in Semantic Acceptability are left blank or not coded in the Semantic Proximity category. Table 2 shows the full array of decision categories in coding Semantic Change.

Table 2

Blank	Miscue doesn't fit conditions for coding
1	Totally incongruous to story
2	Change in subplot
3	Change in *major* incident, character, or sequence
4	Change in *minor* incident, character, or sequence
5	Change: significant but not inconsistent with story
6	Change of unimportant detail
7	Change of person, tense, number, comparative
8	Change in connotation or substitution of a similar name not confusing cast
9	No change in story meaning

The major question in Semantic Change involves how much semantic difference there is between the expected response and the observed response. By measuring the semantic change from the expected response to the observed response and investigating the cumulative frequencies, it is possible to discern the reader's processing strategies in relation to semantics. Conclusions about the reader's comprehension can be generated from this information. By viewing Semantic Change in relation to other categories of the Goodman Taxonomy of Oral Reading Miscues, insights into the reading process itself become available.

As shown in Table 2, key concepts in the decision process concerning Semantic Change involve the story and the message the author is attempting to communicate. The system accounts for miscues that are totally incongruous to the story. Plot, subplot, major and minor incidents, and characterization make up the bulk of the Semantic Proximity taxonomic system. Higher numbers indicate less change, as indicated by category 9, which recognizes a change that does not affect the story meaning at all.

An Example
A relatively simple example below demonstrates the decision process involved in coding in the two categories, Semantic Acceptability and Semantic Change. The material shown was actually read orally, audio tape recorded, and coded. The reader is a primary youngster with some familiarity with the material.

> *Expected Response*
> One day Danny went to the museum.
> He wanted to see what was inside.
>
> > (S. Hoff, 1958, p. 5)
>
> *Observed Response*
> One day Danny went to the museum.
> He *went* to see what was inside.

The reader substituted *went* for *wanted*. Syntactically, the substitution is acceptable with the total passage. This means it receives a 4 in the category of Syntactic Acceptability. A miscue can not be coded higher in Semantic Acceptability than it is coded in Syntactic Acceptability. Assigning a 4 in Syntactic Acceptability means the miscue has enough grammatical fit to warrant a decision at any level in Semantic Acceptability.

Semantically, *went* for *wanted* is acceptable in the total passage so it receives a coding of 4 in Semantic Acceptability. A coding of 3 or 4 in Semantic Acceptability makes the miscue a candidate for coding in Semantic Proximity. Considering the total context of the story, the miscue does not interfere with the story meaning; hence, it receives a 9—no important change in story meaning in the category of Semantic Change. It is the full context of the story that drives one to the conclusion that no important meaning change has occurred. This decision is in contrast with a sentence- or word-bound view that emphasizes the lexical meaning difference between *went* and *wanted*. The coding is shown in Table 3.

Table 3

Category	Code Number	Decision Description
Syntactic Acceptability	4	Acceptable within Total Passage
Semantic Acceptability	4	Acceptable within Total Passage
Semantic Change	9	Acceptable within Total Passage

The miscue we have just coded appears relatively simple to deal with. It is offered as an example to demonstrate the relationship among categories of the Goodman Taxonomy of Oral Reading Miscues. It would be unfair to mislead the reader into thinking that all or most miscues are as uncomplicated to deal with as our example. Most miscues require considerably more analysis, as the full array of coding possibilities in the taxonomic categories shows. Some miscues are candidates for extensive analysis in group discussion, and often, a newfound miscue type suggests a modification of the Taxonomy. The evolutionary quality of the Goodman Taxonomy exemplifies the scientific canon that truth and fact are subject to change, an idea that is particuarly important when studying language.

References

Goodman, K.S. A linguistic study of cues and miscues in reading. *Elementary English*, 1965, **42**, 639-643.

Goodman, K.S. Analysis of oral reading miscues: Applied psycholinguistics. *Reading Research Quarterly*, 1969, **5**(1), 9-30.

Goodman, K.S. Behind the eye: What happens in reading. In K.S. Goodman, & O. Niles (Eds.), *Reading: Process and program*. Urbana, Ill.: National Council of Teachers of English, 1970.

Hoff, S. *Danny and the dinosaur*. New York: Harper & Row, 1958.

Langer, S. *An introduction to symbolic logic*. New York: Dover, 1953.

Ogden, C., & Richards, I.A. *The meaning of meaning*. (8th ed.) New York: Harcourt, Brace & World, 1946.

Peirce, C.S. What is a sign? Three divisions of logic. In J. Buchler (Ed.), *Philosophical writings of Peirce*. New York: Dover, 1955. Original manuscript circa 1897.

Quine, W. The problem of meaning in linguistics. In J. Fodor, & J. Katz (Eds.), *The structure of language: Readings in the philosophy of language*. Englewood Cliffs, N.J.: Prentice-Hall, 1964. Also in W. Quine, *From a logical point of view*. (2nd ed.) Cambridge, Mass.: Harvard University Press, 1961.

Richards, I.A. Powers and limits of signs. In D.R. Olson, & H.G. Richey (Eds.),
    *Media and symbols: The forms of expression, communications and
    education: The 73rd yearbook of the National Society for the Study of
    Education*. Chicago: University of Chicago Press, 1974, 99-121.

Intonation

Bruce A. Gutknecht
The director of the Right to Read Exemplary Teacher Training Project
at the University of North Florida, Jacksonville, Bruce A. Gutknecht is
an associate professor of education, teaching graduate and undergraduate courses.

Background and Assumptions

Changes in intonation are involved in almost all miscues. However, in
the intonation category of the Taxonomy, only the intonation changes
which are part of the direct cause of a miscue are coded.

Intonation miscues involve changes in pitch, stress, or pause
from what is expected. They may occur in combination with miscues
involving word, phrase, or sentence changes. They can be caused
because the reader anticipates a different grammatical structure or is
unfamiliar with the author's structure.

Often, intonation miscues are part of complex miscues in which
the grammatical functions of surrounding text items are changed.

The Taxonomy

The seven categoric decisions dealing with intonation are:

  0 *Intonation is not involved in the miscue.*
     This includes situations where there is no intonation change
     or where the change is an acceptable alternate.
  1 *Intonation within the word(s) of the miscue is involved:*
     Expected Response (ER)   an original project
     Observed Response (OR)   an original pro-ject
     The intonation change makes project a verb meaning "to
     protrude" in place of a noun meaning "a plan."
  2 *Intonation is involved between words within one phrase
     structure of the sentence.*

The intonation shift does not cause changes which cross phrase structure boundries.

ER   came from jungle rivers where ...

OR   came from Jungle River where ...

The intonation shift makes jungle move from an adjective position to a part of a proper name (noun phrase).

3   *Intonation is involved which is relative to the phrase or clause structure of the sentence.*

The intonation shift causes changes which cross phrase and/or clause boundaries.

ER   Tomorrow we must crown a Miss America who has buck teeth, cash in Las Vegas, abandon our calling cards, and list everyone in *Who's Who.*

OR   Tomorrow we must crown a Miss America who has buck teeth, cash in Las Vegas, abandon our calling cards, and list everyone in *Who's Who.*

The deep structure of the ER is *we must cash in,* while the deep structure of the OR is *and who has cash in.* Cash becomes a noun in this intonation miscue.

4   *Intonation is involved which is terminal to the phrase or sentence.*

E R   None of us ever figured out why he chose the pet he did.

OR   None of us ever figured out why. He chose the pet he did.

5   *The intonation change involves a substitution of a conjunction for a terminal punctuation or the reverse.*

E R   The boys fished and then they cooked their catch.

OR   The boys fished. Then they cooked their catch.

6   *The intonation change involves direct quotes.*

E R   "Tom," said Mother.

OR   Tom said, "Mother."

Structural Levels

Rudine Sims
In the School of Education, University of Massachusetts, Amherst, where she is an associate professor, Rudine Sims directs the reading program and teaches courses in reading, language arts, and children's literature.

Background and Assumptions

As the Taxonomy evolved, the researchers discovered that it is not possible to use a simplistic view of a miscue as a substitution, or an insertion, or an omission of one thing or another. What is a substitution at one syntactic level could possibly be an omission at another. The result of trying to solve such problems was the development of five categories which enable us as researchers to examine miscues as possibly involving one or more grammatical constituents.

When miscues are examined in their relationship to the grammatical structural systems of our language, we discover that a miscue can affect one or more structural levels at the same time. The syntactic constituents of our language are interrelated in such a way that a change within one constituent may also cause change in another. A miscue which involves one word, for example, may at the same time alter the phrase structure of the clause in which it occurs.

The Taxonomy

Substitutions, insertions, omissions, or reversals may occur at the submorphemic level, the bound morpheme level, the word level, the phrase level, or the clause level. Each miscue is examined to determine what changes, if any, it has caused at each of these levels.

It will be easier to understand the parameters of each category if they are examined separately:

1.   Submorphemic level. Submorphemic changes are defined as those which involve changes of one or two phoneme sequences within a word. Some examples of miscues involving submorphemic changes are:

Text:	none	bigger	stop
Reader:	known	better	spot

In the first example, the reader substituted one vowel sound for another. In the second, the reader substituted one phoneme sequence for another following the initial phoneme. In the third, there is a reversal of phonemes.

2.   Bound morpheme level. Bound morpheme changes may involve inflectional suffixes, contractional suffixes, derivational suffixes, and prefixes. Some examples are:

Text:	girl	small	quickly
Reader:	girls	smallest	quick

In the first example, the reader has made a miscue which involves the plural inflection. In the second, the reader has inserted an inflectional suffix. In the third, the reader has again made a miscue involving a bound morpheme, an adverbial suffix.

3.   Word or free morpheme. A free morpheme is a meaning-bearing unit which can function independently or in combination with other morphemes. A word is a free morpheme or a free and bound morpheme combination.

At the word level, we try to determine if the miscue involves variations of single and multiple morphemes. Here are some examples:

Text:	train	your	crowded
Reader:	toy	yours	crawled

When the reader read *toy* for *train*, he substituted a single morpheme word for another single morpheme word. In the second example, the reader's miscue, *yours*, is composed of two morphemes, while the text word, *your*, has only a single morpheme. In the third instance, the reader has substituted one free morpheme for another within a longer word.

Interestingly, some young readers are not clear about what oral units are words, and have difficulty relating their oral words to graphic items. For example, when a child consistently says *gimme*, he may not recognize the two graphic items *give me* as the same structure.

4.   Phrase level. A phrase may be a noun phrase, a verb phrase, or an adverbial phrase. A phrase may be represented by only one constituent. When a reader reads *the dog* for *the yellow dog* he has substituted one phrase structure for another. A noun phrase which had consisted of a determiner, an adjective, and a noun now consists of just a determiner and a noun.

5.   Clause level. To be involved at the clause level, a miscue must in some way·change the clause structure of the sentence. For example, when the reader read *I arrived when he was there*, for *When I arrived he was there*, he altered the dependency relationship between the two clauses. The first clause, formerly dependent, became independent.

It was stated earlier that these levels are interrelated. In order to clarify that notion, we can examine another set of examples.

1. Text: the striped pajama *top*...
   Reader: the striped pajama *tops*...
2. Text: put the bottle *into* his hand...
   Reader: put the bottle *in* his hand...
3. Text: I never *once* saw the tube move.
   Reader: I never saw the tube move.
4. Text: I put my mouth *almost* on his ear...
   Reader: I put my mouth *close* to his ear...
5. Text: His voice was pitched *a little higher* than usual...
   Reader: His voice was pitched *with a little anger* than usual...
6. Text: This Harry, I thought, *he* is very refined.
   Reader: This Harry, I thought, is very refined.
7. Text: I remember trying to hold my breath, but *when* I couldn't do
   that any longer...
   Reader: I remember trying to hold my breath, but I couldn't do that
   any longer...

In the first example, when the reader substituted *tops* for *top*, he inserted a phoneme, making a submorphemic level insertion; he included the plural morpheme, making a bound morpheme substitution; and he substituted one word for another at the word level.

In the second example, the substitution of *in* for *into* not only involves the omission of a two-phoneme sequence at the submorphemic level, but also the insertion of a free morpheme at the word level.

In the third example, the omission of *once* is not only the omission of a word, but also the omission of an adverb phrase.

In the next example, the substitution of *close to* for *almost on* presents the substitution of one phrase structure for another.

In the fifth example, a word has been inserted, another has been substituted, and the phrase structure has changed.

The omission of *he* in the sixth example is the omission of a word and also of a noun phrase.

In the final example, the omission of the word *when* is not only the omission of a word, but causes a change in dependency in the clause structure. The second clause becomes an independent one.

The preceding examples were selected in order to illustrate the interrelationship between the structural levels. While the examples are all actual miscues made by one reader, the relationship would be even more apparent if they were examined in the total context in which they occurred.

Proficient readers who are making effective use of the syntactic structures in their reading strategies tend to make more miscues involving phrase and clause structures than young beginning readers who may be paying more attention to individual words.

While most miscues are involved in some way at the word level, they quite frequently are involved at some other syntactic level, also. What may appear to be at first glance a mispronunciation may have occurred because the reader was dealing with one of the syntactic constituents of the sentence, and not specifically with one word. In order to gain a fuller understanding of the reading process and of the miscue phenomena, one must examine miscues not simply as changes involving individual words, but as phenomena which occur in a total language context.

Grammatical Categories

Peter D. Rousch
An Australian, Peter D. Rousch is dean of the School of Teacher Education at Riverina College of Advanced Education, New South Wales.

The Goodman Taxonomy permits observations of the reader's ability to handle grammatical characteristics of individual words encountered. The basis for this aspect of the Taxonomy was a modified Fries model that enabled observations to be made on surface characteristics of grammatical features. As it was necessary to make judgments concerning the underlying structure of these surface features, a system permitting deep structure observations of these was incorporated into the model.

Grammatical categories include noun, noun modifier, verb, verb modifier, function word, and words that defy classification (indeterminate). Allied with these categories are filler and function features that permit refinements within categories. For example, in the sentence, *I went with him*, the word *him* would be categorized as a noun, occupying the pronoun filler and functioning as an object within the prepositional phrase.

An example of the category, function and filler classifications for noun and verb, follows:

Category	Filler	Function
1. Noun	1. Common	1. Subject
	2. Proper	2. Direct object
	3. Pronoun	3. Indirect object
	4. Verb derived	4. Appositive ·
	5. Phrasal unit	5. Address
	6. Word as word name	6. In adverbial or other prepositional phrase
	7. Quantifiers and ordinals	7. Subject complement
	8. Adjective as noun phrase	8. Object complement
		9. In a phrase of intensification
2. Verb	1. "Be" forms	1. Active
	2. Transitive	2. Passive
	3. Intransitive	3. Imperative
	4. Infinitive	4. Subjunctive
	5. Proverbs	

It should be noted that comparisons between expected and observed responses can occur at the word, phrase, or clause levels. In regard to the grammatical categories, our concern is with the word level, where an attempt is made to clarify variations between expected and observed responses as these relate to categories, fillers and functions.

This aspect of the Taxonomy serves a dual purpose. It is possible to gain insights into whether a reader is able to operate with a strong awareness of the grammatical features of the text in so far as his or her ability to substitute words of the same grammatical categories, as denoted by expected responses, is concerned. A tendency to substitute a disproportionate percentage of, for example, noun modifiers with nouns would point up a likely weakness in coping with the noun modifier category in the reading situation. Similarly, it is possible to note the extent to which certain fillers or functions are a potential difficulty.

The second purpose of this section of the Taxonomy relates to the insights it provides into potential problems inherent in reading materials. The practice of controlling vocabulary, and then injecting newly-taught words into the text in profusion irrespective of their grammatical characteristics can be a source of confusion for young readers. For example, consider the use of the noun adjunct *circus* in the following:

> We crept into the *circus*
> tent. We saw all the
> monkeys swinging on the
> bars.

If *circus* has been introduced as a noun in preceding sections of the story, or a reader is not familiar with its use as a noun adjunct, the shift to the noun adjunct form in the example sets up a number of possible reactions by the reader:

1. He might disbelieve that two "nouns" can occur together, and choose to omit one, for example:

> We crept into the circus.
> We saw . . .

2. Still disbelieving, he might come up with

> We crept into the circus.
> Then we saw . . .

In this instance, graphic similarity between *tent* and *then* coupled with the likelihood of *circus* being a noun result in the rendition suggested.

3. Or, the student might read

> We crept into the circus.
> Tent. We saw . . .

as if *tent* cannot possibly occupy any role other than forming a sentence of its own.

Of course, apart from pointing up the need for authors of books for young children to be aware of the need to rationalize a varied use of grammatical features, the example highlights a corresponding problem found frequently in primer materials, namely the tendency for these materials to be written as if each line is a complete sentence in its own right. The use of the noun marker *the* at the end of the line instead of *circus* as the terminal would encourage the reader to move into the later text in a way that would force him to look for further information there, rather than allow him to believe that he had completed the sentence with a likely noun in its usual end-of-line position.

We also have the opportunity in this category to observe the nonword:

Expected Response: I hurried home before it was too late.
Observed Response: I $humed home before it was too late.

Here the reader used graphic information and produced the nonword $humed which is classified as a verb. It would be identified as intransitive in the filler situation and as active in the function situation. We get this information from the inflection (ed) and also from the contextual situation in which the word appears.

Semantic Word Relationships

Peter D. Rousch

Observations of the reading process reveal that the substitution miscues at the single-word level may reflect synonymity to varying degrees. Previous categories of the Goodman Taxonomy have reflected a hierarchical classification of miscues. The semantic relationships existing between words, as reflected in the semantic word relationship category, are classified not hierarchically but rather in a way that permits comparison of the meaning carried by the expected and observed responses at the single-word level only, without consideration of the meaning within the entire minimal terminal unit. This is to say, only the relationship between single-word responses is considered in this category.

In the reading process, words possess a semantic relationship in the mind of the reader in such a way that it is possible for the actual or anticipated occurrence of one item to cause the production of a related item. In the example:

Expected Response: The animal tried to escape.
Observed Response: The bear tried to escape.

the substitution of bear for animal might have been cued by prior context, by processing animal and coming up with bear. On the other hand, it is possible for a reader to come up with a substitution that has no semantic relationship with the expected response as in the example:

Expected Response: The boys ate the *fruit*.
Observed Response: The boys ate the *fort*.

Although the latter example would be indicative of lack of insight into the story line, substitutions at the semantic level can vary considerably from expected responses yet still preserve the spirit of the original. This has been observed in discussions on semantic acceptability and semantic change. A precise knowledge of single-word connotations is not necessary in a process that employs a restructuring of the syntax used by the author. Similarly, when an expected response such as:

She could stay *that* way because *nothing* has *any* weight in space.

is read as:

She could stay *the* way she did because *everything* has *no* weight in space.

The preservation of meaning through restructuring, plus substitutions that vary from zero to close semantic relationship with the original, reflects a strong awareness of meaning without close attention to individual words.

The Taxonomy permits a semantic classification over fourteen discrete areas as follows:

0 The two items are unrelated.
   ER   She rang the bell.
   OR   She rang the bean.

1 There is primarily a syntactic relationship with minor semantic association to a prior or subsequent word or to the word itself.
   ER   It was a bad go of malaria.
   OR   It was a bad go for malaria.

2 There is a strong sequential semantic association to a prior or subsequent word or to the word itself.
   ER   ... smeared thick with face cream.
   OR   ... smeared thick with ice cream.

3 There is an association to a homophone or homograph.

ER   bare ⟶ bear   ER   read ⟶ red
OR   wolf ⟵   OR   blue ⟵

4 There is a shift to a generic term from a specific term.
   ER   apple   train
   OR   fruit   toy

5 There is a shift to a specific term from a generic term.
   ER   chemical
   OR   cyclamate

6 The term in the text and the term in the miscue have common
   semantic attributes.
   ER   I stood beside him.
   OR   I stood behind him.

7 The words are antonyms.
   ER He was awake.
   OR He was asleep.

8 The words belong to a semantic pair.
   ER   Mr. Brown is his father.
   OR   Mrs. Brown is his mother.

9 The ER and OR are variants of the same word.
   ER   bitten   near
   OR   bit   nearer

10 There is a slight difference in connotation.
    ER   He walked home.
    OR   He went home.

11 The ER and OR are similar names but there is no confusion of
    characters.
    ER   Harry Pope
    OR   Henry Pope

12 The words are synonymous within the text.
    ER   headlamps   moment   mother
    OR   headlights   minute   she

13 The words are synonymous in other contexts but not in the
    present one.
    ER   He taped the battery to the ruler.
    OR   He taped the battalion to the ruler.

14 There is some semantic relationship between the ER and OR
    but it is not parallel.
    ER   handed   become
    OR   handled   come

What We Know about Reading

Despite the recent breakthroughs in research which have created new insights into the reading process, some speakers at professional meetings still preface their remarks with comments such as this: "Since nobody understands how reading works, therefore..." As researchers, we are a little tired of hearing such comments from people with credentials and degrees and published programs for reading instruction. But the real problem is that this assumption that no new knowledge about the process of reading exists becomes a justification for almost any kind of program, and, in fact, in reading almost anything has been tried.

We researchers are not saying we know everything about reading. Many times when we listen to kids reading, they do something that we haven't anticipated at all. Language is complicated, and there is a lot to be understood about it.

What we want to share is what, at this point, we do understand about reading. Our contention is that we're too far along as a profession, in terms of knowledge, to justify programs that are not based on any understanding of what has been learned over the past decade about how language works and how it is used and particularly how this knowledge pertains to reading. In sharing with you what we understand about reading, we will also be rather free in indicating what we think this means for school programs.

General Reading Instruction

What We Know about Reading

Kenneth S. Goodman
The former director of reading miscue research at Wayne State University, Kenneth S. Goodman is currently a professor of education at the University of Arizona and president of the Center for Expansion of Language and Thinking. In 1975, he received the David H. Russell Award for Distinguished Research in the Teaching of English from the National Council of Teachers of English.

The parable of the blind men and the elephants offers an apt analogy to the ways in which reading has been viewed in the past. Just as each blind man limited his definition of an elephant to his own superficial experience with its overt characteristics, so reading has been defined by narrow, superficial, observable aspects. The blind man who approached the leg called it a tree; the one who touched its side called it a wall; the one who grasped its tail thought it a rope. In reading, some look and see only words, hence for them reading is a matter of attacking words; some see letters and the sounds they represent, so reading is phonics; some see patterns of letters, so reading is spelling. Some stand at the end of reading and proclaim that reading is thinking. Even had the blind men combined their impressions into an eclectic view of the elephant it would remain superficial. An elephant is certainly not two walls supported by four tree trunks with a hose at one end and a rope at the other.

One must develop a theory of the elephant which makes it possible to interpret superficial observations and get at its essential nature, its elephantness. It's not that the blind men are wrong in their observations; it's their unwillingness to infer from their data the essential unity which underlies it that is the problem. Our research has above all else had as its goal to seek out the unity in reading, to infer from observation of reading behavior the process that underlies the behavior.

From every vantage point we could find, we have looked at the miscues readers produce. We have created a taxonomy to clarify the interrelationships between the parallel observations. We have constructed a model and theory of the reading process to predict and explain what we have observed, and then we remodeled the theory and reconstructed the model on the basis of further observations. Though we can not see into the heads of readers and observe their minds at work, we are not blind.

Certain basic premises provide a foundation for the understanding of reading which we've built. One of these is that **reading is language**. It's one of two receptive language processes. Speaking and writing are the generative, productive language processes. The other receptive language process is listening. Reading and listening, at least for the literate, are parallel processes.

Readers are users of language: that's another key premise. They use language to obtain meaning. Through seeking to comprehend the writer's meaning, they in fact construct the meaning, through a process which is strongly dependent on their own experience and conceptual development. In reading, meaning is thus both input and output, and the persistent search for and preoccupation with meaning is more important than the particular meaning the reader arrives at. *What* message the reader gets is less important than the fact that the reader is trying to get a message. What message the reader produces is partly dependent on what the writer intended, but also very much dependent on what the reader brings to the particular text.

It's a constructive process, this search for meaning. As users of language, children learning to read their native language are already possessed of a language competence and an ability to learn language which are powerful resources, provided that literacy is treated by schools as an extension of their natural language learning.

Simply speaking, reading researchers in the past have treated reading as if it were something new and foreign, and in the process they have lost the opportunity to capitalize on the immense language competence that children have before we ever see them in school.

Here's another premise: **language is the means by which communication among people is brought about**. It's always, therefore, in close relationship to meaning. When it's divorced from meaning it is no longer language. It becomes then an intriguing, manipulable, abstract system. You can play games with language apart from meaning, but it is no longer language. If that intriguing system is fragmented into sounds or letters or patterned pieces, it quickly loses its power even to intrigue and becomes a collection of abstractions.

The significance of regarding language as the means and meaning as the end in language use is that it explains why language is learned easily, why young children are able to treat language as if it were part of the concrete world, why meaningful language is easier to learn, to remember, to manipulate. It also explains why instructional reading programs that begin with bits and pieces abstracted from language, like words or letters, on the theory that they're making learning simpler in fact making learning to read much harder. The very sequencing that we thought we were doing to make the learning simpler turns language into something that isn't language anymore. The kids treat it, then, not as concrete learning, but as abstraction.

I'm digressing from my central concern for the reading process to point this out because I want to emphasize my conviction that there is no justifiable gap between theory and practice in reading. Sound practice can only be built on sound theory. Theory which is impractical is bad theory, and much of current practice is bad because it is not based on an examined, coherent, defensible theory of reading. Too much has been done in reading by blind men who have quickly decided that the elephant is a tree trunk and run home to create a method and materials for training elephants.

We've learned that certain atheoretical commonsense notions are totally inappropriate to understanding the reading process. One such commonsense notion is that accuracy in and of itself is important in reading. That seems so logical. A second related to the first is that being careful to perceive, recognize, and process each letter or each word is necessary to successful reading. I don't know how many times I've had teachers say to me: "After all, how can you read a sentence if you don't know all the words in it?" Those are commonsense views and like most commonsense views they come from superficial observation of reality, not totally invented, of course, but the kind of superficial observation that the blind men were engaging in.

Our theory tells us that these commonsense notions are wrong, and our research confirms our theory. Effective and efficient readers are those who get to meaning by using the least amount of perceptual input necessary. Readers' language competence enables them to create a grammatical and semantic prediction in which they need only sample from the print to reach meaning. They already have the language competence to do that. Psycholinguists helped us to understand this by demonstrating that readers can not possibly be reading language a letter or a word at a time, since the time it takes to do that far exceeds the time the reader actually devotes to the given sequence. Through their miscues children helped us to understand this by demonstrating their driving concern for structure and meaning, even in the first grade, even from the very beginning, as soon as they catch on to the fact that reading is language and that it is supposed to yield meaning.

Some kids get distracted from this understanding; some kids have a little trouble finding their way back to it; but we keep noticing it even in the least proficient readers: this compulsion to try and find some meaning somewhere. They can leap to meaning while only touching base in print.

In reading, as in listening, the language user must continuously predict underlying grammatical patterns because it is from these that meaning may be decoded. Essentially meaning relates to grammar through clauses and their interrelationship.

> It must have been around midnight when I drove home, and as I approached the gates of the bungalow I switched off the headlamps of the car so the beam wouldn't swing in through the window of the side bedroom and wake Harry Pope.

The paragraph above is the beginning of a story that we have used extensively with tenth graders in our reading research; it's from a short story, "Poison," by Roald Dahl. This first paragraph is composed of a single sentence in which the author has done a very interesting job of creating a setting for his story. There's a lot of information here that isn't of vital importance and yet it creates a background against which things are going to happen. How did he get all this into a single sentence? The first sequence, *It must have been around midnight*, is a clause. Now we come to another clause, *when I drove home*. Two basic statements are combined in such a way that we get the idea of time and we get the idea of what's taking place at the time because he uses *when* to join them.

But now the author is going to join the main clause, which is *It must have been around midnight* with another main clause. How does he do that? That's what the *and* is there for. However, before he gets to the next main clause we have another dependent clause introduced by *as.* So we have a main clause, a dependent clause, a conjunction, then another dependent clause and then another main clause: *It must have been around midnight/when I drove home/and/as I approached the gates of the bungalow/* (and here comes the next main clause) *I switched off the headlamps of the car.* If one omits the *and* there, as some of our readers have done, there isn't any particular problem, in fact *and* is a kind of optional element. One might ask, since it isn't necessary, why the author chooses to put it there in the first place. Had he written this in a high school English class or a freshman composition class his teacher probably would have written "run-on sentence" and crossed out *and.* Somehow the author feels the necessity to keep you propelled forward, to give you the feeling that this is all a kind of unity.

But now read the same sentence keeping the *and* but leaving the *as* out. What happens now? *It must have been around midnight when I drove home and I approached the gates of the bungalow.* One can either put an *and* in, (we've had kids who've done that) or one can go back and figure out what went wrong. The point is that in order to get meaning from this sentence one must work through the grammatical structure and one must somehow get at the clauses and their interrelationship. That's really what's significant about the concept that readers have to get to deep structure here; they have to go beyond the surface; they have to see those underlying relationships that are not even sentence relationships.

It is our conclusion that the sentence isn't nearly as important a unit in language as linguists have been saying. The trouble is that instead of looking at language, they've been looking at sets of sentences that they made up. In the task of looking at kids reading real stories, we've had to deal with paragraphs like this and we've become aware that what really is important is the clauses and their relationships, whether within or across sentences. Every teacher is familiar with the kid who shifts clauses when reading a sentence that starts with a left-branching clause. For instance, suppose that a sentence started: *As I approached the gates of the bungalow I switched off the headlamps of the car so the beam wouldn't* . . .

Now if the subject reads: *It must have been around midnight when I drove home as I approached the gates of the bungalow* . . . , he is treating the *as* not as dependent on the clause that follows it but on the clause that precedes it, which means a subtle kind of change.

Teachers have tended superficially to think that these shifts occur because the kids don't see the punctuation. But the problem in reading is that the punctuation comes at the end and one already must have made a prediction about what is being dealt with before one gets to the punctuation. Instead of indicating when to end the sentence, the punctuation, at best, simply confirms whether the reader was right or wrong in the initial decision of what kind of structure is being dealt with. The sentence above is a complex sentence from a short story that wasn't written for reading instruction. We found it in a twelfth-grade literature anthology but it wasn't written for twelfth-grade literature anthologies either.

Here's a sentence that was written for reading instruction: "See Spot run." It could come from any of a number of basal readers. It illustrates how the same process is operating with this short sentence.

How does a child get to the meaning of this sentence? People who developed reading programs and who were obviously trying to get the best knowledge they could into their programs thought that the psychologist had given them proper advice when he said the main problem is exposure to words, that you control the number of words you introduce, and once you introduce a word you use it as often as you can. The problem is that psychological theory treats language as a bag of words. The notion was that once a word is introduced it is learned through repetition. Basal readers avoided inflected forms in primers because they're new words (so they didn't use *sees*, they used *see*).

But since this type of sentence first appeared first-grade teachers have been aware of an interesting phenomenon. A kid could read these words from flash cards and have difficulty reading the three-word sentence. Let's analyze that as we did the more complicated structure. What's the subject of this three-word sentence: *See Spot run?* My second-grade teacher said it was "you understood." I don't know if she understood what that meant. A transformational grammarian now has translated that. What he would say is that there is, in the deep structure, a subject, and the subject is *you*. Well, not really, because *you*, after all, is a pronoun that represents some noun which has already been identified. When do you use *you?* When one person is addressing another and the subject is identified because of the situation of the discourse. In the book, however, there might be a preceding word like *father*. "*Father! See Spot run.*" What does *you* represent then here? Father. Which just happens to be the word which precedes *see*.

The child must dredge up from the deep structure the missing subject. How does he know he's supposed to do that? He will know if he recognizes this as a grammatical pattern in which the subject you is deletable. How does he recognize that? Sentences that start with verbs are often imperative. He has the language competence to know that. If his mother says, "Take out the garbage," he understands because he recognizes that command form, and he knows that the deleted subject is you and that in this case you is himself. But notice that what we're saying is that in order to get the subject of the sentence, he must recognize this as an imperative grammatical pattern. He must predict the pattern from the start.

Now that we know the subject is you, what verb goes with that subject? This is a rather odd sentence: verb-noun-verb. So the reader has to do what we were doing up above in that longer sequence; he has to identify what amounts to two clauses and their interrelationship. The first clause is (you) see (something). The whole second clause, not just Spot, is the object of that verb see. You see (something), and the something is: Spot run.

We've got another problem. Why do we have a verb that doesn't have an s on it following a noun that's third person singular and which is clearly the subject of the verb in that clause? Again the reader must go to deep structure and say that the underlying clause is really Spot runs. How do we get from Spot runs to Spot run? We do it by two transformations; first we make an infinitive out of the verb, and instead of Spot runs it's Spot to run; and then we apply another deletion as we did with the you, and we get from See (Spot runs) to See Spot to run and then See Spot run. Run is really an infinitive with the to deleted. The funny thing about this is not how complicated it is, but how many kids don't have trouble reading it, even though this is a complex pattern with very little meat on the bones. In contrast to the earlier sentence, if you miss anything here you're really out of luck. But, still, many kids learned to grasp this pattern in listening. If a kid can understand his mother when she says, "Take out the garbage," he can understand See Spot run.

The problem with that three-word sentence, then, is not so much that kids can not understand it but that it throws a number of complicated curves at them, one being the invisible subject. It is just at this early point that textbooks should be, instead, maximizing children's ability to predict by presenting more common and more natural sentence patterns. As a matter of fact, the text probably should not have used *see* (which was chosen here because it had already been introduced as a word). It should have said something like *watch* or *look at*, which would then have sounded more natural and been more predictable.

What do kids do with that sentence when they have to read it? One possibility is to read it as a series of three words. Teachers may teach kids to do so by emphasizing accuracy. When the kid says *See* and then there is a long pause, the teacher may say *Spot*. The kid may not have been wondering what the word was, he may have been trying to figure out what it was doing there. Inadvertently what the teacher teaches him is to say the word even if it doesn't make sense to him.

If the focus were on meaning rather than identification of words, there wouldn't be as many reading problems. There's no way to get to the meaning except through the clause relationships. But don't misunderstand the significance of this. What we have to understand is that the search for meaning is itself what makes it possible for the reader to predict the grammatical structures. None of us, even at our current stage of education and linguistic sophistication, can go very far getting into these complicated descriptions while we're trying to understand what somebody's saying; in fact, it works the other way around.

A little girl who was learning to read said it well. She read something that her mother didn't believe she could read and her mother asked, "How did you know that?" The little girl said, "It just popped into my mouth." That's what happens with language. With the focus on meaning, the control over the grammatical system is so well developed that the meaning actually pops into one's mind, and the words, then, into one's mouth. The reader doesn't need to say, "Oh, I see. That is a clause embedded into another clause which is functioning as the object of the verb *see* with the deleted subject *you*." She doesn't have to consciously say that and yet she's automatically processing that information. She thinks she's attending only to the meaning and yet obviously she can't get to the meaning without processing the language.

The meaning makes possible the prediction of the structure *if the* reader is concerned for meaning. One can then try on grammatica structures for fit, that is to see if they do in fact yield something tha makes sense, and then accept and decode them or reject and correc them to an alternate pattern. Decode here means get to meaning.

Somehow the idea became current in reading circles that written language was a code but oral language wasn't. Somehow oral language by virtue of its primacy was something other than code. If you didn't speak English, would you get any meaning from what is issuing from a speaker's mouth? There's no meaning being exchanged in speech. The speaker is simply producing sound and the listener is processing that sound and creating for himself a meaning; but what exchanges between them is a code. No intrinsic meaning is in any of the noises the speaker makes, any more than in the scratches or print on this page. Code to code is recoding; in order to go from code to something else you have to be going to meaning.

We're going to need to understand that concept if we're going to get away once and for all from the misconception that somehow one can divide reading into a physical, mechanical act of translating print to speech and a cognitive act of going to meaning.

Research has demonstrated that readers, proficient or otherwise, can not really be going from print to oral language and then to meaning. Very early readers learn to do in parallel fashion with reading what they have learned to do with listening; to go from code, this time in a graphic form, to meaning. Most literate adults can do that much faster than they can produce speech.

In our research we're trying to get beyond reading performance to a competence which can not be directly observed. We can't see the reading process happening; we can not tune in on it directly; we must infer it from some kind of external behavior.

But how can comprehension, which is the end product, be inferred? All along I've been emphasizing meaning as input, meaning as output, and meaning as what makes the whole thing go. When we try to find out, after the person has read, what he understood, we're dealing with one or another kind of measures of his performance. It is a great mistake to equate that performance with the competence itself.

That's what is so objectionable about the current interest in reading tests that's been brought about by accountability programs and by behavioral objectives programs. Such programs assume that getting a kid to perform in certain ways in fact makes that child a reader. If teachers were asked, they would make clear that kids perform without competence and have competence without performance. For example, someone says to you, "The marlup was poving his kump," and asks you comprehension questions such as: "What was the

marlup poving?" "What was the marlup doing to his kump?" Has your
comprehension been measured because you answered the two questions correctly? Did you understand that nonsense sentence? What
happens to kump when it gets poved, particularly by a marlup? The
point of course is that that's precisely what a lot of comprehension
questions are like. What we're getting is the child's underlying
linguistic competence. She can manipulate grammatical structures.
But we aren't in fact getting any insight into what she learned as a
result of her reading, which is what we think we're getting at.

This problem is not one our group feels we've solved, but we
think we have a grasp of it which we want to share with you. This
represents research recently completed.

Figure 1 shows five groups of readers in eighth and tenth grades.
All of them read Story 61. Four of the same groups read a second story,
Story 60. The figure indicates the percentage of the miscues those
readers made which we were able to code as syntactically and
semantically acceptable or syntactically acceptable but not semantically acceptable. Story 61 is one that even our high group found
somewhat difficult.

The left column in each pair represents the syntactic acceptability of their miscues. The right column represents the semantic
acceptability. Things can be syntactically acceptable and not make
sense, but they can't be semantically acceptable unless they're
syntactically acceptable. So it's not a surprise that the former is lower
than the latter.

Notice the stepladder effect (on Story 61) when you look at our
high tenth-grade group, our high average tenth-grade group, our low
average tenth-grade group, our low tenth-grade group, and our high
eighth-grade group. The high eighth graders look quite a bit like the
high average tenth graders; in fact, they come up a little higher in the
syntactic acceptability. But each tenth-grade group is successively
lower.

Story 60 is the Roald Dahl story referred to earlier. Notice how
much more similar the groups are. In this story where the conceptual
load isn't as great, where there isn't as much to keep track of as in the
harder story, semantic acceptability and syntactic acceptability are
much more similar and the high eighth-grade group comes up to just
about where the high tenth-grade group is. This figure does not show a
measure of performance *after* reading, it shows reading *as* it takes
place. It's still performance, but we're asking ourselves: "When the kid

produced the miscue, did it make sense?" That gives us an indication then of how much attention to and concern for meaning each reader is showing and how successfully that reader is able to stay with meaning.

In the less complex story, the groups are more alike, but the harder material with heavier conceptual load takes its toll. You also notice that, though there is more gradation between the lowest and the highest group in the semantic acceptability on Story 61, there still are some pretty difficult sentence structures in the complex story and

Item	Groups									
Grade	10	10	10	8	10	10	10	10	8	10
Ability	L	LA	HA	H	H	L	LA	HA	H	H
Story Number	59	60	60	60	60	61	61	61	61	61

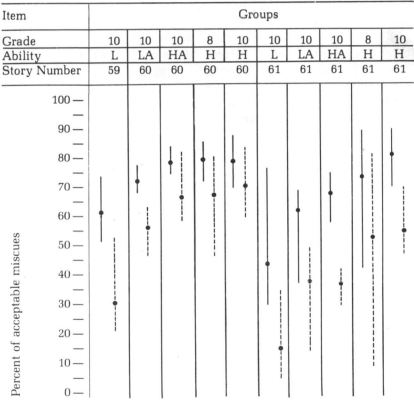

L Low ability   • Mean
A Average ability   ____ Syntactic acceptability
H High ability   _ _ _ Semantic acceptability

Fig. 1 Percent of syntactic and semantic acceptability of miscues by student readers (range and mean by groups)

without the ability to handle meaning that syntax gets too hard to manage.

When we put two things together we come up with something that we've labeled *comprehending*; not comprehension but comprehending. It looks as if comprehending, the concern for meaning while reading, can be measured by taking the percentage of miscues that are originally acceptable semantically and adding to that the percentage that aren't semantically acceptable but which are corrected. Those that are fully semantically acceptable plus those that are corrected to make them acceptable give us a percentage of miscues which we call the comprehending percentage.

Figure 2 shows the range for five groups; the 10L group read only Story 61, the harder story. They didn't read Story 60. Instead they read another story which is from an eighth-grade book. The range on Story 60 ("Poison") for our 10H group in comprehending is from about 67 percent up to about 94 percent with a mean of 77 percent. All the students in this group were doing a lot of comprehending, either because the text makes sense with their miscues or they corrected. Percentage of correction doesn't necessarily have to be high to achieve that, if in fact their miscues are successful in the first place in retaining meaning. The 10H group with the more difficult story still has some pretty high comprehending activity going on, but the range has slipped to 55-95 percent with a mean of 70 percent. The group has a much greater spread than on the other task.

The 10HA group has a high range and mean for Story 60 (74-92 percent, M = 81 percent), but on Story 61 the whole range falls to 42-55 percent, with a mean of 51 percent. The 10HA group is not comprehending as well; they're not as able to get to the meaning or to do something about it when they lose the meaning.

The range for the low average group overlaps the higher tenth grade in comprehending: For Story 60, it is 63-88 percent with a mean of 75 percent, but on Story 61 comprehending range drops to 21-64 percent, with a mean of 43 percent. The difference in reading competence shows on the harder story.

There were kids in the low average group who did better in comprehending than kids in the high average group, or in the high group. This finding has considerable significance, because what we used for grouping these kids originally was their percentile ranking on a standardized reading test. What you see is that some kids who are not particularly high achievers on standardized reading tests do as well in this measure of retaining meaning or correcting to get meaning as the high achievers. Even the low group with the difficult story still overlaps the low average group.

The 8H group comes up as high as the 10H group but has a wider range on Story 60. Their mean, 78 percent, is almost the same. On the harder. story the range of the 8H group becomes very wide, 18-82 percent, and mean drops to 57 percent.

The point this data emphasizes is that we can, by looking at

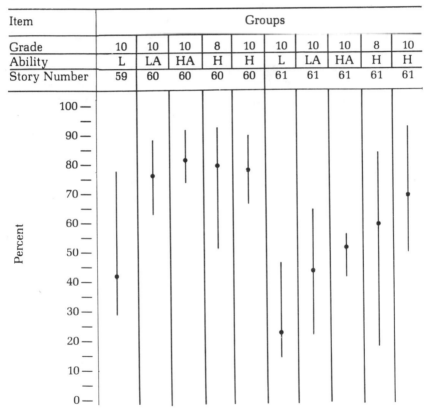

Item	Groups									
Grade	10	10	10	8	10	10	10	10	8	10
Ability	L	LA	HA	H	H	L	LA	HA	H	H
Story Number	59	60	60	60	60	61	61	61	61	61

L   Low ability   H   High ability
A   Average ability   •   Mean

Fig. 2 Comprehending scores of eighth and tenth graders (range and mean by groups). Comprehending score = percent of semantically acceptable miscues added to percent of semantically unacceptable miscues that are successfully corrected.

reading in process, by judging the miscues that kids produce in terms of their effect, get some powerful insights into how each reader is operating: we can get at his or her basic competence.

To summarize, what we know of how readers operate is something like this: First of all, more proficient readers make better miscues; they're better miscues not in the sense that we like them but in terms of their effect. They're less likely to produce unacceptable grammar. Furthermore, more proficient readers have an ability to recognize when their miscues need correction. When a reader is correcting a lot of miscues that don't change the meaning and *not* correcting a lot that *do* change the meaning, there is a pretty powerful insight that he's operating on a wrong model, that in effect he's not very efficient because he's wasting a lot of time trying to achieve accuracy that's unnecessary, while not being able to handle the situation where he loses the meaning.

The difference between more and less proficient readers is not a difference in the reading process but in how well they are able to use it. Our research has made it possible to infer from their miscues the control that readers are exercising over the reading process. It should also provide a basis for instructional procedures designed to improve that control.

Some General Implications Concerning Specific Taxonomy Categories

P. David Allen

In the previous section, each category of the Taxonomy was discussed in order to clarify the assumptions underlying the category as well as to present its purpose. Discrete data regarding each category are valuable, but it is only when the categories are related to each other that the data begin to generate significant implications regarding the reading process, as well as implications for reading instruction.

This portion of the volume generally is concerned with the inter-relationship of the various categories. However, it is felt that some categories merit special attention. The categories discussed in this chapter are correction, graphic and phonemic proximity, intonation, and semantic word relationships.

Correction

It is difficult to talk about correction behavior without examining its interaction with other systems operating in the reading process. As isolated data, correction percentages do give us some information about the reader's use or non-use of such a strategy, but it is only when we examine correction behavior in relation to such information as graphemic and phonemic proximity, syntactic acceptability, and semantic acceptability that the correction phenomenon takes on full significance.

An interesting concept that has come out of the research is the notion of syntactic and/or semantic dissonance. The fact that something a reader has produced does not sound like real language or does not make sense causes him to reprocess the information. This reprocessing, or correction behavior if you will, is most frequently cued by lack of syntactic and semantic fit of the miscue with the text. Generally, if the miscue fits syntactically and semantically and is in alternate form, the reader is less likely to correct it than if the miscue lacks syntactic and/or semantic fit. The following examples illustrate this point:

Miscue is corrected:

ⓒ learned to
I leaned on the baby bed.

Miscue is not corrected:

can
You could get a sponsor.

Also of interest here is the finding that miscues which are partially acceptable structurally and semantically tend to be corrected by the reader more often than miscues which are totally acceptable. Particularly, miscues which fit with the portion of sentence preceeding the miscue but do not fit with what follows the miscue are those which tend to be corrected. Again, this can be seen in the corrected miscue shown above.

Readers are successful in 75-90 percent of their correction attempts. This is again indicative of the strengths the reader brings to the task. The percentage of successful correction attempts strongly implies that teachers need to provide children with an opportunity to correct themselves.

Correction behavior is not closely related to graphemic or phonemic proximity. There is some evidence to indicate that a strong reliance on graphemic and phonemic cues results in a low percentage of correction attempts. If the miscue is in close graphemic or phonemic proximity to the expected response, the reader is not motivated to correct the miscue.

There is a relationship between the percentage of correction attempts and comprehension ratings. Generally, readers who have low comprehension scores show a tendency to make few correction attempts. On the other hand, readers who have high comprehension ratings behave in two ways. They either show a very high rate of correction attempts or a very low rate of correction attempts. It seems to depend largely on the reader's individual mode. Some proficient readers seem to find it unnecessary to correct but show evidence of silent correction when they encounter the same expected response further along in the text and read it correctly. Other proficient readers do find it necessary to correct, and do so before proceeding. There is some evidence that this is related to developmental levels of the readers. Young children and older children who are proficient readers tend to correct less frequently than those in middle grades. Fourth-grade proficient readers in particular exhibit a greater tendency to correct. This could be related to a desire to please the teacher by demonstrating awareness of a miscue.

Miscues that result in intonationally unacceptable readings are most frequently corrected, while miscues which are totally acceptable in the intonational category have a low percentage of correction.

There is a low percentage of correction attempts on dialect miscues. Such miscues are acceptable to the reader, and thus the need for correction is not apparent to the reader. Possibly, when dialect miscues are corrected, it is due to the reader's understanding that there are divergent dialects. Such correction attempts may also be cued by a reading teacher's insistence on correct English. ("I want to hear those endings!")

It would seem that just as reading is behavior which is cued and miscues are a part of this process, correction of miscues is also a systematic natural part of the reading process. Specific kinds of cues related to miscue production trigger correction behavior. Accepting the position that correction is a natural part of the reading process poses several implications for reading instruction. Chief among these is that teachers need to provide readers with every opportunity to develop correction strategies. Obviously, teaching with an emphasis on words or parts of words does not give readers an opportunity to use all of the cue systems they are able to bring to bear on the reading process. This can also be said of such devices as the tachistoscope, which prevents readers from regressing, reprocessing and making a new prediction about the reading. The process of reading is used to get meaning from the printed page. All of the strategies, including correction, which enhance the deriving of meaning from print need to be encouraged if fluency in reading is the objective of instruction.

Graphic and Phonemic Proximity
These categories allow the researcher to compute the means which may be examined separately or compared. Findings revealed by calculating these means include these: first, mean graphic proximity is higher at all developmental levels than mean phonemic proximity; second, phonemic proximity tends to follow patterns set by graphic proximity levels, but it is substantially lower than graphic similarity; third, the consistently higher graphic proximity level indicates that graphic input has more influence on the choice of an oral response than the phonemic cue system; and last, readers at all levels are proficient at establishing relationships between the graphic and phonemic cue systems.

Two important implications of these findings deserve mention. First, the findings raise questions about assumed differences in traditional teaching techniques. Look-say, phonics, and structural analysis techniques force the reader to focus on graphic input; that is, they are alike in their teaching emphasis. Second, teachers need not teach readers "their sounds." Readers bring a complex and highly developed sound system to the reading task and are quite proficient at relating it to the graphic cues within the total context of language. On the other hand, growth in reading is retarded when individuals are asked to distort their language in drills which isolate the phonemic and graphic systems from functioning language contexts.

Intonation
The implications suggested by examining the data generated in the intonation category suggest that while a reader's intonation is acceptable, the syntactic and semantic acceptability of the oral reading of children who are beginning readers or who are experiencing some reading difficulty can be quite low. There is also evidence the readers can produce acceptable intonation even when they fail to comprehend. Acceptable intonation is not the same as preferred

intonation. It can be slightly awkward with hesitation and still be acceptable within English patterns.

It appears that some teachers feel that intonation miscues are caused because the reader does not perceive the punctuation marks. If this were true, how is it possible to know the correct intonation to use while reading a question or exclamation? Does the reader look first to the question mark or exclamation point at the end of the sentence, and then go back to the beginning of the sentence to begin reading? It is more likely that the question marker at the beginning of the question causes the reader to use proper intonation.

The reader's correct anticipation of the structure used by the author cues correct intonation. It is when the reader is unfamiliar with the structure used by the author, or when the reader predicts a different structure than that used by the author, that intonation miscues occur. The number of times readers use incorrect intonation is small when compared to the number of times correct intonation is used.

Even readers who are having a problem with the author's syntactic structures give evidence that they are able to use syntax when they place terminals into the text in order to mark off the ends of phrases or clauses.

Many of the intonation miscues involve direct quotations. This problem arises from the lack of enough information in the text to identify the speaker and from long and confusing dialog carriers. *Said* is an easy dialog carrier for readers to identify. Words like *smiled* and *laughed*, when used as dialog carriers, can lead to confusion for the reader.

Semantic Word Relationships
Because reading is not a word-by-word activity, one wonders about the value of vocabulary items found in the testing situation where it is assumed that if readers can substitute a word for another word semantically, they will be able to understand the wider context of the passage. It is interesting that children are able to handle meaning by manipulating syntax so that word-for-word level is not necessary to meaning retention. It is impossible to make all decisions about semantic relationships by simply comparing words; this semantic aspect is not an absolute. We must consider reading in a contextual situation and forget about making judgments on a child's ability to say, "This word means this word," in isolation.

A reader's failure to produce miscues synonymous to expected responses might only be a reflection of marked structural changes that do not affect meaning. There is some evidence that more proficient readers avail themselves of cueing systems at the word level as well as at the wider level of context. On the other hand, any over-reliance on vocabulary tests as valid predictors of reading success fails to consider the syntactic-restructuring and meaning-preserving strategies that proficient readers bring to the reading task.

The Three Cue Systems

Reading is a sampling, predicting, confirming process during which the reader makes use of three types of information—or cue systems—simultaneously. These three cue systems are graphophonic, syntactic, and semantic. The fact that the reader uses the cue systems simultaneously is important. While this interrelationship of the cue systems is crucial to the understanding of the reading process, each will be dealt with separately.

#1—Graphophonic

Dorothy M. Menosky
An associate professor of education, Dorothy M. Menosky teaches courses in research and reading, practicum, and psycholinguistics of reading at Jersey City State College.

When we talk about the graphophonic cue system, we are referring to the complex set of relationships between the graphic respresentations (such as the shapes of letters and spelling patterns), and the phonological representations of the language. Simply: shapes and sounds.

Using the Goodman Taxonomy, each substitution miscue is coded for both graphic and phonemic proximity. The range for both categories is from zero (no proximity) to nine (high proximity).

Listed below are five substitution miscues which would be coded for graphic and phonemic proximity. Each miscue is a substitution for the word *canary*.

Text: He had a *canary* in a cage.
OR 1   He had a *bird* in a cage.
OR 2   He had a *carrot* in a cage.
OR 3   He had a *cannery* in a cage.
Text: The *canary* sang sweetly.
OR 4   The *carrot* sang sweetly.
OR 5   The *carried* sang sweetly.

Using the High, Moderate, and Little or No Proximity category grouping established by Harris in her chapter on graphic and phonemic proximity, the above miscues can be categorized as follows:

Miscue	Graphic	Phonemic
canary/bird	L	L
canary/carrot	M	M
canary/cannery	H	H
canary/carried	M	M-H

Qualitative judgments can be made concerning miscues if we analyze data across categories. Two measures of quality are syntactic acceptability and semantic acceptability. The accompanying list shows that if we apply these additional measures, certain observations can be made.

Sentence with Miscue	Graphic Prox.	Phonemic Prox.	Syntactic Accept.	Semantic Accept.
He had a bird in a cage.	L	L	Full	Full
He had a carrot in a cage.	M	M	Full	Partial
He had a cannery in a cage.	H	H	Full	No
He had a carried in a cage.	M	M-H	No	No

Now we can see that the best miscue is the one with no graphic or phonemic proximity. This miscue, *bird*, had full syntactic and semantic acceptability. The least successful miscue was *carried*, which lacked both syntactic and semantic acceptability. It should be noted that the graphic and phonemic proximity ratings for *carried* were higher than for *bird*. It should also be noted that graphic and phonemic proximity have little to do with miscue quality.

During the reading process, the reader must anticipate the syntactic and semantic structures which the author intended; in other words, he or she must guess what's coming next. Obviously, the reader doesn't use every cue that's available. The perception and identification of every cue is unnecessary. Not only would this result in a waste of time, but it would actually "get in the way" of the reading process. Instead, the reader needs only to sample from the wealth of information available. Those of you who are reading this article did not identify every letter, every sound, every grammatical function, and every syntactic structure. If you had, you would probably still be on the first paragraph.

During the activities of sampling and predicting, the reader has both the graphemes and related phonemes available as cues, inter-acting with the other cue systems—bolstering and reinforcing one another.

The graphophonic cue system has two very important functions. While the reader is predicting, the graphophonic cues can provide some hint which convinces him to go on with his prediction. The graphophonic cues also provide that extra, or added, information which helps the reader to correct a miscue which doesn't sound right or doesn't make sense to him. For example, a friend of mine was reading aloud from a menu which featured French fried or mashed Idaho's. She read: French fried or mashed potatoes. Because my friend's concern was with semantics, and because her miscue made perfect sense to her, she went right on, never looking back at that word Idaho's, in spite of the fact that she had not correctly utilized all of the graphophonic cues.

When I read a newspaper column headline which declared: Jesus Christ to be honored, that same concern—with semantics—caused me to look back again, gather more graphic cues, and then read the headline correctly as: Justice Christ to be honored.

Referring now to my previous statements: that graphophonic cues can provide some hint that convinces the reader to go on with his prediction, and that graphophonic cues can provide added information for correction purposes, there was more than enough graphic and phonemic similarity between Justice and Jesus in front of the word Christ to convince me that the sentence read Jesus Christ to be honored. But, because it didn't make sense to me—I couldn't figure out how they could honor him now—I went back for more information.

For my friend, and for me, the graphophonic cues played roles that were both similar and different. The important thing is that we were able to use these cues, along with the other cue systems, to acquire the information we needed in order to get meaning from what we had read.

The research has shown that as readers develop they move toward an increased consideration of syntactic and semantic concerns, and away from graphic and phonemic concerns. Some interesting things happen, though, when readers are asked to handle material of varying difficulty. In one study, readers were given a succession of stories to read, each more difficult than the previous one. As the stories got harder, the readers produced miscues with closer graphic and phonemic proximity.

The same thing happened when a group of tenth graders were asked to read a story and a magazine article. The magazine article was more difficult for them. The style of the author consisted of long, clause-within-clause type sentences, so the syntax was difficult for the readers. Although the topic, the generation gap, was a familiar one, the semantics proved difficult because of the author's use of satire and his references to experiences beyond the ken of the readers. And finally, everything was complicated by the fact that the article contained a number of words and phrases which were completely unfamiliar to the readers. For example:

> When the scales start falling from their eyes, I suspect that
> many of today's adults will eventually join with their children in
> the fight against the men with goiters for cerebrums who want to
> do us in.

In one sentence we have phrases such as "scales falling from their eyes," and "do us in," as well as the words *goiters* and *cerebrums.*

The miscues produced during the reading of this article showed that these tenth graders were making a greater use of graphophonic cues than they did when they read the story. More than that, when their use of syntactic and semantic cues bogged down and when they were confronted with unfamiliar words, these readers shifted to a greater use of phonemic cues. In all cases, readers who were not overly concerned with phonemic cues had substitutions that were closer to the text graphically than phonemically.

Readers apparently find it more useful to rely on visual cues than on matching phonological cues. This is not surprising in a process that uses visual output. All of the readers, except those who had been trained to be word bound or phonics bound or both, tended to be more concerned with syntactic and semantic features of the language than with graphic and phonemic features. When their miscues produced unacceptable syntactic or semantic structures, the readers made successful corrections by looking back at graphic cues.

The largest number of unsuccessful corrections occurred when readers, unable to make use of syntactic or semantic cues and confronted with unfamiliar words, attempted to "sound out" those words.

In terms of the reader's ultimate goal, the graphophonic cues are of less importance than the other cues. When readers make use of the cue systems interrelatedly and simultaneously in their search for meaning, the syntactic and semantic cue systems dictate the use of the graphophonic cue system.

The graphophonic cue system is indeed important, but its significance lies in the relation to and interaction with the other cue systems. What is important for the reader, then, is not the constant use of graphophonic cues nor the exact use of graphophonic cues. What is important is the reader's ability to judge when it's necessary to make use of these cues.

Phonics problems are not the cause of kids' inability to read a piece of written material (unless by "phonics problems" we mean the overuse of this strategy). But graphophonic cues are useful for readers who integrate and interrelate the cue systems, and who, in their simultaneous processing of these cues, are able to make decisions about importance, and therefore use the cues that are necessary when they are necessary.

The miscue research has clearly indicated this interplay between cues. Readers were not merely engaged in matching letters and sounds; they were involved in the complex psycholinguistic process of reading.

#2—Syntactic

Carolyn L. Burke

Because language is composed of three interrelated systems, it is impossible to consider the syntactic system without dealing with the other two. In fact, our only means of checking for success in the operation of one system is to verify it in relationship to the others. We can demonstrate this interdependence by considering the varying support available to the reader when words are read in or out of context.

When we read words from a list, our choice of available language cues is quite limited.

canary
Sven
drag

We can hope to recognize the word instantly. Or, we can use graphophonic strategies to sound the word out and hope that we then recognize it as an item from our oral language vocabulary. But in either case we are left with no verification for what we have produced, no external support for our decision. When reading in context, our choices are expanded. If we produce an item that looks and sounds like what is written, we verify by testing its syntactic and semantic acceptability. If what we produce is syntactically acceptable, it can be verified in relation to semantic acceptability and graphophonic information. When what is produced is syntactically and semantically acceptable, it can be verified on the basis of graphic similarity. The successful application of one system is measured by the functioning of the other two systems.

Now let's examine our three list items as they occurred in context and generated one set of miscues (reader-produced variations from the text).

1. She was a small yellow canary, hanging very still in the air.
2. I don't understand what's wrong with her, said Sven.
3. ...I could scarcely drag myself out of bed.

These miscues—*care* for *canary*, *seven* for *Sven*, and *drug* for *drag*—are graphically and phonemically similar to the text items. In fact, in the case of *seven* for *Sven* the reader has come as close to what was expected on the page as is graphophonically possible for an English speaker. However, if the reader fails to ask two questions:

Does what I've produced sound like language? (syntax)
Does what I've produced have meaning sense? (semantics)

there will be no way of verifying the attempt.

In the three examples above, the graphophonic system has been applied with some demonstration of effectiveness. Only testing the usefulness of its application against the functioning of the syntactic and semantic systems will generate any reappraisal of the products. On the basis of the two questions these three miscues should be judged unacceptable and an attempt made to correct. And that, in fact, is what the readers who made these miscues did do.

Effective readers tend to recognize unsuccessful miscues—ones that produce syntactically and semantically unacceptable structures —and to attempt to correct them. Correction attempts, once made, are generally successful in producing fully acceptable structures. Restated, this means that the reader's concern for interrelating the cues of all three language systems is the critical variable in generating semantically acceptable structures. But the concern for acceptability and the effective application of verification strategies in no way implies the exact reproduction of the text.

This relationship between acceptability and exactness can be explored by examining a second set of miscues generated out of the same text.

                            cardinal
1. She was a small yellow canary, hanging very still in the air.

                                      Steve
2. I don't understand what's wrong with her, said Sven.

                        draw
3. . . . I could scarcely drag myself out of bed.

These miscues—*cardinal* for *canary*, *Steve* for *Sven*, and *draw* for *drag*—are of the kind which a reader will tend not to correct. Having produced the structures this way, the reader will be satisfied with the results and continue on. The reader has gone through the same process as that which occurred with the first three examples and has verified what was produced on the basis of the three language systems. What was produced looked like what was on the page, it made language sense to the reader and it had an acceptable meaning. The result of the verification process was a reader decision that there was no reason to reprocess this information. We can effectively apply the verification processes open to us as readers and find that what is produced is not exactly what was in print. Reading is not an exact process.

The three language systems function fully only when they function interdependently. While meaning is the system shared by all communication processes, it is the syntactic system which is unique to language. The syntactic system acts as the exchange through which the three language systems interact, and it offers the fundamental support to the reading process. We can consider this relationship on the basis of three points of information.

Point 1: Beginning readers bring a strong sense of grammatical structure to the reading process. This competency is demonstrated by their ability to retain the grammatical function of miscued items. For example, in one of the sentences which we have already examined,

cardinal
She was a small yellow canary, hanging very still in the air.

the reader's miscue, *cardinal*, retains the noun function that *canary* filled in the text. Even at points where the reader is having difficulty dealing with the intended meaning, a sense of the structural relationships can be maintained.

Perspective on the strength and significance of this grammatical sense can be gained by examining the relative ability of average readers in the second and sixth grades to retain the grammatical function of miscued text items. Information gathered in one such experiment is compiled in Figure 1.

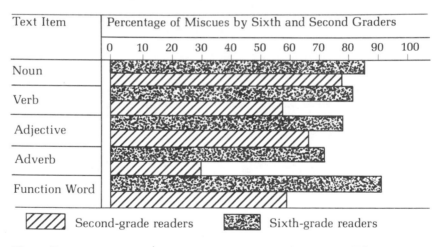

Text Item	Percentage of Miscues by Sixth and Second Graders
	0 10 20 30 40 50 60 70 80 90 100
Noun	
Verb	
Adjective	
Adverb	
Function Word	

▨ Second-grade readers   ▨ Sixth-grade readers

Fig. 1 Percentage of miscues retaining grammatical function of the text item.

The primary message which the figure conveys is that the ability to apply a sense of grammatical structure is well developed in the second graders. The growth over the next four years is minimal compared to that which the beginning readers have already experienced. More detailed examination provides other interrelationships embedded within this general picture.

For both groups of readers, the percentage of retention varies depending upon the grammatical function of the text item, as shown in Figure 2. The grammatical functions can be ranked according to their relative difficulty for the second and sixth graders.

Miscues by Second Graders		Miscues by Sixth Graders	
Grammatical Function	Retention (%)	Grammatical Function	Retention (%)
Noun	77	Function word	94
Adjective	66	Noun	86
Function Word	60	Verb	84
Verb	57	Adjective	77
Adverb	32	Adverb	70

Fig. 2 Ranking of retention of grammatical function for average second- and sixth-grade readers

Not only are the second graders less proficient at maintaining grammatical function, but the relative difficulty which specific functions present varies from that experienced by the sixth graders. The rank order presented by the sixth graders closely reflects the basic predictability of the various functions within English. In this regard the sixth graders present much the same profile as that of any proficient adult reader. Let's briefly explore this syntactic predictability by discussing the most and least frequently retained grammatical functions.

Function words—all of the prepositions, determiners that come before nouns, in fact, all of the words which are not nouns, verbs, adjectives or adverbs—are the most frequently retained. The explanation for this can be glimpsed in the very term used to describe them, "function." These words are the glue that holds the language together. They announce the phrase and clause structures as they are strung together in sentences. Since a limited number of structural patterns are repetitively used within the language, they become highly predictable.

Although readers have great facility in retaining function words because they are structurally predictable, these words hold minimal semantic meaning and are easily interchangeable, one with the other.

> about
> ~~of~~
> "I have an idea for a TV program," he said.

Therefore, a number of miscues are made on function words, but these miscues do not necessarily alter the syntactic structure or disturb the semantic acceptability of the sentences in which they occur.

Adverbs are the least frequently retained function for both the second and sixth graders. This seems directly related to the adverb's ability to move within sentences without changing the essential meaning of the sentence.

> He ran *happily.*
> *Happily* he ran.
> He *happily* ran.

There is no one familiar position in which the reader can expect to find an adverbial. Because of this, all readers exercise less predictive power when handling adverbs and are bound to produce more syntactic miscues in relationship to them than to other grammatical functions.

Now it becomes interesting to examine a couple of the instances in which the second graders do not reflect the relative predictability of grammatical functions within the language—verbs and function words. At least one explanation can be sought in the structure of the material which they are frequently asked to use. In the instance of verbs their earliest reading experiences often involve such structures as:

> See Spot run.
> Come here.
> Look at my toy.

Substitutions of *Sally* for *See* are to be anticipated if we assume that the young reader will make intuitive use of the syntactic predictive powers developed as a speaker. The noun phrase in the initial sentence position is the most prevalent structure.

The possible explanations for function words are not as obvious as the one for verbs, but probably result from a combination of factors. The first is that the initial introduction of function words is not made until the third pre-primer of many basal series. By this time the young readers have learned not to anticipate such a structure in print. The second is that many of these same programs focus the reader's attention upon individual words instead of larger structural units. This frequently makes children's initial reading attempts closely resemble word calling from lists, limiting them to recall or graphophonic strategies. Under these circumstances the miscue produced tends to be a graphically similar word previously taught but with no necessary syntactic or semantic relationship to the text. Yet a third factor has to do with the young language user's own lack of experience or flexibility with specific syntactic structures.

Beginning readers quickly demonstrate facility in handling the grammatical structures of their language. This is a strength which they bring from their oral language development. The more clearly they see speech and reading as alternate expressions of the language process and the more they are encouraged to use their language intuition, the more rapid will be their initial growth as readers.

Point 2: The syntactic acceptability of miscues is always significantly higher than is their semantic acceptability. A reader's ability to retain the grammatical function of a text item (Point 1) actually is a result of that reader's attention to the phrase and clause structures of language. Individual items do not have grammatical functions.

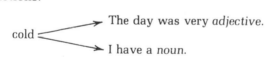

cold → The day was very *adjective.*
→ I have a *noun.*

It is only by combining one's intuitive knowledge of language structure with syntactic cues from the material already processed that a reader can make predictions concerning the grammatical function of the item presently being processed.

That this is the case is demonstrated by the fact that 71 percent of the miscue-containing sentences generated by average second graders and 74 percent of those generated by average sixth graders are syntactically acceptable. (Included in these figures are sentences containing more than one miscue.)

They took pictures of (their) mother wearing her ^pretty party clothes.

So the picture was sent to the contest which took place in Mr. Vine's ^the Wahn's

Candy Shop.

down and looked
I sat looking down at Andrew.

Even as these readers vary from the structure provided by the author they tend to remain within the confines of the available structures of the language.

The strength of this grasp of the grammatical units of language is further demonstrated when the readers' ability to maintain the semantic acceptability of the same sentences is examined—43 percent for the second graders, 44 percent for the sixth graders. While syntax is generated from a finite set of rules and structures, meaning relationships are infinite and therefore less predictable.

Point 3: Miscues involving grammatical transformations tend to cluster around pivotal points in sentence structure. Sentences are composed of combinations of phrases and clauses. The syntactic sequence within any one of these units is more predictable than are the possible combinations among them. These junctures where one structure ends and another begins can be viewed as pivotal points in the sentence. Think about the various syntactic patterns which can conclude a sentence starting with the noun phrase *The boy...*

   ... whistled in the dark.
   ..., who was left, hid in the closet.
   ..., without another thought, waited for her return.

At such pivotal points there are no cues from the right hand side of the sentence (the portion already read) which will allow the reader to unerringly predict the upcoming structure, even when that reader might have accurately predicted the meaning that the author intends to convey. This gives added significance to the percentages previously mentioned, for syntactic and semantic acceptability of miscue-containing sentences read by average second and sixth graders (second graders: 71 and 43 percent respectively; sixth graders, 74 and 44 percent).

The most effective reader, making adequate use of all available language cues, can be expected to produce miscues involving grammatical transformations of the author's structures. Thus effective readers can be distinguished from less effective readers, not by the number of miscues made but by the fact that effective readers' miscues tend to cluster at pivotal points in sentence structure and to represent alternate patterns available within the language. Samples from average sixth graders demonstrate this language facility.

A miscue such as: *And her mate followed her* in place of *And her mate followed after* is completely acceptable. The reader departed from the text at the point where it was possible to produce an alternate structure. And, in fact, this particular miscue is very common for children from the fourth through sixth grades, where they are not as familiar with handling the adverbial in this position.

In the miscue: *Chip was hungry and had expected food but he sat facing the sheep*, the child is predicting that the verb structure in the second clause is going to look like the verb structure in the preceding clause, and in fact it could have been so: *Chip was hungry and had expected food but he had sat facing the sheep.*

In yet another story used for miscue research there is the sentence: *Besides, our teacher says if you know how to think and know enough words to express your thoughts, there isn't anything you can't say or do.* A miscue pattern which became typical for the sixth graders reading this story is as follows: *Besides, our teacher said, "If you know how to think and . . ."* At a point where the author could have chosen to go to direct speech he chose to continue in narrative form. The readers did not, and very neatly transformed the structure into a dialog carrier and direct speech by a simple shift in intonation. No other changes were needed, and the reconstructed sentence was perfectly acceptable.

Moving dependent clauses from one sentence to another was also quite frequent and, again, is a demonstration of a pivotal structural point. *She turned once more to the tent halting after a step or two, when she saw Chip lying a few feet away. She trotted to him, sniffing at his still head, whining close to his ear, pawing his shoulder.* One small intonation shift and the reader has produced: *She turned once more to the tent halting after a step or two. When she saw Chip lying a few feet away, she trotted to him, sniffing at his still head, whining close to his ear, pawing his shoulder.* Some young readers have produced as many as twenty or thirty such miscues within one text.

At points where the language offers structural options, proficient readers will always produce some grammatical transformations. It even seems possible to conclude that such miscues will increase or diminish for a given reader, depending on similarity with the author's written dialect and/or that reader's growing familiarity with a particular author's structural style.

In conclusion: The syntactic system can be pictured as that point at which thought processes and language processes merge in deep structure. If the reader recognizes language as a specific instance of meaning-gaining and recognizes reading as an expression of language, then the finite nature of the syntactic system and the intuitive control of it developed in oral language usage are immediately available to the reader. Perhaps the single most important question which readers can ask, basic to the rest of their attack upon written language, is: Does it sound like language?

#3—Semantic

William D. Page

No productive discussion of semantic cue systems in reading can ignore the fact that meaning and knowledge are interrelated in the process of comprehending print.

Knowledge is the beginning and the end of the reading process. The reading process begins with the author's thoughts, which include his or her knowledge *of* the world and *about* the world (S. Langer, 1953, p. 22). Knowledge *of* the world includes the author's sense impressions, the feelings and images that resist encoding in language forms. What sets the reading process in motion is the author's decision to encode his knowledge *about* the world in writing for readers to encounter. The reader's will to construct knowledge from reconstructed meanings guides the reader's part in the reading process. The end in view for the reader is comprehension, the result of "... the successful processing of three kinds of information: graphophonic, syntactic, and semantic" (K. Goodman, 1970, p. 29). We are concerned here with semantic information and its organization into a system of cues in the reconstruction of meaning for comprehension.

Comprehension is a basis for thinking about semantic cues in reading. When we try to test comprehension, we often think of a matching process. Something that the author does is to be matched with something that the reader does. This presents problems for behavioral research because most of what the author and reader do is not observable. We can not look into the brain and observe it working.

The elements of the process include the printed material, internalized sentences, phrase and clause relationships, analogies or meanings, and personal knowledge. Each has a dual existence in the thinking of the author and the reader in the communicative process called reading.

The *Goodman Model of Reading* (K. Goodman, 1970, pp. 30-31) organizes the elements—events, decisions, and systems of reading—into a complex web of interrelationships. Extracted from this complex, and placed in linear form in Figure 1, at the risk of oversimplification, are five key forms: knowledge, meaning, deep structure, internal surface structure, and external surface structure.

The author's knowledge is transformed into analogies, the basis of people's ability to represent their thoughts (S. Langer, 1953, p. 30). In Figure 1, representation through analogy is called meaning. Deep structures or clause relationships are assigned to meanings using the author's language rules. Once deep structures are assigned, individual authors can select from their repertoire of surface structures the specific ways in which they want to express themselves. A pre-writing post-semantic state called surface structure (W. Chafe, 1971, p. 43) is shown in Figure 1. The transformation from internal to external surface structure is the production of writing.

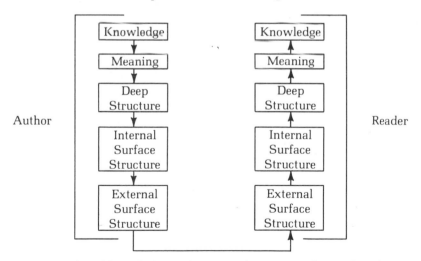

Fig. 1 Transfer of knowledge and meaning between author and reader

The reader, upon encountering the author's work—the observable surface structures we call writing or printed material—constructs his or her own knowledge of the author's thoughts. The end in view for the reader is the construction of personal knowledge, but the means for this end are no simpler than the process the author waded through to produce the writing.

Readers capture visual images of the surface structures in sensory store, holding them just long enough to fill the limited capacity of their short-term memory with selected samples. The reader, like the author, is engaged in a selection process based on the manner in which the reader's inquiry has been organized. Once the visual images are internalized, the reading process is again hidden, as it was with the author before writing occurred.

The reader's language is the organizer, because language is so automatic from constant use that it can permeate both short-term memory and long-term memory with remarkable facility. While the samplings of surface structures are held in the reader's short-term memory, the reader is able to process them using information from the long-term memory. Deep structures—phrases and clausal relationships—are assigned to the samplings. The rules of the reader's language determine the deep structures he assigns.

Dialect divergence between the author and the reader makes it unlikely in ordinary reading that a precise match will occur between the deep structures assigned by the reader and the deep structures of the author. Only through specialized training, as in a scientific discipline, can deep structures be precisely reconstructed. For a precise match, both the author and the reader must have had common experiences in their training, as in the case of a medical doctor and a pharmacist. Most reading occurs outside the realm and methodological constraints of a discipline.

The deep structures are what readers work with to produce analogies in their attempts to reconstruct the author's meanings. From these reconstructed analogies, the reader can infer. The inference process is constructive rather than reconstructive, since it produces personal knowledge that is uniquely the possession of the reader. Just as portions of the author's knowledge do not lend themselves to encoding in language, the reader's personal knowledge includes thoughts, ideas, and impressions from his or her reading. The reader's inferences are interrelated with previous experience. Though no precise match between the author's knowledge and the reader's knowledge is probable, these two instances of knowledge are, in fact, the beginning and the end of the reading process.

When reading is viewed as a search for knowledge, a psycholinguistic guessing game (K. Goodman, 1967), productive parallels with the inquiry process can be found. Inquiry includes an encounter with information, the construction of predictive and explanatory hypotheses, tests to verify, modify, or dismiss the hypotheses, and the production of statements interpreting the findings. The interpretive statements are knowledge, the result of inquiry. The reader engages in these same operations.

Analysis of the reader's correction performance brings the semantic cue system into focus as a strategy of verification in the reading process. Miscue analysis permits assessment of the way the reader uses graphophonic, syntactic, and semantic information to verify his guesses. The observation categories that yield direct insights when viewed in relation to one another are: Correction, Graphic Proximity, Phonemic Proximity, Syntactic Proximity, Semantic Proximity, Syntactic Acceptability, and Semantic Acceptability.

By seeking out the patterns of produced miscues, it is possible to piece together the elements of process. The underlying theory that reading is inquiry provides a grid of decision structures that guides and predicts the patterns. Treating the information categories—graphophonic, syntactic, and semantic—as cue systems that function as verification strategies is one productive tactic for generating insights. Consider the following example of how the patterns can be structured in relation to correction performance.

A miscue can be viewed as a guess that the reader seeks to verify by using graphophonic, syntactic, and semantic information. Once the miscue occurs, it is a candidate for correction by the reader. If the reader corrects a miscue, we know that the miscue was a source of dissatisfaction. The dissatisfaction results from the reader's unsuccessful verification attempt. Analysis of graphophonic, syntactic, and semantic characteristics of corrected miscues reveals the tools the reader is using to verify guesses.

Similarly, the uncorrected miscue reveals to some extent the verification strategies in *disuse*. A semantically and syntactically acceptable miscue might be graphophonically divergent and still not be corrected. This suggests the reader is using the syntactic and semantic cue systems and ignoring the graphophonic system. The following uncorrected miscue produced by a young reader is an example.

Expected Response
"I'm sorry they are not real," said Danny.
"It would be nice to play with a dinosaur."

(S. Hoff, 1958, p. 10)

Observed Response
"I'm sorry they are not real," said Danny.
"It would be nice to play with one."

The substitution of one for a dinosaur does no syntactic or semantic injustice to either the sentence or the story. Yet, the graphophonic match between the expected response and the observed response is absent. The reader is using the syntactic and semantic cue systems to predict, generate, and verify the oral response. At the same time, the reader is disregarding the graphophonic cue system either consciously or unconsciously.

A miscue reveals the strategies the reader uses. By conjugating the logical possibilities, miscue analysis generates insights into specific characteristics of a reader in relation to specific reading material, as well as producing insights into the reading process itself. Figure 2 represents a pattern of possibilities.

Note that Figure 2 shows the miscue as a candidate for verification using three cue systems; graphophonic, syntactic, and semantic. Verification attempts result in satisfaction yielding no correction attempt, or dissatisfaction yielding a correction attempt. No correction attempt is also shown as resulting from the reader's inability to form a correction attempt because no cue systems are operating effectively.

Once a correction attempt occurs, it can be classified as successful, partially successful, or unsuccessful. All three of these alternatives are shown as candidates for verification using the same three cue systems. The complexity of the recycling process is evident, as it is in the more comprehensive Goodman Model of Reading (K. Goodman, 1970, pp. 30-31).

The semantic cue system is not independent of the other systems. In reading, the reconstruction of meaning is a function of the integrated use of the systems, despite the linguistic traditions of attempts to compartmentalize phonetic, graphic, syntactic and semantic structure (W. Chafe, 1970, p. 69). Recognition that the cue systems are inter-related is crucial to understanding reading and improving reading

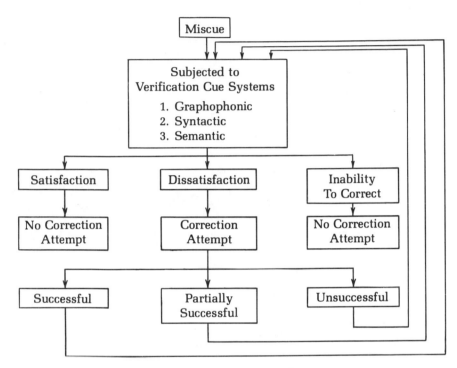

Fig. 2. Possible reader strategies for dealing with miscues

instruction. Despite the fact that we *can* train a potential reader to respond to the graphophonic information while ignoring the syntactic and semantic information, we must ask whether or not that kind of training leads to the objective of reading: comprehension.

References

Chafe, W. *Meaning and the structure of language.* Chicago: University of Chicago Press, 1970.

Goodman, K. Reading: A psycholinguistic guessing game. *Journal of the Reading Specialist*, May 1967.

Goodman, K. Behind the eye: What happens in reading. In K. Goodman and O. Niles, *Reading: Process and program.* Urbana, Ill.: National Council of Teachers of English, 1970.

Hoff, S. *Danny and the dinosaur.* New York: Harper & Row, 1958.

Langer, S. *An introduction to symbolic logic.* New York: Dover, 1953.

Strategies for Comprehension

Yetta M. Goodman
A faculty member at the University of Arizona, Yetta M. Goodman teaches courses in child language development, children's literature, language arts and reading. She is the coauthor of *Reading Miscue Inventory—Procedure for Diagnosis and Evaluation.*

A strategy is a plan which an individual makes to overcome the obstacles in his or her way, to reach a desired goal. In order to plan the best strategy, the individual must know as much about the lay of the land as possible. He must be aware of his own strengths—capitalize on them and minimize his weaknesses. When reading, the student's desired goal is meaning. In order to gain meaning he must have all the language systems (graphophonic, syntactic and semantic) intact and available so he can make the best judgments possible as he overcomes the obstacles of getting at the author's message.

These decisions or judgments each reader makes about how to handle aspects of reading during the act of reading are strategies. All readers show evidence of using reading strategies, but the difference between the poor reader and the proficient reader is that the proficient reader is much more effective in making accurate judgments in choosing appropriate strategies.

As she reads, the proficient reader corrects when she has predicted grammatical or semantic information which is not confirmed by subsequent information. She employs meaning-seeking strategies when she encounters words she has never seen or heard before by using the grammatical and semantic cueing systems. She recognizes name slots and is able to construct a thorough understanding of a character's personality and lifestyle even without being able to pronounce the name. (Remember Rodion Romanovitch Raskolnikoff in *Crime and Punishment* by Dostoyevsky.)

Proficient readers develop and use these strategies and are successful in their use. However, the less proficient readers sometimes need help to support any effective reading strategies they develop as well as to eliminate the ineffective strategies interfering with developing reading proficiency. This aid can be provided in the form of reading strategy lessons. Reading strategy lessons focus on certain problems which an individual reader has, but the problem is embedded within a strong contextual setting in order to provide the reader with all the language cueing systems needed to build effective use of reading strategies. As my colleague Carolyn Burke and I have worked with children helping them support their developing strategies, we have organized a paradigm of reading strategies set forth in the grid on page 96 (Y. Goodman, Burke, and Sherman 1974).

In developing the paradigm we have organized all the strategies around three major ones: predicting, confirming and comprehending. Predicting strategies are those which the reader employs when he samples, selects, and predicts, from any one or from an integration of the three language systems. Confirming strategies are those which the reader uses when he asks himself if what he is reading sounds like language to him and if it makes sense. In addition, confirming strategies include correction strategies which a reader uses as he confirms or disconfirms as he reads. Comprehending strategies include the complex process of integrating the meaning the reader is receiving with the knowledge he brings to the reading task.

The three major strategies are placed on the horizontal axis of the paradigm. On the vertical axis are listed the three language systems. The graphophonic system deals with the graphic display and its relationship to the sound system of the reader. The syntactic system deals with the grammatical cues which the reader employs as he reads, and the semantic system deals with meaning. The language systems and the reading strategies operate in an interrelated fashion. While the reader is dealing with any one of the individual strategies, all the other strategies and systems are still operating. We have isolated the strategies in order to examine them in greater depth and to provide greater insight into reading instruction. Some of the strategies may ultimately fit better under another category of the paradigm or may fit under all categories of the paradigm. The paradigm is merely used to highlight the specific reading strategies which need to be emphasized for a particular reader for instructional purposes. In addition, it is hoped that the paradigm will be used as a basis for further discussion and continued research.

When using a reading strategy lesson with any reader, the teacher must have evidence that the reader needs support in that particular area. There are some strategy lessons which might be beneficial to most readers, but in general, giving readers help when there is no evidence of need may interfere with a reader's appropriate development of reading strategies. This suggests, of course, that the teacher's appraisal of the reader's performance is extremely important. The

GRID OF READING STRATEGIES

	PREDICTING	CONFIRMING	COMPREHENDING

GRAPHOPHONIC	I. Uncommon Spelling Patterns
	  A. Eye Dialect
	  B. Foreign Words and Phrases
	II. Graphic Variations: Personalized
	  A. Print Variations
	  B. Format Variations
		I. Initial, Medial, and Final Graphic Cues: Personalized	

SYNTACTIC	III. Grammatical Function: Word Level
	  A. Nouns as Names for People
	  B. Nouns as Place Names
	  C. Alternative Names
	  D. Titles Preceding Names
	  E. Varieties of Grammatical Functions
	IV. Indicators of Direct Speech
	  A. Dialogue Carriers: Word Level
	  B. Dialogue Carriers: Phrase Level
	  C. Omission of Dialogue Carriers
	V. Complex Grammatical Structures
	  A. Phrase Structures
	  B. Clause Structures
	VI. Derivational Bound Morphemes: Personalized
		II. Punctuation
		  A. Question Markers
		  B. Hyphens
		  C. Commas
		III. Habitual Association
		  A. Thought/Through
		  B. Then/When; What/That
		  C. Varieties of Habitual Associations	

SEMANTIC	VII. Relational Words or Phrases
	  A. Causal Relations
	  B. Contrastive Relations
	  C. Time Relations
	VIII. Negatives
	  A. Contractions
	  B. Context
	IX. Style and Mode
	  A. Type of Material
	  B. Story Line
	X. Pronoun Antecedents
	  A. Male-Female
	  B. Varieties of Pronouns
		IV. Discriminating Significant from Insignificant Information
		  A. Informational Material
		  B. Story Material
		V. Does This Make Sense?
		  A. Correction: Rethink/Reread
		  B. Continuing to Read
		VI. Developing Meaning Through Context
		  A. Synonym Substitution
		  B. Building New Concepts
		  C. Nonword Substitutions: Personalized
			I. Developing and Integrating Concepts
			  A. In Informational Material
			  B. In Story Material
			II. Developing Theme or Generalization
			  A. Through Inferences
			  B. Through Comparisons
			III. Integrating Plot
			  A. Organizing Events
			  B. Development
			IV. Integrating Characterization and Setting
			  A. Who Is Telling the Story?
			  B. Getting to Know the Place
			  C. Relationship of Characterization and Setting to Action
			V. Understanding Motive
			  A. Inferring Humor and Pathos
			  B. Detecting Significant Subtleties
			  C. Propaganda or Point of View

teacher must be able to determine the strategies with which the reader needs help. Miscue analysis would be of great benefit for such diagnostic purposes. Also, teachers must use their professional judgment about what written material could best support the development of a particular reading strategy. They need to select written material that provides the linguistic and conceptual setting which has the appropriate controls to help the reader develop the appropriate strategy.

A strategy lesson may be carefully written by the teacher or may be selected from already prepared material. The material should be a short story or article which meets the criteria of good writing. It must contain language which is familiar to the reader. The grammatical structure should be unambiguous and the meaning must be clear. Concepts and ideas must be within the understanding of the reader as well as interesting to him or her.

At this point, I would like to explore in greater depth a few of the strategy lessons suggested in the paradigm.

Predicting Strategies

Often in written material, authors use "eye" dialect to indicate the socioeconomic class or national origins of a character. Sometimes, they actually use foreign language words or phrases to give more emphasis to setting or characterization. Authors either use the foreign language units or try to more closely represent the character's oral speech by changing the spelling of particular words. Examples of "eye" dialect include *I'm gonna get ya* or *zee sveet babee*. Foreign language units might appear as follows: *Carol said, "Vamanos, we really must hurry,"* or *If we don't meet in Amsterdam in September, "quelle tragedie"* then *I'll see you at Christmas time.* Most proficient readers develop strategies to handle these types of reading situations and are often able to explain the meaning.

The unusual language unit is initially predicted by using graphophonic cues and noting that the language represented is not similar to the rest of the author's language or that the spelling patterns are unfamiliar. There are, however, some readers who are disconcerted by these. They tend to sit and look at these sections, trying to sound out the words or phrases until someone can help them. Others simply give up, read no further, and decide that this particular piece of writing is too difficult. Therefore, a reading strategy which would help the reader predict or anticipate non-English graphic units or "eye" dialect might prove helpful to readers who have not developed effective reading strategies in such settings. This particular strategy is best taught whenever students first encounter "eye" dialect or foreign phrases in their readings. Comic strips are good for this use. The teacher should help the readers understand the phenomenon through questions:

1.   How does the author let you know that the word or phrase is not like others in the story?

2.   What cues are there, when you look at the word or phrase, that it won't be English? (This might lead to an examination of non-English spelling patterns which could not possibly exist in English.)

Confirming strategies become involved as the reader explores additional cues which substantiate his hypothesis that the author used a foreign word or "eye" dialect. As readers become more proficient, they might explore the language background the author might be presenting, based on cues from the rest of the story.

Lessons which focus on predicting strategies using the syntactic system might help the many readers who do not have appropriate strategies to handle unfamiliar names. These readers need to be convinced that pronouncing the name is far less important than knowing that a particular language unit is a name and then searching for information about the person or thing being named. Such readers need to know that it is acceptable to supply a substitute name until they find out what any particular name might be. (Some they may never meet again and never know.) The first chapter of Mabel Leigh Hunt's story Little Girl with Seven Names (Hunt, 1936) could be an excellent story to use. The little girl, her uncle and parents are introduced in the first chapter. Two pages are devoted to describing the little girl before her name is introduced. Uncle Mark's name appears before you know much about him: "As for her name, truly there were so many words in it that only one person ever called her by all of them. That was her Uncle Mark. And he did it just to tease."

Readers must be helped to focus their attention on references in the story to the little girl and build an understanding of her; references to her uncle and what he is like, and references to the other characters. The readers can be encouraged to select semantic cues which are also available to construct a picture of the characters. No emphasis should be placed on the pronounciation of Melissa Louisa Amanda Miranda Cynthia Jane Farlow.

Reading strategy lessons can also help readers who are not predicting semantic information. Pronouns or titles like Mr. and Mrs.

are often confused by the inexperienced reader. By using a blank for a pronoun slot, a reader can be encouraged to use preceding context in order to predict the appropriate prounoun. It is important for the strategy lesson to have carefully delineated characterization so that there is little ambiguity regarding the antecedents. The following is the beginning of a teacher-prepared reading strategy lesson for a reader with such problems.

> Bobby Scott and his mother were walking through the woods. Bobby was scared. He had heard that wild cats roamed the woods. Bobby's mother held _____ hand tight. _____ moved closer to _____ mother when an owl called out. _____ Scott was tall and strong and Bobby knew she wasn't afraid. As _____ moved closer to _____ mother, he wasn't as scared as he had been.

Confirming Strategies

Often readers who are not using reading strategies effectively confuse two words which look very much alike. They are usually using graphic information and not confirming the choice of word with additional use of syntactic and semantic cues. Sometimes these words have the same grammatical function and related meanings, which makes it even more difficult for readers to overcome their confusion. Examples of habitual associations include brought/bought and for/from. Concentrating on letter-sound correspondence does not help the reader develop confirming strategies which they rely on syntactic and semantic information.

The best way to help the reader overcome habitual associations is to write a strategy lesson with only one of the two confused words included. After the reader has learned to handle one of the habitually associated items in context, then the other one can be written into another reading strategy lesson. It is important to write the story so that the other habitually associated item cannot fit grammatically nor make sense to the reader. Examples of the beginnings of two reading strategy lessons developed for a reader with a thought/through habitual association follow:

> Billy sat looking out of his window. He was thinking. He thought about a party he went to Saturday night. He thought about the good time everybody had. The go-carts were fun. The engine in his go-cart stopped. He thought it had stopped because someone got dirt in it. "I'll have to send Zachary a thank-you note for the good party," thought Billy.

The reader demonstrated his ability to handle the word *thought* through the use of a number of strategy lessons. At that time another story with the word *through* was given to him.

> Billy ran into the house through the front door as fast as he could.
> He threw his coat on the couch as he went through the living room.
> He was really scared. As he ran through the hall he saw that the
> door to his bedroom was closed. Who could have closed it?

Often readers who confuse *through* and *thought* also have a problem with *though*. Since *though* is not common in the conversation of children, it is especially difficult for such readers to predict and confirm when they encounter *though* in reading. The use of *though* in a reading strategy lesson should be avoided as long as possible until the teacher has provided a variety of oral language experiences using *though*. Reading stories with *though* in them will also provide the young readers with experiences which will help them know how *though* is used in a variety of settings.

Another confirming strategy which some readers need help in developing has to do with the use of the semantic system to confirm the significance or insignificance of any particular word. Some readers need to understand that words are not equally important and that there are often contextual clues that indicate which items are most significant. A reader might read a passage such as the following, which has a number of words unknown to him or her. Through discussion the reader determines which words can be omitted while retaining meaning.

> Today is my birthday. I had a good time at my party. My mom
> called us all to the table. "It's time for cake and ice cream," she said.
> We had a delicious chocolate cake. The ice cream was yummy.
> Then I opened my presents. My favorite present came in a huge
> gigantic box. I couldn't even see the top of it until my dad put the
> big box on the floor. Inside of the huge box I saw two roly-poly
> puppies . . . . They were playing with each other. Now they are
> both playing with me.

Comprehending Strategies

Most readers who are not using effective reading strategies are not fully aware that the main goal in reading is to gain meaning. Comprehending strategy lessons should help focus on the process of gaining meaning. In the previous strategy lesson, if the reader decides that gigantic is not too important but the h-u-g-e might be since it appears twice, the teacher might ask the reader if there is anything in the story that tells him what h-u-g-e means. If meaning is his main purpose the reader may be able to say that h-u-g-e probably means big and that gigantic might mean something like big, too.

Readers need to know that sometimes you have to read a whole story to find out what a word means. When a word or idea is significant to an author he will find ways to tell you more about it if you keep reading through the story. In a short story, "Poison," Roald Dahl builds the concept of *krait* for his readers. The following sentences are excerpts from the story which refer to the *krait* only. Stop after you read each section and ask yourself what picture you have of *krait*. See what ideas go through your mind as you use your background and experience to gain the author's meaning. Some of you will probably not pronounce *krait* the way the author might, but you have the concept by the end of the story.

> A krait! Oh, Oh! Where'd it bite you?
>
> It's on my stomach. Lying there asleep.
>
> Then out of the corner of my eye I saw this krait sliding over my pajamas. Small, about ten inches.
>
> They hang around people's houses and they go for warm places.
>
> The bite is quite deadly, except sometimes when you catch it at once; and they kill a fair number of people each year in Bengal, mostly in the villages.
>
> I was going to be ready to cut the bitten place and try to suck the venom out.
>
> Shall we draw the sheet back quick and brush it off before it has time to strike?
>
> "It is not safe," he continued, "because a snake is cold-blooded and anesthetic does not work so well or so quick with such animals."

Conclusions

Reading strategy lessons help the reader focus on meaning. The main strategy which a reader must employ is continuously asking, "*Does this make sense to me?*" Each strategy lesson must be selected or written with this in mind. Since making sense to the individual is a unique aspect of reading, preparing the same strategy lesson for all the children in a classroom will prove fruitless. Strategy lessons must be used only with readers who need additional support with a particular strategy. Some problems apply to a large number of readers, and one lesson may easily be adapted for a small group or for a number of individual readers as the need arises. The significant thing, however, is that the teacher has an extremely important role to serve. The teacher must know enough about language and the reading process to be able to detect where a student needs support and then to select well-written material or write new lessons which will support the development of effective reading strategies.

References
Goodman, Y., Burke, C., & Sherman, B. *Strategies in reading*. In preparation.
Hunt, M. L. *Little girl with seven names*. Philadelphia: Lippincott, 1936.

Modes and Materials

Dorothy M. Menosky

The reading process involves the interrelationship of all these elements:

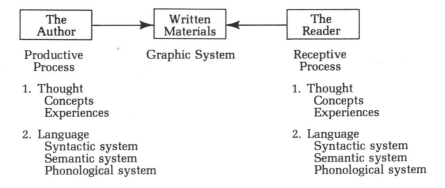

The author's language patterns and some of the past experiences of the author are represented by written materials. Reading, then, is an active process which involves a constant interaction between the reader and the text.

Because the author and the reader contribute varying language structures and experiential backgrounds to the reading process, they must communicate "long distance" across these variations. The reader has to predict the syntactic and semantic structures which the author intended. At those points where the distance between the author and the reader is greatest—where the language patterns and experiences differ most—the reader finds the material least predictable. As the predictability of the material decreases, the chance for confusion or misconception increases. For example, if you were to read an article about cameras and the use of fast film you might think, unless the term is explained, that fast film moves quickly through the camera, or enables you to click the shutter at a greater rate of speed. Those of you who might be smiling as you read this probably know something about fast film; those of you who thought the idea of quick movement made sense probably don't have the information in your experiential background.

Because there is always *some* gap between the author and the reader, reading is not a totally accurate process. Nor is reading a single, monolithic, solidified process. The writer has available a variety of writing formats or styles. A counterpart for the reader is an appropriate reading mode. For example, we read *The Happy Hooker* or *The Exorcist* differently from a research report or a journal article. When we read a new recipe or a how-to-do-it book or the directions for putting kids' toys together, we read carefully because a miscue could be costly.

An opposite approach is utilized when we read street signs, or read an article in order to find one particular item or quote. For these tasks we quickly scan the material, looking for key words.

Somewhere between these two extremes is the type of reading we do most. But even then, one person's soda is another person's pop; and what may be a couch to one, is a davenport to another, and a sofa to still another.

We know that thought and language develop together in a relationship that is interdependent. We also know that the understandings and concepts we develop are both limited and expanded by the experiences we have. Similarly, experiences limit and expand our language. When, therefore, reading instruction is begun by building upon the language and experiences of children, they are allowed to make use of the competencies they already possess. Children come to school equipped with a wonderful tool—their language. Unfortunately, some teachers, who might ordinarily be great experimenters and innovators in regard to educational products not only do *not* make use of children's language, they don't want the kids to use it either. In order to have effective learning, we know that new understandings must be based upon already established ones. It makes sense then to begin with the language and experiences of the child.

When considering modes of reading and materials for reading, three important suggestions should be kept in mind:

1.   Children need a variety of reading materials—not only for interest, but for different purposes.

2.   Experience stories should be written, and they should be written in various styles and formats.

3.   Materials should be meaningful and concept centered.

These suggestions call for a relationship between reading and all of the other language arts, as well as a close relationship between reading and the entire curricular spectrum. The following science experiments are examples of how this might be done. Students are asked to read, to actively engage in a happening, to discuss, and to write.

Curds and Whey

You will need:
    a glass
    milk
    vinegar
What to do:
    Fill the glass ¾ full of milk
    Fill it the rest of the way with vinegar.
    Do not shake or stir it.
    Watch what happens.

Rockets

You will need:
    a small plastic bottle with a snap top
    a set of measuring spoons
    vinegar
    baking soda
What to do:
    Fill the bottle ½ full of vinegar.
    Add ¼ of a teaspoon of baking soda.

Put the top on tightly and quickly.
Stand back.
Watch what happens.

Within these projects we have aspects of reading, speaking, listening, discussing, writing, spelling, science, and mathematics. (Even primary teachers can teach and apply fractions, because now there is a *reason*.)

Another example involves the use of noncooking recipes. These include all of the aspects already mentioned for the science experiments, plus some new experiences and concepts.

Peppermint Pats

You will need:
        4 cups confectioner's sugar
        2/3 cup sweetened condensed milk
        3 drops green food coloring*
        ¼ teaspoon peppermint extract*
        measuring cups and spoons
        flour sifter
        waxed paper
        bowl
        spoon
        fork
        * *any* color and *any* flavor may be used. Red bananas are fun.

What to do:
        Sift confectioner's sugar onto a piece of waxed paper.
        Measure 4 cups.
        Mix milk, flavoring. Shake 3 drops of coloring onto spoon first.
        Then mix it well.
        Beat in sugar gradually. Mix smooth with hands when the candy gets stiff.
        Form into 30 small balls. Place on waxed paper. Flatten with fork tines.

We can use science experiments, recipes, and how-to-do-it projects with a variety of directional materials in which all areas of the language arts are incorporated. Teachers should consider all of their class activities to see if language expansion is possible. When, for example, the class goes for a walk, instead of just collecting leaves, a map of the neighborhood might be made. In art, the students might design their own stamp. This necessitates reading about stamp design and gathering information about the subject of the design. Some students may want to get into philately; others may start letter-writing clubs.

Commercially prepared materials need not be ignored, but we must ask ourselves some important questions about those materials: What about that gap between the author's input and the reader's input? Besides language and experiential background, what concepts are presumed? What concepts are presented? How are the concepts presented?

Unfortunately, some teachers think the concepts presented in a book—such as a geography text—are "automatically" learned by their students just by having them read the chapter and answer the questions at the end of that chapter. This, of course, is a gross misuse of the material. If the material doesn't provide enough clues for that building, the reader cannot learn from reading it.

We might compare this idea to spelling and word games. You have to know the rules, i.e., you have to know how to spell, or break words into syllables, etc., in order to win the game—or even to play the game. The game doesn't teach those skills. The same thing happens with some content reading materials. If the reader already has the concept, she can answer the questions at the end of the chapter. If she doesn't have the concept, the material usually doesn't give it to her. Therefore, she can't answer the questions at the end of the chapter.

For example, an economics book states, "The president believed that the best method is one of priming the pump." If you don't already know that "priming the pump" means to add water to what is already there in order to cause the flow to begin, you can't know how this idea can be applied to money. And if you think that priming refers to painting with a primer coat, you might think, as one reader did, that priming the pump means to paint a picture of what is going on in regard to economic situations.

In all fairness, it should be noted that materials written by students can have the same problems found in commercial materials. Problems can arise when teachers use children's writing for other students to read. These student-produced materials often provide no context and no redundancy. Further, individual children differ in their experiences. In short, when teachers become the publishers—using kids' writing for kids—they are often guilty of the same mistakes made by commercial publishers.

When we are looking at other modes of reading, it might be a good idea to look also at math story problems. There is some evidence that students who are word bound can't get past the struggle to identify the words in the story problems. Although these students may be good at computations, they can't get to the "meat" of the problem. They never find what it is that needs to be computed.

One of my colleagues gave me the example of a math story problem which asked students to compute the cruising speed of a boat. Those students who didn't understand *cruising speed* couldn't find any meaning in a math story problem which wasn't long enough to provide any clues. They stayed on a word level rather than looking for the problem to be solved.

We need materials, then, which enable students to learn how to find key phrases such as: how many, how far, what percent, etc. We need materials which present math story problems within the concepts already familiar to the readers. Again, we should make use of the reader's language and experience.

It doesn't harm a student, by the way, to have words in his reading vocabulary which he doesn't pronounce in the expected manner. This is common to all proficient readers. What *is* important is that readers develop a *concept* for a significant word or phrase, regardless of pronunciation. All materials, student-produced, teacher-produced, or commercially produced, must provide for the development of these concepts.

Implications for Reading Instruction

P. David Allen

Reading miscue research has given us insights into what is happening during the reading process. As a result of the research, a number of generalizations can be stated about the reading process. Although these generalizations have been referred to throughout the previous chapters, it might be helpful to restate them here prior to a discussion of reading instruction.

1.   Reading is an active process by which the reader reconstructs the message of the writer. This reconstruction assumes that the reader has arrived at the same or comparable meaning as the author's intended meaning.

2.   Whereas the deep structures may be the same, the author's surface structure (print) may not be the same as the reader's. It is also possible for an oral reader to produce a surface structure identical to the author's without arriving at the same meaning.

3.   Three cue systems are available to readers as they process the material they are reading. These cue systems, graphophonic, syntactic and semantic, are interrelated, and the various miscue studies indicate that proficient readers at all levels use all of the systems.

4.   Proficient readers develop and use a set of strategies in order to reconstruct the writer's message. These strategies fall in the general areas of predicting, confirming, and comprehending.

5.   Related to the strategies of predicting, confirming, and comprehending is the strategy of correction. Correction behavior offers important insights into reading competence.

Miscue Research and Current Reading Instruction

In view of these generalizations, we are therefore compelled to voice our concern about some of the current practices in reading instruction.

Our basic concern is the preoccupation with letter-sound or graphophonic relationships. Such preoccupation may cause the teacher to ignore the other cue systems completely. It is as though teachers believe that once these letter-sound relationships are learned there will be no further trouble ahead for the young reader. One is reminded of the segment on the Electric Company show in which the character slowly sounds out a printed warning, and keeps sounding it out until it makes sense, only to be too late to avoid the impending disaster. One thing our research has taught us is the fact that you don't have to be able to pronounce every word in order to read for meaning. Certainly as adults we don't, and there should be no reason why we would expect beginning readers to do so. There is the danger, also, that the letter-sound relationships will be taught solely—at the expense of the other cue systems available to the reader.

Another concern would be the preoccupation with the so-called word recognition, or word attack, or word identification skills. The term *recognition* here can present a peculiar problem in that underlying it is the assumption that the child already knows the word. *Word attack* is a somewhat more accurate term, and perhaps *word identifi-cation* best states the purpose of teaching this set of skills to a reader. Our concern here is with the emphasis on *word*. It was stated above that it isn't necessary to be able to pronounce every word in order to read for meaning. The statement could be extended to ". . . to pronounce, recognize, and/or identify every word in order to read for meaning."

The emphasis on skills in reading programs seems to be built on the notion that if these are taught sequentially and if they are dealt with in some careful, systematic manner, the child will become a good reader. From this notion comes the assumption that we can determine the reading capability of the child by measuring his or her ability to perform these skills, often in isolated testing situations. We then say that inability to perform x number of skills indicates the child is a poor reader, or that the ability to perform x number of skills indicates the child is a good reader. Either assumption is a dangerous one.

Our next concern is also related to skill instruction. It seems then that if it is these skills that are measured, we must teach them—often at the expense of reading instruction. It is possible for children to sit through hours of skill instruction without ever really getting the chance to read! This is inexcusable. The writer once observed a teacher spend twenty minutes teaching a skill to a reading group that had indicated at the beginning of the session that they knew the skill(r-control) by reading a list of words correctly from the board. She ended the session by saying that there would not be any time left to read.

The next set of concerns are teacher-related. In fact, they might be appropriately called "areas of teacher interference." These would include unnecessary prompting, insisting on super-correct oral reading, discouraging guessing, not allowing readers to regress, and confusing reading instruction with other areas of instruction such as "correct pronunciation."

In each of these areas the teacher is "short-circuiting" the child's ability to deal with the reading process. Often the slightest hesitation on the part of the reader will trigger the teacher (or other members of the group) into providing the child with the word. Hence the child is often unable to utilize his own strategies at the point where they are needed.

The insistence on precise oral reading can be even more damaging. Our research has demonstrated that a proficient oral reader will often produce a different surface structure from the author's. If the meaning of the passage has not been altered, there would seem to be little excuse for the teacher to be constantly interrupting the reader. Even if the meaning were changed, the teacher should allow readers the opportunity to discover this for themselves. Our research shows that children will often do just that, given the opportunity.

Related to precise oral reading are the next three areas of teacher interference. Children are often discouraged from guessing. If anything, children should be encouraged to guess. The strategy of predicting has been referred to throughout this book. One of the purposes of reading instruction should be to produce readers who are able to make intelligent guesses or predictions about what they are reading. The reader who stops reading and looks up at the teacher and says, "We haven't had that word yet!" is expressing a real need for such a strategy.

Similarly, not to allow children to regress may be depriving them of the chance to utilize their confirming strategies. All of us regress as we read—for the purpose of clarification, for correction, or for any number of reasons. There is no reason why the developing reader should not be allowed to regress.

Finally, we are concerned about the tendency to confuse reading instruction with other areas such as instruction in enunciation or "correct" pronunciation. A child who reads *crick* for *creek* does not have a reading problem. Unfortunately, the fact that his dialect may be different from the teacher's dialect may be a problem for him, but it is not a reading problem and should not be treated as such. The little girl from Boston who reads *idear* for *idea* in Kansas, the little girl from Kansas who reads *warsh* for *wash* in Ohio, and the little black girl from Illinois who reads *so* for *sore* in Illinois have all read correctly. It is at this point that the teacher's attitude becomes such an important factor in reading instruction. His or her knowledge and understanding of language differences and the nature of language is crucial to the self-esteem of these children and their chances for becoming proficient readers.

Recommendations for Reading Instruction
In discussing our concern about current instructional practices in reading, we alluded to some recommendations for reading instruction. It may be fruitful to outline some further recommendations, based on our research findings.

Emphasizing the strengths a reader brings to the reading task
It has been stated that a child comes to school as a competent user of language—a language that has served him well to this point.It is also a language that has developed because of a need to communicate and of a perhaps greater need to order his world. Reading (and writing) should be regarded as a further extension of this development, not as a complete new set of communication skills. What is perhaps more important is that a child needs his existing language on which to build new competencies, new understanding, and new concepts. Any program which ignores this language or, worse, negates it is doomed to failure.

Providing more opportunities for children to read
It seems ludicrous to make such a statement, but it is possible for a great deal of "reading instruction" to take place without having the children actually read. Skills taught in isolation, words taught in lists, and other such practices lead to such conditions. Our subjects have shown us again and again that they are capable of teaching themselves as they work their way through a story or article. More importantly, they are dealing with the real rather than the contrived. If they do run into problems, it is then possible to develop strategy lessons that will help in overcoming them. And as it has been pointed out, these strategy lessons always involve the reader in a real reading situation.

Another point for teachers to consider is the need to involve the student in reading situations outside of the formal reading instructional periods. Reading in the content areas such as mathematics, social studies, and science should be an integral part of any reading program at any grade level. And yet, it is quite common to find classrooms where these content areas are not dealt with at all, particularly science and social studies because "they can't read the material." In such classrooms, therefore, reading is often taught all day long, and sometimes not too successfully.

Emphasizing strategies rather than skills
It may be thought that *strategy* as we have discussed it is just another label for *skill*. This is not the case. While it is true that the comprehending strategies in the Goodman-Burke paradigm resemble the higher-level comprehension skills found in most textbooks and

basal programs, the important difference centers on the "word-getting" skills commonly referred to as word recognition, word attack, or word identification skills. Yetta Goodman uses the term *meaning-seeking strategies* when she discusses what a child must employ when he encounters words he has never seen or heard before. Therein lies the crucial difference. If a child can tell us without being able to pronounce it that a *ewe* is a mother sheep; if a child reads *asked* instead of *queried*; and if a child reads *Steve* instead of *Sven*, he is indicating that he is indeed capable of employing meaning-seeking strategies.

Another important difference is that strategies are taught as they are needed by individual readers and not necessarily taught indiscriminately to everyone at a given point in a program.

Finally, two overriding strategies that all readers need to employ are the constant asking of two questions: *Does what I read sound right?* and *Does it make sense?*

Implications for Teachers
The above recommendations may be discomfiting for many teachers. They seem to violate many of the sacred tenets of reading instruction. Teachers are reluctant sometimes to give up the security of a word list, a skill lesson, or the right to correct a child who has not read what was printed on the page. They may be even more reluctant to write down exactly what the child has said on an experience chart or to admit that those darn tests aren't always right. But there are those teachers who have marveled at what Johnny just did to that sentence when he read orally or feel that Suzie, for all her preciseness, just doesn't seem to understand what she has read. For those teachers, what we have said makes sense and sounds right.

Special Areas of Investigation

Developing Reading Proficiency

Yetta M. Goodman

Reading development is growth toward becoming a proficient reader. A proficient reader is one who is both effective and efficient when processing written language information. According to K. Goodman, the effective reader is one who is successful in constructing meaning while reading. He is comprehending and integrating meaning into his own conceptual framework as he reads.

The efficient reader is able to integrate meaning while using the fewest possible cues from the graphic display. A reader's proficiency develops in relation not only to the three language cueing systems but also in relation to some general learning principles. The process of becoming an effective and efficient reader never ceases, but is continuous as the reader encounters new and unfamiliar material.

Discussing reading development is complicated by the many uses of the term *development*. Development can refer to maturing physically as well as becoming more proficient in any particular aspect of learning. There are some second-grade readers who are more proficient than some tenth-grade readers. Yet the tenth grader who is less proficient than a certain second grader is nevertheless a more proficient reader than she was in the second grade. The tenth grader is able to understand more complex concepts than the second grader. In order to distinguish age from reading proficiency, the phrase "as a reader gets older" will be used to indicate age maturation and the phrase "as a reader develops proficiency" will be used to indicate more effective and efficient reading.

This discussion of developmental trends in readers as they acquire proficiency, and of these trends as they relate to age is based on the analysis of the reading miscues of six youngsters who were taped at regular intervals for a period of seven years, from 1966 to 1972 (Y. Goodman 1967, 1971, 1972). In addition, data from the other reading

113

miscue studies (K.S. Goodman and Burke 1968, 1973) as well as similar research carried on by Marie Clay (1967) in New Zealand have been used to support developmental trends.

General Developmental Data

From the beginning of reading instruction in school, readers make use of all three of the language cueing systems (graphophonic, syntactic and semantic). The following excerpt from one child's reading is used to underscore this developmental principle. It was read by Franklin, who was in a first grade where a language experience approach to reading was used. The teacher never gave direct instruction in phoneme-grapheme correspondence. Reading instruction in this classroom took this form:

1.   The teacher read aloud to the children daily.
2.   The teacher worked with small groups where children read their own and other children's own dictated stories.
3.   The children were encouraged to read in the classroom library.
4.   The children listened to audiotapes of trade books while they were reading along in the same books.

Franklin had never seen the material prior to reading it. His miscues are marked.

1.   Here is a little red toy.   *train*

2.   Here is a big blue toy.   *airplane*

3.   Come in here for a toy.   ©c– / *train*

4.   Look, Sue.

5.   Here is a big toy.   *train*

6.   It is a big blue airplane.

7.   And look at the little train.   Ⓐ

8.   Look here! Look here!

9.   I see the toy for me.   Ⓐ *airplane*

10.   It is big.

11.   It is blue.

12.   It is the big blue airplane.   © *little*

13.   Here is the airplane for me.

14.   See Pepper and the big toy. *(A)* *bear*
15.   It is the (toy) for Pepper. *(C)* *lit-*
16.   Look at Pepper and the big toy. *little bear*
17.   I see Pepper.
18.   And I see the big toy. *bear*
19.   It is the toy for Pepper. *bear*

The parts of the story Franklin read without miscues suggest that he had an adequate awareness of the integration of the language cueing systems without direct instruction. This evidence is supported in a more observable way through his miscues. In his substitution of *train* for *toy*, he used initial consonant clues (formal instruction was not necessary for him to learn to use sound-letter correspondence). Every one of his substitution miscues retained the same part of speech as the text word.

All the substitutions were semantically related to the story. There were pictures to supply Franklin with some of the meaning. The pictures show a blue airplane which is smaller than many of the other toys. The bear in the picture which is pointed to by the child in the story is smaller than Pepper, the dog, who is sitting next to the bear. Franklin read the words *little* and *big* in lines 1, 2, 5, 6, 7, 10, 14 and 18. In lines 12 and 16 it was the concept of size based on his knowledge of toys and animals involved in the miscues which gave him clues, not his recognition of the words.

He retained the grammaticality of the language structures and the meaning in those miscues. His other miscues involved nouns. Franklin had to make choices about which nouns to replace for *toy*. He was using meaning, not only picture clues, since he had the option of a *red* train, plane, umbrella, ball, socks, chair, and doll. He had the choice of a *blue* bed, chair, sweeper, ball, and bus. His rejection of some of the nouns and his choice of *train*, *airplane*, and *bear* indicate Franklin's concern for meaning as he was reading.

His substitutions for *toy* also indicate the degree to which background, experience and language knowledge are related to reading. In the retelling of the story, Franklin was able to tell the researcher that the children were playing "with their toys" in answer to the question: "What are the children playing with?". He knew the word *toy* and used it orally. *Toy* seems to be an easy word, often used in primers or pre-primers. It seems to be easy graphically since it is short and has a common spelling pattern related to *boy*. It seems to be easy grammatically because it is a common noun in a common noun position. However, conceptually a child should not be expected to predict a word like *toy* in the positions it is found in the above excerpt. *Toy* is generalization. Children say, "They play with their toys." or "They clean up their toys." but a specific toy is called by its name: *plane*, *bear* or *train*. Some words, used because they seem grammatically and graphically simple, may actually be too difficult for the reader because they represent a misconception or a complex conceptualization.

Readers are able to produce substitutions, omissions, insertions and reversals of words, phrases and clauses as they read. Substitutions are in most cases the commonest miscue types, omissions are next, insertions third; reversals always represent the smallest percentage of miscue types for *all* readers, including those children labeled perceptually handicapped. Reversal miscues for all readers number less than 1 percent of all miscues. The percentages of miscue types, however, are not as significant as the qualitative differences among these miscue types as readers get older and develop proficiency.

In beginning reading, substitution miscues tend to be real words. Often the substitutions will be limited to words the reader has seen in print. It seems as if beginning readers expect only words which they have already encountered. As proficiency develops, readers begin to substitute nonwords or real words which they may never have encountered before in their reading. As readers get older they begin to substitute nonwords or more complex real words, even if they do not become very efficient readers. A reader's proficiency can sometimes be examined if the same unknown word appears a number of times in the text. The reader will indicate that he knows he does not know by substituting a variety of nonwords often with high graphic sound similarity. He may attempt various real words or build up context until he can actually produce the word expected in the text. The variety of these strategies indicates levels of proficiency and gives insight into the strategies a reader uses in attempting word recognition.

Omissions by a beginning reader tend to be omissions of words the reader suspects she does not know. In rare instances, a beginning reader is so tied to "knowing the word" that her percent of omission miscues may be larger than her substitution miscues, since she only reads the words she recognizes. As a reader gets older but has not developed very much proficiency, the percentage of omission miscues will decrease as she plods along, reading each word, producing substitution miscues rather than omissions. As a reader develops proficiency, she tends to omit known words which are not significant to the meaning. These may be omissions of function words like *the* or *and* between two independent clauses. Or these may be omissions of redundant features. For example, in some early reading materials, it is not uncommon for a phrase like *old apple tree* to be repeated five or six times. After the initial reading of the phrase, the reader knows the description of the tree and retains this information even if at subsequent readings she omits *old* or *apple* or both. Phrases like *he said* or *John said* are often omitted by proficient readers once the reader knows who is carrying on the dialogue in the story. The story retellings often give added evidence that the readers who are developing proficiency retain meaning even when they omit such words or phrases.

Insertions tend to increase as a reader begins to develop proficiency, although insertion miscues generally account for less than 10 percent of all miscues. Insertion miscues are not frequent in the reading of less proficient readers. When a reader begins to produce insertion miscues, the teacher has some evidence that reading proficiency is beginning to develop.

Reversals within the word are very infrequent for all readers. These include substitutions like *was* for *saw* and *on* for *no*. These tend to disappear as readers get older and develop proficiency. As a reader develops proficiency, he uses confirming strategies so that if he does predict a reversal, he will correct if the reversal has not produced an acceptable language structure. Reversals of two words or phrases are more common than reversals of letters within words. These include phrase substitutions like *mother said* for *said mother* and *they laughed heartily* for *they heartily laughed*. Such phrase-level miscues almost always retain meaning and indicate the reader's use of predicting strategies. Nonetheless, reversals are not a significant part of reading miscues for any reader.

Miscues do not disappear as readers develop proficiency; rather the miscue types change qualitatively as readers become more proficient.

Developmental Data: The Graphophonic Cueing System

For almost all readers on the 0-9 graphic and phonemic similarity scale, the mean similarity score stabilizes at about 5. Only low first and second graders may have a mean score as low as 3 on the similarity scale. All substitution miscues tend to have at least some letter-sound similarity about 90 percent of the time. For almost all readers, the graphic score is somewhat higher than the phonemic similarity score, which means that readers tend to obtain cues from configuration to a greater extent than from the sound-letter relationships.

Readers in early grades use initial letters and, to a lesser extent, final letters to determine their word attack. A sample of Franklin's second-grade reading reflects his teacher's instructions to him to be concerned with sound-letter relationships. Compare the following with his first-grade reading above.

Bird   doll   muggy   newp   hair
But the old toys (did) not make the new doll happy.

First and second graders who do not produce the average mean of 5 on the graphic and phonemic similarity scale seem to be relying on one of two different strategies. Some decide that part of the reading process is to continue to tell the story and make sense without use of the graphic print. They ignore much of the graphic display at certain points in the text in order to produce meaningful language units. Althea was in the second grade when she produced the following example:

                      mother
The little boy ran to the woman.
© How
  "Oh, mother! Here you are!" he said.

(uc) 2. helped me
      1. help me find you   mother she took
Ted\begin to walk away. But the woman said to him, "Do

       (uc) 2. will to
       1. will take
not go! I\want to thank you.
      good friends
We are going to the show.
(uc) 3. Would you let me go to the show?
    2. We will leave now to the show.
    1. We will
    Will you let me take you to see it?"

The children who produced this kind of reading strategy relied on it for two or three sessions (about six months) at the most and then returned to the pattern of making greater use of graphic display.

Another group of children with a low phonemic-graphic similarity mean score used graphic display but confused the configuration of one word with another and habitually produced a substitution miscue which had no graphic similarity to the text word. Substitutions of *the* for *and* and *is* for *said* will be recognized by primary teachers as such commonly confused words. Concentrating on phonics or word recognition reinforces these associations. Placing them in context and helping the reader become concerned with the meaning of the sentence can help to separate habitual associations of unrelated words.

As readers get older, regardless of developing proficiency, they produce miscues which have closer phonemic and graphic similarity to the text. This is true of all readers and does not seem related to test scores, reading methodology or reading effectiveness. Nonwords which readers produce are especially good evidence of the development of closer proximity between the expected and observed responses. When a reader produces a nonword, he or she uses the graphic display to produce a place holder. It should be pointed out, however, that syntactic elements like word inflections are often retained as part of the nonword. See the following examples:

Grade Level at Which Miscue Was Produced	Observed Response	Expected Response
2	muggy	monkey
2	newp	new
3	foo	few
3	rooshed	rushed
4	anshun	ancient
5	ongle	uncle
5	exterically	excitedly
6	abrusion	outburst
6	orgunate	originate
7	reasonableance	reasonably
7	accualting	acculturating

Although they tend toward closer phonemic and graphemic similarity between their expected and observed responses, proficient readers also produce larger numbers of miscues with *no* graphic or phonemic similarity. These are not corrected if the rest of the context confirms the acceptability of the miscue.

Examples: I said as calmly as I could
                 that

There in the dry, dead leaves he saw a little fawn.
           there was

If the reader rejects her prediction, she will tend to correct miscues which have little or no phonemic or graphic similarity.

Examples: Might as well study word meanings first.

"Let's see what we can find in the S's," I said.

All readers use the graphophonic cueing system to predict and select appropriate cues toward gaining meaning and to confirm predictions which may seem unacceptable. Efficient readers use the graphic display as little as possible. Less efficient readers tend to use more of the graphic display and do not seem willing to risk abandoning this inefficient strategy. Even the proficient reader begins to make greater use of the graphic display when the going gets tough and when the semantic and syntactic cueing system is destroyed.

Developmental Data: The Syntactic Cueing System

From the very beginning of reading instruction in school, children show evidence that they bring their own knowledge of the syntactic system of language to their reading as well as respond to the grammatical system of the written material. The Goodman Taxonomy of Reading Miscues analyzes the grammatical information apart from semantic information. The categories of syntactic acceptability, syntactic change, grammatical function, transformation, and the various "levels" categories examine the reader's ability to handle grammatical information.

The differences in data between the syntactic and semantic systems indicate that for all readers the syntactic system of language is more easily controlled at any point than the semantic system. Such differences may also occur because syntax as a finite system is well learned during early childhood, while the semantic system, which is tied to the development of concepts and ideas, is more complex and continues developing into adulthood. Another reason may be the control of the graphic input, which limits the reader to substitutions on the word or phrase level in oral reading, while the meaning of the substitution might have a broader range of definitions. In the phrase *the beautiful hat* here are many words which can replace *beautiful* and *hat* and change the general meaning of the phrase to *the bountiful hat* or *the beautiful cap*. However, the words retain their *exact* grammatical functions.

For less proficient readers, the same words are easier to identify when they are in more common grammatical slots than when they appear in less common grammatical slots. The following excerpts (not continuous text) from a story Franklin read in third grade will substantiate this point. The numbers at the left indicate the occurrence of the word *circus* in the text:

1.   It looks like a circus monkey. *(trained)*
2.   "Circus bear!" said Ted. *(Trained)*
3.   "Are they circus balloons?" *(trained)*
    Then they will know
4.   The circus is coming. *(train)*
    "All the boys and girls in Green Hills *(© ... Mrs.)*
5.   will get circus balloons." *(© with ... trained)*
6.   "He is in the circus," said the man. *(© ... © a ... circ—)*
    "I came to tell the boys and girls
7.   The circus is coming." *(© clown ... gone)*

A number of readers made miscues in this story similar to those of Franklin. When *circus* appeared in the less common adjective position, (1, 2, 3, 5) the readers were unable to identify the word and either omitted the word, replaced *circus* with adjectives or possessives like *colored, trained* or *children's,* or produced nonwords with adjective intonations, e.g., *circsus.* When the word appeared in its more common noun position (4, 6, 7) most of the readers were able to read the word as expected. As readers develop proficiency they are able to handle the less common grammatical units. They may still predict the more common item but will correct their miscues on the basis of subsequent language information.

"We could use ether . . . chloroform ∴." *(© either ... or)*

Miscues reflect a reader's knowledge of grammar through the retention of inflected features of words even if the word does not appear to be a meaningful one. The nonwords listed earlier in this chapter indicate that even when readers produce nonwords they tend to inflect these words in order to retain acceptable grammar in the sentence. In the example of Franklin's reading above, he read *trained* for *circus* whenever the word *circus* appeared as an adjective. This is the only way *train* can be inflected and remain an adjective. In the fourth occurrence of *circus*, when it appears in a noun position for the first time, Franklin deletes the *ed* and substitutes the noun *train*. The reader's ability to produce miscues which are syntactically acceptable increases with proficiency and is generally consistent regardless of the difficulty of the material. This is not the case in terms of semantic acceptability. The following table indicates the mean percent of syntactically and semantically acceptable miscues for eighth and tenth graders who read the same two stories:

Table 1
Miscues of Eighth and Tenth Graders

Student Grade & Ability	Miscues					
	Syntactically acceptable			Semantically acceptable		
	Story 1	Story 2	Difference	Story 1	Story 2	Difference
10H*	89%	80%	9%	73%	47%	26%
10HA	78%	66%	12%	54%	28%	26%
10LA	71%	57%	14%	47%	20%	27%
8H	78%	71%	7%	58%	38%	21%

H = High ability, HA = High average, LA = Low average

Story 1 was easier for all readers than Story 2, but regardless of readers' ability, the difference in syntactically acceptable miscues between stories 1 and 2 was no greater than 14 percent for any group of readers. The difference in semantically acceptable miscues, however, was no lower than 21 percent even for the most proficient group of readers. More than half of all the miscues were syntactically acceptable even for the more difficult story and even for the least proficient readers.

Transformations that involve alternate acceptable structures increase qualitatively as a reader develops proficiency. Beginning readers who are not efficient make few transformations, since they stick close to the print. As readers develop proficiency and begin to select graphic information and predict on the basis of their selection, transformations increase in number. With proficiency, transformations will generally produce acceptable language structures.

Developmental Data: The Semantic Cueing System

Developmental data on the use of the semantic cueing system must be tied to conceptual development as well as to aspects of comprehension. Differences in reading materials affect the semantic cueing system to a greater extent than any other cueing system. The experiental background a student brings to the reading material must be taken into consideration during any discussion of semantic cueing systems. Until we understand to a greater extent the way meaning and concepts are acquired through oral language, there will be limitations on our understanding of the function of comprehension in reading.

Examining retellings of a story which readers have read over a period of time gives insight into development in comprehension. As readers get older they can better understand the material they are reading. Life's experiences give readers who lack proficiency the needed background to gain greater understanding from reading material, even if they do not use their strategies very efficiently. At the same time, lack of life's experiences limits the young reader who is making proficient use of reading strategies.

Fausto read "Sheep Dog" in May 1968, at the end of third grade and again in May 1970, at the end of fifth grade. "Sheep Dog" is a story in an eighth-grade literature anthology, which was read and used in the larger miscue research studies by low tenth graders, average eighth graders and high sixth graders. Fausto's miscues per hundred words, his syntactic acceptability score and his phonemic and graphic proximity scores on both readings of "Sheep Dog" were within the ranges of sixth and eighth graders who read the story. However, in his 1970 reading of "Sheep Dog," 60 percent of all miscues resulted in no loss of meaning to the story, whereas in his 1968 reading, only 26 percent of his miscues resulted in no meaning loss.

After being asked to retell the story in May 1968, Fausto recalled: "Well, they heard he was so hungry he couldn't lie still. He went to search for food. But at first he couldn't find any food no matter what and he would never tend the sheep."

Although the information presented by Fausto is correct in terms of recall, the cause and effect relationship between the dog's hunger and his inability to tend the sheep was not revealed through the retelling. After some additional questioning by the researcher, who asked who "they" were and who "he" was in relation to the above retelling, Fausto answered, "I don't remember what I was trying to say .... I haven't thought about the story yet." Additional questions about additional characters or events did not elicit further response.

In May 1970, however, Fausto not only retold the story in greater detail, recalling main characters and major events, but he was able to interpret from the story that the herder "might have died of starvation." When asked by the researcher, "What makes you think that?" he replied, "He'd been alone. He might have died of old age ... a heart attack." The story itself does not make clear how the herder dies, but Fausto used many semantic cues from the story to show that through his life's experiences he could infer reasons for death which were implied but not spelled out in the story. A further discussion between Fausto and the researcher indicates mature gathering of semantic cues in the 1970 reading which is not at all evident in 1968.

> *Researcher:* How was the whole thing resolved? Did Peggy ever get any food?
> *Fausto:* Yeah, she got some grub, I think.
> *Researcher:* What's grub?
> *Fausto:* I don't know.
> *Researcher:* What do you think it is?
> *Fausto:* I believe, probably a nickname for something.
> *Researcher:* What would you guess?
> *Fausto:* I don't know ... a snack or something.
> *Researcher:* Who gave it to her?
> *Fausto:* These two men. They came when they saw trouble.

For readers who have not developed reading proficiency, there can be a snowballing effect in miscues and the reader tends to grasp at semantic cues in short linguistic sequences. Meaning becomes fragmented, although the reader can still often discuss some of the meaning from the written passage. The following passage from a newspaper article read by Franklin in June 1971 is a good example of this point. This excerpted example includes the second and third paragraphs and the last two paragraphs of a newspaper story on baseball, Franklin's favorite sport.

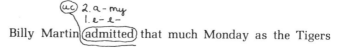

Billy Martin admitted that much Monday as the Tigers

spent their day off wondering when Jim Northrup and (Aurelio)
Rod—
Rodriguez will be ready to return.

Mickey Lolich, with a personal two-game losing streak to
worry about meets Milwaukee's talented rookie Bill Parsons
in Tuesday's home opener.

Here is the play which the Tigers and Willie Horton claim
cost them four runs in the first inning of their Sunday loss to
Chicago.

The Tiger left fielder claims the fan interfered with him,
causing him to drop the ball.

The second paragraph in the above example indicates how Franklin can grasp at semantic cues in short linguistic sequences to gain meaning. This single-sentence paragraph has six miscues which disrupt the meaning of the sentence. Nevertheless, the reader is able to produce *Tuesday home game* for *Tuesday's home opener*, a fragmented piece of the sentence which indicates an attempt to get at the meaning. At the same time Franklin is able to handle the names, which are difficult for most readers unless they have had extensive experience with the sport. The last two paragraphs indicate that as Franklin gained the author's intent and related it to his own experiences, his miscues become acceptable. All the miscues in the last two paragraphs are semantically and syntactically acceptable in Franklin's dialect.

Conclusions

It is generally agreed that maturation or development is built on earlier growth. Yet when it comes to reading, much research and teaching methodology reflect the notion that the child is an empty slate. Instead of building on the language competencies a reader brings to school, abstract units of language are often presented as the initial stages in learning to read. The potential reader in the United States lives in a print-oriented society. Everywhere in our culture, all children, whether in affluent homes or in poor homes, have been interacting with print media from the moment they begin to watch TV, go for walks in their neighborhood or go to the store or market with older siblings or parents. It is at these early moments that reading acquisition begins. However, since we tend to be controlled by the notion that reading starts in school through formal instruction, there are few research studies dealing with reading acquisition in preschoolers.

Most educators operate on the assumption that children learn most easily moving from the concrete to the abstract. The concrete of language is its wholeness. The concrete of language is the interaction between speakers in a shared setting with the major purpose being communication. The sound system of language without the grammatical system which gives organization and structure to meaning is abstract—so abstract that the scientists who study the sound system argue about its existence, its description and its variations. Yet many reading programs operate on the premise that it is perfectly logical to start beginning reading by teaching the most abstract aspect of language—the system's smallest units.

No one pronounces isolated out-of-context sounds or words for an eight-month-old baby and expects this to help the baby to learn to speak. Yet beginning readers are often provided with abstract sounds and words and then have the task of placing these abstract units back into the language as a whole.

All of our research supports the basic assumption that when reading takes place, even at the earliest moment, all three systems of language must be intact in order for the reader to understand that reading is language and that the purpose of reading is to get at the author's message.

In reading miscue research, there is *no* evidence that reading proficiency develops gradually and continuously in an upward direction for any one reader. Werner and Kaplan (1952) define this as saltatory development: "Mental growth, rather than being conceived as a straight increase of achievement, is here seen as a sequence of rises and declines of processes, subserving such achievement."

This principle is especially useful in terms of reading development because it provides for the many variables which help make up the complexity of the reading process. In order to understand the saltatory nature of developing proficiency in reading, one must keep in mind (1) the personal, emotional and physical factors of the readers; (2) different instructional approaches; (3) the concept load of the material;

(4) the interest of the reader; (5) the experiential background of the reader in relationship to the setting, time, characterization, plot and theme of the reading matter; (6) the style of the written material; (7) the complexity of syntax; and (8) the subject matter.

The interrelationship of these factors helps explain why some readers are able to read more difficult material with greater proficiency than less relevant material written at a lower reading level, or why some readers can read a twelfth-grade literature selection with greater understanding than a popular magazine article.

Although readers generally tend to progress toward greater efficiency, every reader experiences situations in which, at some given time, he or she can handle one piece of material more effectively than another because of an interrelationship of the factors mentioned above. Even the most proficient adult reader can be illiterate when faced with some specialized reading material. A child develops in many aspects of learning, simply through life's experiences. These processes of development are complex for teachers, psychologists, linguists, and educational researchers to understand and study, but seem to come easily to the learners. These include learning to walk, talk, conceptualize and categorize. Reading, too, is indeed complex, but as we understand its complexity and become aware of the ability of the human mind to deal with its complexity, we may discover that learning to read is easy.

References

Clay, M. M. The reading behaviour of five-year-old children: A research report. New Zealand Journal of Educational Studies, 1967, 2, 11-31.

Goodman, K. S., & Burke, C. L. Study of children's behavior while reading orally.(USOE Final Report, Project No. S425, Contract No. OE-6-10-136) Washington, D.C., United States Department of Health, Education, and Welfare, March 1968.

Goodman, K. S., & Burke, C. L. Theoretically based studies of patterns of miscues in oral reading performance. (USOE Project No. 90375, Grant No. OEG-0-9-320375-4269) Washington, D.C., United States Department of Health, Education, and Welfare, March 1973.

Goodman, Y. M. A psycholinguistic description of observed oral reading phenomena in selected young beginning readers. (Doctoral dissertation, Wayne State University) Detroit, Mich.: University Microfilms, 1967. No. 68-09961.

Goodman, Y. M. *Longitudinal study of children's oral reading behavior.*
    (USOE Final Report, Project No. 9-E-062, Grant No. OEG-5-9-325062-
    0046) Washington, D.C., United States Department of Health, Education,
    and Welfare, September 1971.
Goodman, Y. M. Quantitative and qualitative reading diagnosis. *Reading
    Teacher,* 1972, **26**(1), 32-37.
Werner, H., & Kaplan, E. The acquisition of word meanings: A developmental
    study. *Monographs of the Society for Research in Child Development,*
    1950, **15** (51). Evanston, Ill.: Child Development Publications.

What We Know about Dialects and Reading

Rudine Sims

Our research is based on a view of the reading process in which readers are seen as using their knowledge of their language system, their experiences, and their concepts when interacting with the written material. Since authors have used their language systems, experiences, and concepts to produce the written materials in the first place, there cannot be an exact match between the reader's and the author's systems and experiences; some mismatch is inevitable.

The language forms which we classify as dialect can differ from other dialects, such as the researcher's or the author's, in a few ways. There are phonemic differences, syntactic differences, and semantic differences, or differences in choices of lexical items. There are also differences in intonation patterns, which we haven't dealt with because we do not yet have adequate information about them.

For the readers in our studies, most dialect miscues involve phonemic level dialect differences. These miscues are those, for example, in which a reader renders w-i-t-h as *wif*, or h-e-l-p-e-d as *hepped*. Such miscues have been shown in our research to have no effect on the reading process. They cause no change in structure or in meaning, and therefore are seldom corrected, except when readers feel that the situation calls for some special supercorrect reading style, as when a teacher has repeatedly admonished a child to "pronounce all the endings."

Reactions to such pronunciation differences are often quite

strong, but frequently are the result of attitudes toward the social status of the speakers or their dialects. Reaction to Bostonian *pahk* is likely to be more tolerant outside of Boston than reaction to *desses* for desks, in spite of the fact that one makes no more difference than the other in the reading process.

Other dialect-involved phenomena are coded in our studies, and we have been able to gather some information concerning them. When the inflectional system of a dialect speaker differs from that of the author, the reader frequently makes miscues in which he uses his own inflectional system in place of the author's. Thus, readers produce third-person singular verb forms with no apparent *s*, or past tense forms without apparent *ed*, or possessives apparently without *'s*.

We have found that there appears to be a developmental pattern in the occurrence of such miscues. Beginners, who often are very word conscious, tend to have few such miscues. As they become slightly more proficient readers, and begin dealing effectively with syntactic structures and leaning less heavily on graphic cues, they tend to make more such dialect miscues. However, their ability to accommodate to an author's writing style grows with their proficiency, and when they become highly proficient oral readers, structural dialect miscues tend to disappear in their oral reading.

Dialect Speakers in the Classroom

There has been a good deal of concern recently over the possibility that children who speak a nonstandard dialect when they come to school may have particular difficulty learning to read because their language system differs from that of the material they are expected to read.

I recently completed a study in which second graders read two stories, one in standard English, and a different one in black dialect. The results do not support the contention that speaking a nonstandard dialect interferes with learning to read standard English. My findings may be summarized as follows:

1.   Readers shifted to a special oral reading style when reading aloud. This style more closely approximated standard English than their speaking style as recorded in their retellings. The following are samples of some of the nonstandard dialect features to be found in some of the retellings:

He told him that *wasn't none of his sock*.
Laura didn't have on *nothing but one* sock.

> *They* grandmother whipped them.
> *It look like* to me a snake.
> The other boy *had done lost* one of his socks.
> They take this thing that *be on* the street.

The italicized features are generally associated with black dialect. In his Detroit dialect study, Walt Wolfram found that adult speakers of black dialect also tend to more closely approximate standard English in their reading than in their speaking. This shift seems to imply that these children have, at minimum, receptive control of standard English (*A Sociolinguistic Description of Detroit Negro Speech* (Washington, D.C.: Center for Applied Linguistics, 1969).

2.   The readers made miscues which shifted from one dialect to the other. That is, when reading dialect materials, they shifted frequently to standard English forms, and when reading the standard materials, they shifted to black dialect forms. Some examples follow:

> *Black dialect to standard English*
> Text: Ollie *say,* "Boy, give me my sock."
> Reader: Ollie *said,* "Boy, give me my sock."
> Text: ...and it *start to bleeding.*
> Reader:...and it *started to bleed.*
> Text:...and the people...*gets* mad.
> Reader:...and the people...*get* mad.

> *Standard English to black dialect*
> Text: Ollie *pointed* to Leroy.
> Reader: Ollie *point* to Leroy.
> Text: Ollie *said,* "Leroy, give me my sock."
> Reader: Ollie *say,* "Leroy, give me my sock."

3.   The stories with the highest percentages of dialect miscues were the dialect stories, and therefore those miscues involved shifts from black dialect to standard English.

4.   There was a lack of consistency in use of dialect forms by these readers. In one sentence, a reader may have read *point* for *pointed,* in the next, she may have read *pointed* for *pointed.* Lack of consistency does not, however, mean any lack of organization in the dialect. It is simply a reflection of the fact that the reader is dealing with two dialects at the same time.

5.   Most of the dialect miscues in this study were phonemic miscues.

6.   There were no important differences in reading performance which could be attributed to dialect differences in the stories. The

reading process was the same in both kinds of stories. Any differences were between groups of readers or between the two stories as reflected in both versions.

Implications

What we have learned about dialect seems to imply the following:

1.   If speakers have, at minimum, receptive control of a language system, they can learn to read that language.

2.   The concern of teachers needs to be for understanding the dialect system of readers, so they know when the child has actually arrived at meaning and translated orally into his own dialect and when he is using inefficient or unproductive reading strategies. Translations into dialect are high-quality miscues, and need not cause concern on the part of the teacher.

3.   There is no need for the creation of dialect specific materials for wide scale use in teaching beginning reading to speakers of nonstandard dialects. This is not to negate the possible use of the new trade books, such as John Steptoe's *Stevie*, which reflect the everyday, nonstandard language of their characters. Such books may be fun to read or listen to, and are not meant for reading instruction, which is the issue here.

4.   Reading is not really "talk written down." Every reader, no matter what his dialect, must adapt to written language styles which differ from oral language in general, and from his own language in particular. This includes speakers of standard dialects, and I say dialects, plural, because there are various standard dialects. Witness the dialects of John F. Kennedy, Lyndon Johnson, and Richard Nixon.

The rejection of a need for dialect specific materials does not negate the hypothesis that the closer the language of the material comes to the language of the reader, the easier the reading task, especially for beginning readers. This hypothesis still holds, but it is obvious that the best way to reflect both the reader's language and his experiences is to record experiences as he brings them to the classroom. His language system is intact, systematic, organized; his experiences are known, and it is those two considerable strengths which will stand a reader in good stead as he begins the process of learning to read.

Testing

Peter D. Rousch

In this period of accountability, performance contracting, and competency-based instruction, it is inevitable that reading tests come under the close scrutiny of researchers. Rather than offering solutions to the problems inherent in current reading tests, I shall confine my comments to three significant areas:
1.   How we view tests of performance in the light of our research into reading as a language process
2.   What we consider to be an alternative to the present performance tests
3.   What we have discovered about some aspects of performance tests while working with children

First, how do we view performance tests of reading? Basic to the theory that reading is a language process is a view of the reader, even the child reader, as a competent language user. Our research verifies that the young reader uses his intuitive knowledge of language to process the graphophonic, syntactic, and semantic features in a manner that reflects his understanding of the material he is reading. Our interest is in evaluating the reader by using a model of competence based on the language knowledge used by the child as he reads, rather than a performance-oriented test.

Why this distinction? Psycholinguistic research convinces us that children do not learn language in small pieces, or in a way that enables them to eventually put the pieces together and arrive at a coherent language form. Yet performance tests of reading seem to assume that this is precisely how language is acquired. To verify this, we need only consider the separate so-called skills that comprise subtests of many reading tests. Such instruments assume that proficiency in the language process that is reading can be acquired as a consequence of proficiency in a number of disparate skill areas. If a child understands what he or she reads, even on a performance test of reading, it is puzzling that teachers should be exhorted to "teach, test, reteach and retest word attack skills until they are mastered so that these skills come up to the child's comprehension level." The purpose of reading is to get meaning, and if a child is able to achieve this without scoring well in areas labeled attack skills, it may be that tests for the latter are at least poorly structured and most likely irrelevant. I would make only three further points about tests of this kind:

1.   They are incompatible with a view of reading as a language process.

2.   They are not based on a theory of reading specifically, or language development generally.

3.   They ignore the language competence of the child, preferring to see him as one whose oral language needs to follow a pattern in order for him to read successfully.

As for alternative means of coping with evaluation, I have already made reference to the child's ability to process material meaningfully. Miscue analysis enables us to make decisions on the quality of deviations from the text. As a child reads, we can make judgments on the acceptability of her miscues within a semantic framework. If she is endeavoring to understand what she is reading, she will correct miscues that distort meaning. Those that are semantically acceptable within the story she may allow to go uncorrected. It is possible for us to arrive at a comprehending score by totalling the number of semantically acceptable miscues and those that were originally unacceptable but later corrected. I have used the term *evaluation* as distinct from *measuring*. Our interest is not in precise scores but in evaluating the child in the process situation. Comprehending scores do not allow us to put labels on children, but they do permit insights into what the child is doing or failing to do while reading.

What about those children who read so precisely that they don't miscue? Two comments are relevant here:

1.   Psycholinguistic researchers such as Frank Smith and George Miller have pointed up the difficulty of storing information into long-term memory. In order to do this successfully in the reading situation, it would seem to be necessary to refrain from using all the surface features of the material by eliminating redundant information from the graphic array, and processing that which is important to meaning. Smith provides insight into the phenomenon of information processing in his book, *Understanding Reading* (New York: Holt Rinehart & Winston, 1971).

2.   The intonation patterns of careful readers can be observed through miscue analysis, which provides us with cues as to whether

the reader is processing surface structure features to an acceptable deep structure.

Is it possible, then, to structure tests that take into account the language competence of the child? By this I mean tests that don't entail miscue analysis. The only procedure that comes close to this at the moment is the cloze type test that requires the reader to insert words in a text so that the original meaning is preserved. Most of the outstanding work with the cloze has been done by John Bormuth, who has stated that "a detailed analysis of children's comprehension skills showed that in the fourth grade a great many of the children (in the study) were unable to exhibit comprehension of even the simplest structures by which language signals information." (NCTE Convention, Milwaukee, 1968).

Our own research into the cloze reinforces aspects of this view. Fourth-grade children seem to have tremendous difficulty handling the cloze task. Yet we have found that this inability to handle structures is not reflected in the same children's reading, where they exhibit awareness of grammatical and semantic relationships in the quality of their miscuing and correction patterns. Even producers of high quality miscues who are able to retell very well the substance of a story experience this same problem with the cloze. What is even more perplexing is the inability of these proficient readers to perform better on the cloze than those with low quality miscues, whose retelling of the story indicates a comparatively low level of insight into the story line.

Why this difference between the quality of language used in the reading situation and that of the cloze? Probably we need to acknowledge the difference in developmental stages between receptive and productive processes. Young children seem able to use their language competence earlier in the receptive process that is reading than they can in the productive process of writing. It may be that the cloze is more akin to a productive than a receptive language process.

Does our research into testing reinforce the claims of teachers who question reading tests? We do know that background knowledge of the concepts developed in a story influences the quality of miscues and style of reading. A pretest of fourth-grade subjects through use of a picture-discussion task enabled us to classify children from the I.Q. range 90-110 and average reading level as having high or low prior conceptual awareness of a particular story to be read.

The table indicates that cloze scores for these subjects are similar, yet on an oral reading task, subjects with prior conceptual insights used more intelligent verbal behavior. The high conceptual awareness group's ability to process syntactic and semantic features of text material is most marked, and when the trend in correcting semantically unacceptable miscues is incorporated into the comparison between groups, the high group score for total semantic acceptability reaches 83.7 percent, compared with 52.3 percent for the low group. Retelling scores, arrived at by close questioning of subjects on events, plot and theme, are correspondingly different between groups.

Table 1
Prior Conceptual Awareness and Reading Performance in Fourth Graders

Prior Conceptual Awareness	Child	Scores in percent on oral reading retelling task					
		Reading Miscues					
		Syntactically acceptable	Semantically acceptable	Seman-unaccept. (Corrected)	Total	Cloze	Retelling
High group	Tim	56.3	46.9	31.3	78.2	56	68
	Dian	84	76	12	88	—	74
	Dick	64.7	52.9	35.3	88.2	58	—
	Sue	82.8	82.8	13.8	96.6	67	—
	Ben	82	78	12	90	—	80
	Pat	62.7	49.3	11.9	61.2	40	33
	Total	72	64.3	19.4	83.7	55.2	63.7
Low group	Robt.	63.8	11.1	15.5	56.0	53	28
	Shar.	72.4	55.2	10.3	65.5	62	—
	Shirl.	57.5	35	27.5	62.5	60	—
	Dan	62.9	22.9	20	42.9	—	16
	Beth	35.5	30.6	16.1	46.7	—	25
	Ken	35.6	26.7	12.9	39.6	43	12
	Total	54.6	35.3	17	52.3	54.5	20.2

Recent research (1972) by Weber and Meier at the City College of New York indicated that the Metropolitan Achievement Test operated against children with particular thought processes. These children were not confused because they couldn't read, but because they *could read*. They could not accept some of the "correct" answers. During 1971 we carried out a similar study with two standardized tests. Results suggested:

1.   The ability of some children to answer correctly without reading the extracts

2.   The ability of some children to answer correctly by reading only a key word in the extract

3.   Confusion created in the minds of some children who could see possibilities in more than one correct answer

It is not better tests or unbiased tests that we need. Rather, we need to evalute reading by examining it in relation to a theory of reading. This requires us to understand thoroughly the nature of the process. This understanding will lead us to accept the futility of testing away from the context of language, because reading is language.

Learning Disabilities

Bruce A. Gutknecht

Very often, children who are having trouble learning to read are separated from their classmates and put in special groups. Such groups may remain within the regular classroom, but with increasing frequency, they are isolated in a learning disabilities room.

In practice, such rooms have various names, but the children in them have some common characteristics. While their I.Q.'s are average or above, they have experienced failure in learning. Most are two or more years below grade level in reading or some other subject.

Often these children have been evaluated as disabled on the basis of the Illinois Test of Perceptual Abilities, the Marianne Frostig Developmental Test of Visual Perception, the Wechsler Intelligence Scale for Children, the Wide Range Achievement Test, or some other commonly used measure. It may be fair to assume that these instruments are valid and that they were administered correctly, and that competent school personnel have determined that placement in the learning disabilities room is best for these children. But unless teaching programs currently used in such rooms are altered, the children in them are bound to suffer continued failure in reading.

To find out whether children identified as perceptually handicapped differ in their reading strategies from children in regular classrooms, I conducted an analysis of the oral reading of five children

Table 1

Profiles of Children in Learning Disabilities Classroom Based upon ITPA, Frostig, and Neurologist's Comments

Child subjects identified by number	ITPA— psycholinguistic age					Chronological age (years—months)	Frostig—perceptual age					Neurologist's Comments
	Chronological age (years—months)	Auditory reception	Visual reception	Auditory assoc.	Visual assoc.		Test I	Test II	Test III	Test IV	Test V	Perceptual Handicap
901	9-11	9-10	6-07	8-10	10-03	10-00	10-00	8-03	9-00	7-00	8-03	No
*902	11-00	9-02	7-01	8-03	7-07	11-00	7-09	8-03	8-03	8-09	8-03	Yes
*903	10-01	9-02	7-09	6-00	10-03	10-00	9-06	6-06	9-00	8-09	7-05	Yes
904	8-11	8-04	5-02	6-00	6-10	8-10	7-03	8-03	6-03	7-00	8-03	Possible
*905	9-01	5-08	7-04	6-09	8-11	9-01	6-03	8-03	7-00	8-09	8-03	Yes
*906	11-03	8-07	10-10	9-05	10-03	11-03	8-06	8-03	8-03	8-09	8-03	Possible
907	10-08	10-02	10-10	10-06	8-05	10-07	9-06	7-00	7-00	8-09	8-03	No
908	11-06	8-00	10-10	9-09	10-03	11-06	10-00	8-03	9-00	8-09	8-03	No
*909	10-03	9-02	10-10	9-05	6-06	10-03	9-06	8-03	8-03	7-00	8-03	Yes
*910	10-01	10-02	4-10	8-03	7-07	10-03	9-06	8-03	8-03	7-00	8-03	Yes

* = Subjects used in the study.

who were classified as disabled. The child subjects were selected from an upper elementary school learning disabilities room, on the basis of their records on the ITPA and Frostig tests, plus a neurologist's evaluations.

Table 1 gives their scores and those of other members of the learning disabilities class on the ITPA and Frostig tests, along with a neurologist's opinions about the presence of a perceptual handicap.

Using the Goodman Taxonomy, the researcher focused on the graphophonic, syntactic and semantic cues available to the reader confronted with the printed page. For the test, the researcher chose reading materials comparable in difficulty to those the child subjects were currently using. The oral reading of each subject was tape recorded along with the subject's retelling of the story. From the tapes, miscues were identified and comprehension ratings assigned.

Table 2
Reading Task Level, Miscues per Hundred Words
and Comprehension Scores for Individual Subjects

Subject	Reading task level	MPHW	Comprehension
902	2–1	16.2	31%
903	Primer	10.6	60%
905	4	6.7	52%
906	3–1	17.9	63%
909	Primer	25.0	50%

Table 2 summarizes the results for the five children tested: the levels of their reading tasks, their miscues per hundred words, and their comprehension scores.

The major conclusion from this study is that there appear to be only slight differences between the oral reading of children identified as perceptually handicapped and the oral reading of children placed in regular school classrooms.

One difference is in the range of miscues per hundred words. This was considerably higher than that previously encountered in similar research with the perceptually handicapped, using the Goodman Taxonomy. Another evident difference is the high percentage of unsuccessful correction attempts made by certain subjects. These attempts show that the children were using a graphophonic reading strategy. This was frequently unsuccessful, however, because the children seemed to correct on the basis of graphic mismatches, not because they detected disruptions of meaning or grammar. In other words, the children were unsuccessful in reading because they over-used graphophonic cues.

The subjects of this study were having trouble acquiring proficiency in reading. Nevertheless, they were using the same processes as the readers in the regular classrooms. All of the children studied used graphophonic, syntactic, and semantic reading strategies. However, their syntactic and semantic strategies were not sufficiently developed to permit successful reading when the graphophonic strategy did not work. Unless reading programs now being used for learning disabilities classes include instruction in the use of syntactic and semantic context, they are failing the children. If, in fact, these children do have a perceptual problem, one wonders why they are given yet another dose of phonics, which depends heavily on perception.

The findings of this study render the label *perceptually handicapped* suspect. If the reading process of perceptually handicapped children is not much different from the process used by other children, just what is it that they do differently?

These "perceptually handicapped" children—and indeed all children—need a program of reading instruction that will equip them to use syntactic and semantic strategies along with graphophonic strategies. Such a program will include materials with an adequate syntactic and semantic context, from which the children can draw needed cues. When the child can use these strategies flexibly, the only result can be successful reading.

Miscue Research and Diagnosis

William D. Page

Miscue research, the observation and analysis of unanticipated oral reading responses, is causing in-depth re-examination of clinical practice in reading. The observation, diagnosis, and treatment of reading problems is of great concern. The role of the reading clinician warrants revision to account for new knowledge and new insights into the reading process that miscue research is producing. An obvious applicable inroad is the work of Y. Goodman and C. Burke in their *Reading Miscue Inventory* (1972). Of concern here are some less obvious long-range implications of miscue research for clinical practice in reading.

For many, the role of the reading clinician is that of an error seeker. Errors in oral reading, errors on comprehension tests, errors in word recognition, and errors in performing perceptual tasks are persistently sought out as indicators of reading problems. Word recognition scores from oral reading of graded paragraphs are a major contributor to setting a reading level to permit effective reading instruction. The match between the reader and instructional material is crucial (A. Harris, 1970, p. 139).

Since oral reading errors play a decisive role in setting reading levels for reading instruction, it makes sense to critically examine the identification of oral reading errors. Some background is helpful.

At present, controversy surrounds the concept of error. Disagreement exists in two areas: the definition of an oral reading error and the interpretation of oral word recognition scores for setting reading levels. For instance, some widely used published informal reading inventories count repetitions as errors while others do not. Some use instructional level criteria of one error in twenty words while others use different criteria. Some require silent prereading, others do not. What is important here is that a distinct lack of agreement exists concerning the definition and criteria for scoring oral reading errors (W. Powell and C. Dunkeld, 1971; H. Beldin, 1970).

Probing the Reading Specialist
While these disagreements exist, there are some who maintain that a skilled, experienced reading clinician's judgment can rise above the controversies. This amounts to relying on an expert authority, a position which itself has generated controversy (D. Sawyer, 1974). With this tack in mind, the author conducted a brief study to probe experts by sampling their judgments.

Fourteen reading specialists were asked to listen once to an excellent quality audiotape recording of one child slowly reading a single 115-word passage. The reading specialists were provided with a typed script before the listening, to permit them to peruse the passage ahead of time. Then, as the tape was played, they marked the oral reading errors they perceived and counted them. The results were interesting.*

The Errors
One reading specialist perceived one reading error. Two found two. Two recorded three errors. One found five. Three marked six, one marked seven, one eight, one nine, one eleven, and one fourteen. The lack of agreement is devastatingly apparent.

Characteristics of the Specialists
But what of the experiential background of the reading specialists in this group? Did they have sufficient teaching experience? The range of years of teaching experience of the fourteen specialists was from six years to twenty years and the average was twelve. The group did not lack teaching experience.

Teaching experience does not tell the whole story, of course. What is the clinical experience of the group? The lowest number of years of clinical experience for an individual in the group was one year. The highest number of years of clinical experience was ten, and the average was six. This was a group of experienced clinicians.

The credentials of the group require further examination. One could have teaching and clinical experience evident in years of service in a specific position but still not have much experience administering oral reading tests. The lowest number of oral reading tests administered by members of this group was fifty, the average was 513, and the highest number of tests was over twelve hundred. The group was not inexperienced in administering oral reading tests.

We must ask one final question about the characteristics of the group. What training had they had? Did they attend colleges and universities to gain their knowledge of reading tests and oral reading errors? One person in the group held a bachelor's degree from an accredited institution. Eight had received master's degrees. Three held master's degrees plus certicates of advanced study, and two had received doctorates, all from accredited institutions.

*The author is indebted to Kenneth S. Carlson, Ball State University, for aid in gathering the data and conceptualizing the brief study of reading specialists reported here.

Controversy
The past few paragraphs may sound rather tongue-in-cheek and critical of training practices. This is really not the case. The fourteen reading specialists were well trained, better than most school districts can boast, and a group any superintendent should be proud to hire. The fact that they did not agree to any significant degree on the number of oral reading errors simply underscores the existence of controversy. Do we as reading specialists and teachers agree on what an oral reading error is? Apparently we don't.

Reflections on Miscue Analysis
Whenever a reading specialist comes face to face with the decision process concerning oral reading errors, reflections on the definition of oral reading errors and implications for instruction immediately come to mind. The analytic process in reading miscue research forces constant rethinking. Early in the research, the concept of error was set aside. The more productive concept of the relationship between an observed response and an expected response was conceived and used to guide miscue studies (K. Goodman, 1965).

Observed Response and Expected Response
Instead of seeking an oral reading error, miscue research compares the observed response with an expected response. When the two differ, the resulting condition is labeled a miscue. This state of affairs is represented by Figure 1. Note that the decision about the existence of a miscue rests on whether or not the observed response is equal or not equal to the expected response.

Fig. 1 Common sense oral reading error

Underlying Process
Depth analysis of identification of miscues has progressed beyond this recognition that the distinguishing characteristic is a difference between the observed response and the expected response. Miscue research, with its attention to detail, has made it clear that the reader is

interacting with the printed material and that the observed oral reading response is an outcome of this interaction. The significance of this position lies in the fact that an underlying process is recognized (K. Goodman, 1967). That process is the reading process, and the oral reading response is only a glimpse of what is really happening in the reader's thinking. Figure 2 represents this stage of reflection on miscue analysis.

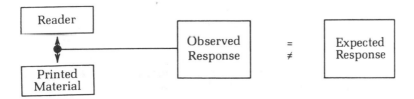

Fig. 2 Second generation miscue

Observer Interaction with Printed Material
The brief study with the fourteen reading specialists cited earlier makes it fairly clear that it is easy to disagree about what has been observed. This is true even after critical examination of definitions of observed oral reading responses.

We can account for one intervening condition by considering the observer's role in relation to the printed material. The expected response (ER) is not a foregone conclusion. The expected response is

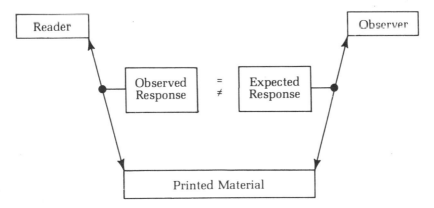

Fig. 3 Third generation miscue

the outcome of the observer's interaction with the printed material, a condition subject to considerable variability. If the dialect, background, and thought processes of the observer differ from those of the reader, and they usually do, the expected response is likely to differ from the reader's observable response. Figure 3 represents this relationship.

Observer's Listening Ability
Miscue research prompts one more step in critically examining the observation of oral reading responses. Consider again the study with the fourteen reading specialists who disagreed on the number of oral reading errors in the passage heard. One factor previously not considered is the variability of the observer's listening ability. It is a fact that listening ability differs among individuals and within one individual under varying conditions. A respiratory infection, fatigue, room acoustics, position in relation to the source of sound, and dialect divergence are some of the conditions that contribute to variation in listening.

An observer, then, is not only generating the expected response by interacting with the printed material, but is also generating the observed response by interacting with the phonological output or the sound produced by the oral reader. Both the generated expected response and the generated observed response are products of the observer's interactions with the elements of the observation situation. Figure 4 represents this fourth and last state of reflection on miscue analysis.

Implications for Clinical Practice
What is happening when a reading clinician listens to an oral reading and marks miscues on a typed script? Insights produced by miscue analysis suggest the situation is anything but simple. We've considered the fact that the expected response is a variable in itself, a product of reading, just as much as the observed response.

Fluent adult readers, including reading specialists and miscue researchers, are not free from the production of miscues in oral reading. *There is no evidence suggesting that the expected response be treated as a constant.* Most clinical practice probably does not include an audiotape recording of the reader's responses. A strong case is made by miscue analysis for the use of such recordings to permit careful, more reliable analysis of oral reading.

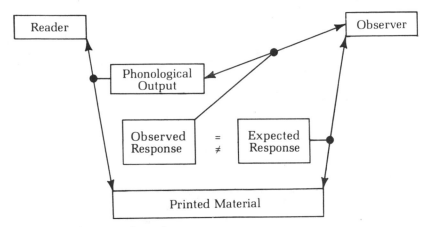

Fig. 4 Fourth generation miscue

Problems of interpreting expected and observed responses generated by the observer in miscue research are the same for the clinician or teacher listening to a child reading orally. Both generated responses are subject to variation. Both must be held in the memory of the observer while a judgment is made. The practice of audiotape recording the reader's oral responses permits the observer to listen and relisten to the performance, thus reducing the problems of remembering and the difficulties of hastily marking the typed script.

Clinical practice must begin to take advantage of more productive systems for analyzing oral reading responses. The theory and the descriptive tactics of miscue research can contribute significantly to the insights of the clinician. Clinicians must bolster their knowledge of how the reading process takes place and how language works. *The Goodman Taxonomy of Oral Reading Miscues* (See Appendix A) and *The Goodman Model of Reading* (K. Goodman, 1970, pp. 30-31) serve as a foundation for insights into the complexities of the reading process.

Long-range implications of miscue research for clinical practice are complex indeed. Three crucial thrusts are evident and warrant continued effort. First, we must approach the analysis of oral reading errors with a good deal of doubt—doubt about our own perceptions, doubt about our definitions, and doubt about our judgments. Second, we must remain aware that oral reading observations are but surface indications of the reading process. Third, we must treat reading as a search for information by the reader, rather than a process of making the sounds we expect. The purpose of reading is not meeting the contrived demands of a clinical situation. Comprehension is "... the only objective in reading... " (K. Goodman, 1970, p. 28).

References
Beldin, H. O. Informal reading testing: Historical review and review of the research. In W. Durr (Ed.), *Reading difficulties: Diagnosis, correction and remediation.* Newark, Del.: International Reading Association, 1970.
Burke, C., & Goodman, Y. *Reading miscue inventory.* New York: Macmillan, 1972.
Goodman, K. S. A linguistic study of cues and miscues in reading. *Elementary English,* 1965, **42,** 639-643.
Goodman, K. S. Reading: A psycholinguistic guessing game. *Journal of the Reading Specialist,* 1967, **6,** 126-135.
Goodman, K. S. Analysis of oral reading miscues: Applied psycholinguistics. *Reading Research Quarterly,* 1969, **5**(1), 9-30.
Goodman, K. S. Behind the eye: What happens in reading. In K. S. Goodman, & O. Niles (Eds.), *Reading: Process and program.* Urbana, Ill.: National Council of Teachers of English, 1970.
Harris, A. *How to increase reading ability.* New York: David McKay, 1970.
Powell, W. & Dunkeld, C. Validity of the IRI reading levels. *Elementary English,* 1971, **48**(6), 637-642.
Sawyer, D. J. The diagnostic mystique—a point of view. *The Reading Teacher,* 1974, **27**(6), 555-561.

Miscue Research and Readability

Laura A. Smith
An instructor in the Teacher Education Division, Wayne State University, Laura A. Smith teaches courses in reading and language arts and supervises student teachers.

Findings of miscue research suggest new bases for judging the readability of classroom materials. They reveal the limitations of today's commonly accepted measures of readability, and have definite implications for future selection of classroom materials in reading as well as reading materials in the content areas.

As part of the reading miscue research project, we were given the opportunity to field test stories and articles being considered for inclusion in a new basal reading series.[1] The sample included children from various areas of the United States who read the materials orally. Their miscues were analyzed and their retellings of the stories were studied. Miscue analysis, retellings, and discussions with the children became the basis for determining how interesting and understandable the materials were to the students.

On the basis of our findings, recommendations were made to the authors concerning the materials. These included possible changes in syntax, vocabulary, and, in some cases, even in the names of characters in the stories.

In our work, we found many factors that seemed to be ignored by readability scales. These factors could generally be divided into two categories: Language Related Factors and Concept Related Factors. This is not to suggest that these two factors did not operate simultaneously.

In the area of Language Related Factors, it seemed not so much a matter of how long sentences were but how predictable they were.

Very long sentences could be read if the grammatical function of words and their meanings were familiar. For example, brown used as a color was not a problem for beginning readers, but when it appeared as a person's name, Mr. Brown, these same readers could not recognize it. They didn't expect it. Brown would not be considered a "new" or "hard" word in a reading series since it was earlier introduced as a color word.

Children who knew the word saddle and could read it when it appeared as a noun, did not anticipate it as a verb and found it more difficult when used as one. In one story at the second-grade level, we found that readers were able to read the word place in the sentence He found him in an open place, but later had difficulty with the word when it was used to mean put in the sentence Place him in a hole in the ground. At the third-grade level, just was a problem when it appeared

1. Scott Foresman Reading Systems, Scott Foresman and Company, Glenview, Illinois, 1971.

with the meaning of *right* in the phrase *just next to the hole in the tree.*
Pipe was less predictable when it appeared meaning *bagpipe* or *piper*
or *piping* than when it appeared with a more familiar meaning.

In each of these cases either the word itself was not expected
... not predictable... or it caused the reader to expect something that
didn't follow.

Very long sentences could be read if the phrases in them were familiar. Such awkward and unfamiliar phrases as *she walks in such a way* and *Charlie turned his attention,* and expressions such as *a gust of wind* and *fat and firm* caused readers more difficulty than either their length or the "difficulty" of the words would suggest. Very often these phrases are the result of translations from other languages or are common forms used at other times or places.

Very long sentences could be read if the phrases were in predictable order both within and between sentences. One of the selections we tried with third graders was from *Winnie the Pooh* (Milne, 1965). It is beautiful when read aloud but children had difficulty predicting such phrase order as *"I've been thinking," said Pooh. "And what I've been thinking is, I think I will ..."* In another story under consideration for second or third grade, the text was: *Jonathan had gone quite a way before it suddenly came to him. He stood still in the snow, feeling cross with himself. You and I know what he had forgotten* (Daigliesh, 1952). This is perfectly understandable in oral language. It is fine for a storyteller. But readers expected the story to continue. They did not expect a personal message from the author. Because the course of action or order was unpredictable, it often caused readers to reread in order to understand what was happening.

Very long sentences could be read if the tense choices were familiar to the reader and predictable in the story. When the author changed from one tense to another, often to make a subtle point, readers tended to change tenses to fit previous structures or to match their expectations.

In one story at the fourth-grade level the text read *I wish this could be from Margaret, thought Janie. But it can't.* The readers tended to change *But it can't* to *But it couldn't* to make it match the previous sentence.

In another story the author tried to make the subtle point that the hero knows that he cannot do what he wanted to do, and writes *I wanted to pipe*. Our readers, ever hopeful, read *I want to pipe*.

Very long sentences could be read if the word order was predictable. Questions and negative statements were not consistently anticipated in the stories. These constructions were often changed to positive statements. If nothing came into the action later to give the reader a clue to his first miscue, the miscue tended not to be corrected.

Sentences beginning with the words *what, where, when* usually caused readers to anticipate questions, and the word order was changed to make a question. This left the reader with a problem of understanding the remainder of the sentence.

The word order in directions and descriptions of processes caused more miscues than stories with a plot. In evaluating a story about Wilbur and Orville Wright, readers had more difficulty reading the descriptions of a giant kite and a mouse trap than with the rest of the story. Further, the readers did not include these descriptions in their retelling. They generally did not understand the descriptions as well as they did the story.

Dialogue and dialogue carriers, also known as direct speech and speech markers, were another area of difficulty. At early levels there were differences in readers' abilities to handle *John said, "I want to go."* and *"I want to go," said John*. A dialogue carrier placed in the middle of what is being said proved even more confusing.

Some authors further complicate this structure by including the name of the person being talked to: *"We must hurry, John," said Mother. "We will be late."* This was often read: *"We must hurry," John said. "Mother, we will be late."* or even *We must hurry. John said, "Mother we will be late."*

The problems encountered with the use of unusual dialogue carriers like *continued, explained, hazarded, replied, retorted, spluttered,* and *bellowed* is probably obvious. But *shouted, cried, screamed* and *smiled* are also problems when used as dialogue carriers. Children expect these words to indicate real actions, not a way to say something.

Simple additions to dialogue carriers like *gloomily, firmly, solemnly, anxiously,* and *briskly* were a problem. Some authors carry the additions further: *said Jonathan full of politeness and hunger* and *"That's all right," Miss Robbins, her earrings swinging, smiled at*

Beezus. "Get your paints and paper. Today everyone is painting an imaginary animal." (Cleary 1955).

We found three Concept Related Factors to be important: (1) the amount of specialized vocabulary, (2) the amount of vocabulary that was unfamiliar to the reader and (3) the complexity of the concept and how well, how thoroughly, it was developed.

The amount of specialized vocabulary is a fairly obvious factor. Unfamiliar words may be sounded out or said in some way, but this is often little help in knowing what the words mean. This is a greater problem for young readers than for older readers because their exposure to specialized vocabulary is often limited. Adults are often unaware that for a child, specialized vocabulary is not limited to *pipers, pipes, chanter, drones, bonnets, clans, tartans, moors, sconces* and *cabers,* but can include *wheeling gulls, crashing waves, canals, waving fields of wheat, pop* or *soda, tennis shoes* or *sneakers, spades* or *shovels.*

Not only teachers but also those who write and select materials for children must remember that there are regional and background differences among readers and that a reader's difficulty with a particular story may be due to limited concepts.

Elementary school science and social studies materials are often difficult for students because they sometimes fail to develop a concept in depth; rather, they present large numbers of facts and details. They are often about as predictable as a grocery list. One second-grade text dealing with turtles told, in thirteen sentences, (1) the names of three kinds of turtles, (2) where each of them lives, (3) how two of them look, (4) what two of them can do and (5) what one of them likes to do. Little of this information would be new to readers who knew about turtles, but much of it could not be read by readers with limited experience with turtles. The readers with limited related experience could not predict or understand *snap at* as an action. And they were not familiar with *ponds, lakes, streams, woods* or *meadows.*

Readers' abilities to deal with any of these factors grow as they become more proficient and better able to handle complex language and concepts. For example, in the area of phrase order, we found that late first graders were more able to deal with the sentence *We can put on a show if we can do it* (a magic trick) than if the phrases were reversed: *If we can do it, we can put on a show.* They seemed to have difficulty holding the initial idea while they read the second idea. But after stating the first idea, *We can put on a show*, they could add the qualification, *if we can do it*. Readers just a year older did not find this a problem.

In dealing with more complex and unfamiliar usages, we found that second-grade readers expected the word *had* to show possession: *He had a hat* or necessity: *He had to go with his father*. When we tried some of Carolyn Haywood's stories with second-grade readers, they expected *had* to be followed by *a* or *to*. Instead they found such phrases as *He had stopped, He had just come*, and *He had never. Had* was not a new word but it caused them to make some false predictions as to what was coming next. At the fourth-grade level we used another author who used *had* as an auxiliary, and we found that fourth graders had no difficulty with *had made*, or *had suggested*. But they did not expect *She had had fun* or *Janie had had plenty of friends*. They tended to omit the second *had* or to go back and reread to see if something were wrong.

Underlying all these findings is the disturbing fact that no existing readability scale takes the reader into consideration. The amount of frustration readers will tolerate depends on their personalities, how proficient they are as readers, how well they think they read, what they expect the reading process to be, and their interest in the material. Readability scales need to deal with both authors' and readers' styles, not just with the printed materials.

References

Cleary, B. *Beezus and Ramona.* New York: William Morrow, 1955.

Daigliesh, A. *Bears on Hemlock Mountain.* New York: Charles Scribner's Sons, 1952.

Milne, A. A. *The House at Pooh Corner.* New York: E. P. Dutton, 1965.

An Afterword and a Look Forward

P. David Allen

The preceding discussions of oral reading miscues offer an overview of the research done at Wayne State University between 1965 and 1974 and also indicate the research that is still going on in the fields of developmental reading, remedial reading, and reading in the content areas. Beyond these fields, research is needed to discover the most appropriate reading materials for instruction and how miscue analysis might relate to the cloze procedure, as a technique for measuring comprehension and as a method for establishing readability.

The Wayne State scholars also broke new ground in the areas of testing, clinical implications, and modes and materials for reading instruction. Their studies form only the beginnings of investigations that need to be broadened and deepened. The sort of psycholinguistic analysis of miscues represented by the Goodman Taxonomy may also be useful for examining oral and written language.

As for the application of miscue research, we have mentioned the Reading Miscue Inventory developed by Yetta Goodman and Carolyn Burke. This inventory, worked out during a project in El Cajon, California, is for classroom teachers to use for meaningful diagnosis and evaluation. Currently projects utilizing the R.M.I. are under way in the Columbus, Ohio and Norfolk, Virginia public schools. These projects represent extensive inservice training efforts. The R.M.I. is also enjoying wide distribution at the college level and is used for education of future teachers of reading. Yetta Goodman and Carolyn Burke are now developing prototype strategy lessons as the next step for meeting individual students' needs as diagnosed by the Reading Miscue Inventory.

A two-year project recently completed by Kenneth Goodman and funded by the National Institute of Education offers an example of the continuing nature of miscue research and its application. This project analyzed oral reading miscues of groups of twelve children from each of eight language groups, reading two stories. At this writing, findings have undergone preliminary analysis and suggest that researchers can learn how bilingual a pupil is from the miscues he or she produces. Readers nonfunctional in English showed more preoccupation with letters and words and less control of syntax, intonation, and meaning.

Of the groups studied, four were speakers of low-status dialects of English—pidgin of Honolulu, black English of rural Mississippi, Appalachian of Cumberland Gap, and downeast from coastal Maine. Preliminary analysis indicates that even pidgin speakers, whose dialect most diverges from standard English, still have sufficient receptive control over the dialect of books that they are not handicapped or disadvantaged in developing literacy.

Patterns were more complex among children in groups whose first language was not English. Spanish speakers from southeast Texas seemed truly bilingual and functioned like monolingual speakers of English in their reading. Samoan immigrants to Hawaii and Arabic immigrants to Detroit showed greater individual variation. Navajos, the most truly American subjects, appeared least bilingual and showed miscue patterns least like those of monolingual English speakers.

Most of the reading researchers whose findings are reported in this book are in universities where their major responsibilities are teaching courses in reading instruction. Clearly, their research has led them to a definite point of view about reading instruction and the preparation of teachers of reading. Their findings have brought them to believe that not just reading instruction but the whole content area known as "general education" needs to be re-examined.

Reading teachers today, no less than language arts teachers and teachers in content areas, need a strong background in the nature of the English language: linguistics, psycholinguistics, cognitive psychology, and language acquisition. We need to decide whether such a background should be taught at the undergraduate or graduate level, and who should be responsible for the courses. But if there is any one specific conclusion emerging from the research embodied in this book it is that we need to examine carefully the preparation of *teachers* of reading teachers, as well as the preparation of the reading teachers themselves.

APPENDICES

Appendix A: The Goodman Taxonomy of Reading Miscues

A Note on the Taxonomy: As Kenneth Goodman explains in his article, "What We Know about Reading," the Taxonomy through which miscue researchers explore the reading process has already been revised several times to take into account new findings. Its evolution is continuing with another major revision, now in process.

The version reproduced here appeared in 1973 as part of a government research project report (Goodman, K. S. and Burke, C. L. *Theoretically based studies of patterns of miscues in oral reading performance.* [U.S.O.E. Project No. 90375] Grant No. OEG-0-9-320375-4269. Washington, D.C., U.S. Department of Health, Education, and Welfare, March, 1973.) This manual and its revisions utilize established computer programs. If teachers or researchers wish to use the manual in research, they may obtain information on the computer programs by querying Dr. Kenneth Goodman, College of Education, University of Arizona, Tucson, Arizona 85721.

On the following pages each of the eighteen categories of the taxonomy are briefly outlined and examples are given. There are some limitations placed on the examples used.

1   There is no consistent way of representing the intonation which has caused us to make specific keying decisions. In some cases punctuation markings and/or the changing grammatical function of the E R items will serve as partial indicators.

2   All of the examples presented contain only one miscue per sentence. While this situation does not always exist in continuous text, it does serve to focus attention within the examples.

3   All of the examples (with the exception of those in the correction category) are presented as if they were not corrected. This is the state in which the E R sentence must be read to answer the taxonomy questions.*

4   All of the examples represent miscues made by children studied in the research. In the instance of a couple of subcategories we have been unable to supply examples.

1 CORRECTION

A reader can produce a miscue and be totally unaware that he has varied from the text. In such instances the reading will continue uninterrupted.

When the reader does become aware of a miscue, he can choose to correct either silently or orally, or he can choose to continue without correcting.

Uninterrupted reading at the point of a miscue can be related to the reader's lack of awareness of the miscue, his use of silent correction or his conscious awareness that he is unable to handle the variation. We have no consistent method devised for distinguishing between these possibilities.

It is possible to note some silent corrections by paying attention to pauses in the reading, by checking miscues made during repeated occurrences of the same word in text, and by comparing miscues made during the reading with successful usage during the oral retelling.

Because our proficiency in identifying silent miscues is sufficient to substantiate their existence but not to accurately tally their occurrences the correction category is used only to tally oral correction occurrences.

The occurrence of a correction or correction attempt is evidence that the reader feels he has made a miscue. In order to correct a reader must repeat material which has already been read. The length of the repetition (whether it involves one or several words) can provide a cue to when the reader became conscious of the miscue and/or the point at which he was able to determine the word.

It is possible for the correction attempt to occur further on in the text either due to repeated occurrences of the word or to the developing semantic context of the reading. Corrections that occur across structures and not with near immediacy to the miscue occurrence will not be coded in this category.

In no time at all Sven's pet was everybody's pet̲.̲ *pup*

pup for *pet* is coded 1.0 (not corrected)

When a complex miscue is involved, the correction category must be keyed on the main line of the miscue only.

He had a smile on his face. *small* |*one* ©

The miscue is *small one* for *smile on* and is coded 1.9 (unsuccessful correction).

0 *No attempt at correction is made.*

She pounded the young tree into (long) strings.

Then he picked up the fawn and carried it home.

When warm weather came,̲ the Whitemoons moved to their summer camp. *to*

1 *The miscue is corrected.*

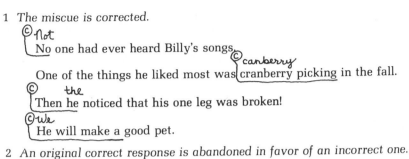

© *not*
No one had ever heard Billy's songs.

© *cranberry*
One of the things he liked most was cranberry picking in the fall.

© *the*
Then he noticed that his one leg was broken!

© *we*
He will make a good pet.

2 *An original correct response is abandoned in favor of an incorrect one.*

(AC) ② ↓
① "You can't prove it!" the hunter said.

9 *An unsuccessful attempt is made at correcting the miscue.*

(UC) *crawled* ②
crowned ①
Then they crowded into the car.

(UC) *creeped*
cr —
Then they crowded into the car.

Additional Notes: Terminal punctuation can be assumed to be corrected when the reader adjusts the intonation of the following structure. ©

We had just never had any pets until Sven Olsen decided he wanted one.

©
Freddie nodded sadly. Sometimes he thought that a scientist's life was filled

with disappointments.

2 DIALECT

Dialects of a language vary from each other through phonemes, intonation, vocabulary and structure. Phonemic and intonation variation almost never result in any meaning or structural changes. Only dialect miscues which involve vocabulary or structural changes will be coded in this category.

For specific substudies phonemic dialect variations can be coded on the Multiple Attempts Taxonomy and under the secondary dialect influence and doubtful subheadings of the general taxonomy.

In substudies which record phonemic variations use a spelling which approximates what was said while retaining as much as possible of the ER spelling. This representation is preceded by a dollar sign ($).

In all other studies, the general rule of thumb is to accept the wide range of phonological variants found in communities as within the limits of the expected response and hence not miscues.

When a miscue has been marked DIALECT it can not be coded under ALLOLOG.

0   *Dialect is not involved in the miscue.* The OR is not recognizable as a distinguishing feature of a specific group of speakers.

1   *Dialect is involved in the miscue.* The OR is recognizable as a vocabulary item or structure which is a distinguishable part of the speech system of an identifiable group of speakers.

ER But the woman said to him, "Do not go."
OR But *the woman, she,* took him, "Do not go."

ER I don't have *any* pennies.   ER He *is* a funny pet.
OR I don't have *no* pennies.   OR He a funny pet.

ER Neither of us *was* there.
OR Neither of us *were* there.

Bound morpheme differences of inflected words. Dialect miscues involving bound morphemes will be treated graphically as having a standard spelling; /help/ and /helpt/ are both spelled *helped* and morphonemically as having null forms of the inflectional endings. The absence of an ending is itself a signal. Hence, *help* (   ) for *help (ed)* is a substitution rather than an omission.

ER helped   ER Freddie's   graphic 3.9
OR help   OR Freddie   bound & combined morpheme 13.11
                                   word & free morpheme 14.18

Bound morpheme differences of noninflected words. Some words register tense or number changes internally (woman/women) while others have neither inflectional nor internal changes (sheep/sheep). It is possible for the reader to become confused over what constitutes the root word (present tense of a verb, singular form of a noun). Where this confusion is habitual to a particular reader it will be marked idiolect (2.2). Where it is habitual to a group of people, it will be marked dialect (2.1). In these instances the reader does not change tense or number by his miscue.

ER sheep   ER women   dialect 2.1 or .2
OR sheeps   OR womens   bound & combined morpheme 13.17

In other instances the reader is not confused over what the root word is, but simply applies alternate rules in order to produce tense or number changes.

ER women	ER men	ER drew	dialect 2.1
OR woman (pl.)	OR mans	OR drawed	bound & combined
			morpheme 13.12

2 *Idiolect is involved in the miscue.* The OR is recognizable as a vocabulary item or structure which is a distinguishable part of the speech system of the reader. It is an example of his own personal dialect but will not be a part of the patterns of his speech community.

ER Elizabeth	ER library	ER refrigerator
OR $Lizabit	OR $liberry	OR $frigerator
(phonemic)	(phonemic)	(morphemic)

3 *A supercorrection is involved in the miscue.* In some instances a reader intentionally uses a word pronunciation which he views as being acceptable regardless of the pronunciation he habitually uses in speech situations. This can be a reflection of what he hears or thinks he hears in others' dialects. It can be a school-taught pronunciation which is an attempt to use a reading dialect or a supposed literate form.

| ER kitten | ER frightened | ER a tree |
| OR kit+ten | OR frighten+ed | OR ā tree |

| ER started | ER the man |
| OR start+ted | OR thē man |

This category will be used on the Multiple Attempts Taxonomy for substudies which include phonemic dialect variations. It will also be used on the general taxonomy if an example of supercorrection which includes structural changes can be identified.

4 *There is a secondary dialect involvement in the miscue.* The OR which the reader produces involves a variation which can be identified as dialect, idiolect or supercorrection.

ER ... learning the ways of the range and the work of a sheep dog.
OR ... learning the ways of the range and the work of *coming* a sheep dog. (*coming* is an idiolect variation for *becoming*)

ER Why were there no coyote fires at night?
OR Why were *not no* coyote fires at night? (*not no* is a dialect form)

ER I could see he was watching to make sure his whispering wasn't disturbing the thing that lay there.
OR I could see he was watching to make sure his *whispers* wasn't disturbing the thing that lay there. (*whispers wasn't* is a dialect form)

Additional Notes: This category is used on the general taxonomy only for substudies which include phonemic dialect variations or if an example of secondary dialect involvement which includes structural changes can be identified.

5   *A foreign language influence is involved in the miscue.* The reader applies to an English word the phonological rules of an alternate language which he speaks.

ER chair   ER busy
OR $shair (French influence)   OR $bissy (French influence)

This subcategory will be used on the Multiple Attempts Taxonomy for substudies which include phonemic dialect variations. It will also be used on the general taxonomy if an example of foreign language influence which includes structural changes can be identified.

9   *Dialect involvement is doubtful.* There is a lack of conclusive information on which to make a definite decision, but dialect involvement is suspected. When "doubtful" is marked the rest of the taxonomy categories are coded as if there is no dialect involvement.

   This category is generally marked only for suspected dialect involving vocabulary substitutions or structural changes. Phonemic variations are included only for specifically designated substudies.

3 & 4 GRAPHIC AND PHONEMIC PROXIMITY

A reader must anticipate the structures and meanings of the author. In so doing both the graphemes and related phonemes of the ER are available to him as cues. The physical shape and/or the sound patterns related to the ER function in determining the reader's choice of the OR.

   The two categories are scored using a zero through nine scale of increasing similarity. The points on the scales are intended to have equal weight across the two categories. Only word level substitutions are keyed.

3 GRAPHIC PROXIMITY

Blank *This category is inappropriate.* The miscue involves:
   a An omission or an insertion of a word.

      ER "Here *take* one," said the man.
      OR "Here one," said the man.

      ER The herder patted Chip and gave an arm signal toward the flock.
      OR The herder patted Chip and gave *him* an arm signal toward the flock.

   b A phrase level substitution in which the two phrases can not be broken down into submiscues.

ER You *do not have to stay home.*
OR You *may go and have fun.*

Or, a phrase level substitution for a single word (or the reverse.)

ER ...is quite a *businessman.*   ER do not
OR ...is quite a *busy man.*   OR don't

c Phrase or clause level intonation changes only. The specific word involved might change its grammatical category but not its spelling or its pronunciation.

ER ...that grew under *water, snails, and...*
OR ...that grew *underwater snails, and...*

ER He still thought it more fun to pretend to be a great scientist, mixing the *strange* and the *unknown.*
OR He still thought it more fun to pretend to be a great scientist, mixing the *strange* and the *unknown*o———➤

ER It was fun to go to *school. When* he wasn't in *school, he* skated with his friends.
OR It was fun to go to *school when* he wasn't in *school. He* skated with his friends.

d Reversal miscues that involve no substitution of ER items.

ER suck the venom out   ER look first
OR suck out the venom   OR first look

0 *There is no graphic similarity between ER and the OR.*

ER the	ER too	ER so	ER huddle
OR a	OR very	OR but	OR moving
ER looking	ER coyote	ER urged	ER had
OR $intellate	OR fighting	OR only	OR been

1 *The ER and the OR have a key letter or letters in common.*

ER for	ER under	ER be	ER accident
OR of	OR ground	OR keep	OR instead
ER with	ER enough	ER ledges	ER made
OR this	OR often	OR glen	OR read

2 *The middle portions of the ER and OR are similar.*

ER zoom	ER took	ER touch	ER explode
OR cook	OR looked	OR would	OR $imploy
ER Elizabeth	ER bold		
OR Isabel	OR glow		

3 *The end portions of the ER and OR are similar.*

ER don't	ER voice	ER sharply	ER uncles
OR needn't	OR face	OR deeply	OR friends

ER taking	ER vegetate		
OR checking	OR $invirate		

4 *The beginning portions of the ER and OR are similar.*

ER perceive	ER may	ER have
OR perhaps	OR might	OR hadn't

ER queer	ER out	ER experiment
OR quick	OR of	OR $exmotter

5 *The beginning and middle portions of the ER and OR are similar.*

ER chloroform	ER walk	ER went
OR chlorophyll	OR walked	OR wanted

ER narrowed	ER morally	ER vapid
OR $nearow	OR normal	OR rapidly

6 *The beginning and end portions of the ER and OR are similar.*

ER twitching	ER pets	ER lamps
OR twinkling	OR puppies	OR lights

ER library	ER uncle	ER must
OR liberty	OR once	OR might

or, the middle and end portions of the ER and OR are similar.

ER eternal	ER cough	ER glanced
OR internal	OR enough	OR danced

7 *The beginning, middle and end portions of the ER and OR are similar.*

ER chemist	ER quickly	ER preconception
OR $chemisist	OR quietly	OR preoccupation

ER thought	ER exclaimed	ER calibrations
OR through	OR explained	OR celebrations

or, there is reversal involving three or more letters.

ER was	ER spot	ER elbow
OR saw	OR stop	OR below

8 *There is a single grapheme difference between the ER and the OR.*

ER squirting	ER batter	ER stripes	ER A
OR squinting	OR butter	OR strips	OR I

ER sister's	ER cloudy	ER made	ER when
OR sisters	OR $cloudly	OR make	OR then

or, a reversal involving two letters.

ER on	ER stick	ER girl
OR no	OR ticks	OR grill

9 *The ER and the OR are homographs.*

ER read (present tense)	ER live (adjective)
OR read (past tense)	OR live (verb)

ER tear (noun)	ER record (noun)
OR tear (verb)	OR record (verb)

Additional Notes: For numbers 0 through 6, one extra point is added when:

a the ER and OR have similar configuration

ER tab	ER dig	ER plug
OR tip	OR dip	OR play

b or when the ER and OR are two letter words which might have no other points of graphic similarity.

ER to	ER he	ER at
OR in	OR it	OR in

When the OR is a nonword, a spelling is created for it by using the spelling of the ER as a base.

ER caperings	ER scabbard	ER vegetate
OR $camperings	OR $scappard	OR $venget

Dialect miscues involving phonemic variations are treated as having standard spelling.

ER	get	ER	with	ER	this
sounds like /git/		sounds like /wif/		sounds like /dis/	
OR	get	OR	with	OR	this

4 PHONEMIC PROXIMITY

Blank *This category is inappropriate.* The miscue involves:

a An omission or an insertion of a word.

ER Soon he returned *with* two straight sticks.
OR Soon he returned two straight sticks.

ER Her hunger made her sniff hopefully under rocky ledges and along the small trails in the sage.
OR Her hunger made her sniff hopefully under *the* rocky ledges and along the small trails in the sage.

b   A phrase level substitution in which the two phrases are not broken down into submiscues.

ER You *do not have to stay home.*
OR You *may go and have fun.*

Or, a phrase level substitution for a single word.

ER businessman   ER don't
OR busy man   OR do not

c   Phrase or clause level intonation changes only. The specific word involved might change its grammatical category but not its spelling or its pronunciation.

ER ... that grew under *water, snails, and ...*
OR ... that grew *underwater snails, and ...*

ER He still thought it more fun to pretend to be a great scientist, mixing the *strange* and the *unknown.*
OR He still thought it more fun to pretend to be a great scientist, mixing the *strange* and the *unknown*⊙——————⟶

ER It was fun to go to *school. When* he wasn't in *school, he* skated with his friends.
OR It was fun to go to *school when* he wasn't in *school. He* skated with his friends.

d   Reversal miscues that involve no substitution of ER items.

ER suck the venom out   ER look first
OR suck out the venom   OR first look

0 *There is no phonemic similarity between the ER and the OR.*

ER huddled   ER so   ER find   ER have
OR moving   OR but   OR allow   OR use

ER had   ER urged   ER sage
OR been   OR only   OR shack

1 *The ER and the OR have a key sound or sounds in common.*

ER keep   ER under   ER often
OR pick   OR around   OR enough

2 *The middle portion of the ER and OR are similar.*

ER tight   ER his   ER knolls
OR lightly   OR with   OR stroll

ER explode   ER ran
OR $imploy   OR had

3 *The ER and OR have the end portions in common.*

| ER higher | ER voice | ER made |
| OR anger | OR face | OR head |

| ER choked | ER taking | ER had |
| OR caught | OR checking | OR did |

4 *The ER and OR have the beginning portion in common.*

| ER stood | ER before | ER have | ER kite |
| OR still | OR because | OR hadn't | OR cap |

| ER experiment | ER lamp | ER who |
| OR $exmotter | OR light | OR he |

5 *The ER and OR have common beginning and middle portions.*

| ER should | ER smiling | ER needn't |
| OR shouldn't | OR smile | OR needed |

| ER setting | ER neighbor |
| OR settle | OR $neighnew |

6 *The ER and OR have common beginning and end portions*

| ER twitching | ER poured | ER being | ER must |
| OR twinkling | OR pushed | OR beginning | OR much |

| ER tearful | ER while | ER library |
| OR $teareeble | OR well | OR liberty |

or, they have common middle and end portions.

| ER calibrations | ER eternal | ER moisture |
| OR celebrations | OR internal | OR posture |

| ER cellar | ER expressed |
| OR curler | OR impressed |

7 *The beginning, middle and end portions of the ER and OR are similar.*

| ER dissidents | ER crowded | ER Maximilian |
| OR descendents | OR crowned | OR $Maxiymilan |

| ER exclaimed |
| OR explained |

8 *The ER and OR differ by a single vowel or consonant or vowel cluster*

| ER grow | ER A | ER stripes | ER sighed |
| OR grew | OR I | OR strips | OR said |

| ER round | ER Tom | ER when | ER cloudy |
| OR around | OR Tommy | OR then | OR $cloudly |

or, there is a morphophonemic difference

E R went   E R pen
OR $wint   OR $pin

or, there is an intonational shift (including the schwa).

E R a   E R contract (v)
OR ā   OR contract (n)

9   *The ER and OR are homophones.*

E R read   E R too   E R heir
OR red   OR two   OR air

5   ALLOLOGS

Allologs are considered to be alternate representational forms for the same
item. Unlike synonyms there is no meaning change involved in the substitution of allolog forms. Both forms are generally available to the same language
user; he uses them in different settings.

0   *An allolog is not involved in the miscue.*

   a   The miscue is coded under DIALECT. (The only exception to this rule is
        5.4—long and short form or syllable deletion/insertion.)
   b   The miscue is coded under SEMANTIC WORD RELATIONSHIPS.

1   *The OR is a contracted form of the ER.*

E R can not   E R that is   E R you have
OR can't   OR that's   OR you've

2   *The OR is a full form of the ER contraction.*

E R won't   E R haven't   E R let's
OR will not   OR have not   OR let us

3   *The OR is a contraction which is not represented in print.*

E R He will not go.
OR He willn't go.

4   *The OR is either a long or short form of the ER.* This must be an alternatve
    available form within the dialect of the reader,

E R airplane   E R Tom   E R because   E R into
OR plane   OR Tommy   OR 'cause   OR in

E R toward   E R round   E R trouser pocket
OR towards   OR around   OR trousers pocket

or the OR involves a syllable deletion or insertion. This must be an alternative available form within the idiolect of the reader.

ER regardless ER refrigerator
OR irregardless OR frigerator

5 *The OR involves a shift to idiomatic form.*

ER The sheep were spreading *over* the sides.
OR The sheep were spreading *all over* the sides.

ER ... reading the words *aloud.*
OR ... reading the words *out loud.*

6 *The OR involves a shift from idiomatic form.*

ER The boss *took in* the camp at a glance.
OR The boss *took* the camp at a glance.

ER He is going *on* nine.
OR He is going *to be* nine.

7 *The OR involves a misarticulation.* This is an inadvertent production of a form for which the reader has another acceptable form.

ER Aluminum ER strings ER brother ER soft-soled
OR $Alunimum OR $shtrings OR $brothy OR $soft-sholed

In instances where the reader has an articulation difficulty and is unable to produce the acceptable form, 2.2 'idiolect' is marked.

6 & 7 SYNTACTIC AND SEMANTIC ACCEPTABILITY

A sentence can be viewed as involving both a syntactic organization and a semantic organization. The effects that a miscue has upon these two systems can be analyzed both in terms of acceptability and of change.

The following two categories are concerned only with whether the OR produces structure and/or meaning which is acceptable within the context of the material.

A reader reacts to the correctness and the expectedness of material in terms of his own dialect. In both of the acceptability categories, the reader's dialect is the norm by which the material is judged.

6 SYNTACTIC ACCEPTABILITY

The grammatical structures forming the sentence must be viewed apart from any semantic meaning which they carry. The view is an abstract one involving possible grammatical function organization. The sentence: "Canaries are very vicious dogs." involves a grammatical organization.

Subject	be	intensifier	adjective	subject
pl. noun	present			complement
	tense pl.			common
				pl.

which is completely acceptable while *canaries* does not fit semantically with the rest of the sentence.

The test for the syntactic acceptability of any word is that an acceptable English sentence be able to be produced with that word in the specified position.

ER Did you see ~~my~~ ^the^ little monkey?

The grammatical function has been changed from possessive pronoun to determiner, but the resulting structure is fully acceptable.

It is possible for the miscue to produce a significant change in grammar which is still acceptable within the context. This category is meant to register only the acceptability of the OR to the rest of the material.

As a reader processes a sentence, it is possible for an initial miscue to cause the need either for a regression correction or for additional changes in the structure in order to maintain its acceptability. Whether or not a reader chooses to make these adjustments provides a cue to his processing of grammatical structure. In determining syntactic acceptability, the entire sentence is read with all uncorrected miscues intact.

The quick eyes of the boss found what Jacob saw, and he shouted, "Don't shoot! That's Peggy."

In coding *that* the sentence must be read:

The quick eyes of the boss found that Jacob saw, and he shouted, "Don't shoot! That's Peggy."

In coding *was* the sentence must be read:

The quick eyes of the boss found what Jacob was and he shouted, "Don't shoot! That's Peggy."

In coding *I* the sentence must be read:

The quick eyes of the boss found what Jacob saw, and he shouted, "Don't shoot! I Peggy."

The structure which is treated as an "entire sentence" is defined by Kellogg Hunt's concept of "minimal terminable unit."

It had been a long day for the dogs/and Peggy limped heavily as she approached the camp. (2 minimal terminable units)

The rays of the setting sun lingered over the high Arizona desert, touching the rocky tip of Badger Mountain and tinting the bold face of Antelope Rim. (1 minimal terminable unit)

0 *The miscue results in a structure which is completely syntactically unacceptable.* The miscue disrupts the structure of the sentence and does not have any possible grammatical relationship with either prior or succeeding portions of the sentence.

ER I couldn't *help* feeling proud.
OR I couldn't feeling proud.

ER My blue airplane *is* not here.
OR My blue airplane *look* not here.

ER *Look* for the red train.
OR *The* for the red train.

1 *The miscue results in a structure which is syntactically acceptable only with the prior portion of the sentence.* It would be possible to complete this segment and produce an acceptable grammatical structure.

ER Billy was delighted that *the* roots had made such beautiful colors.
OR Billy was delighted that *he*/roots had made such beautiful colors.

ER I stood still beside him watching. Harry was watching too and sweating all over his face so it shone like it was smeared thick with face cream.
OR I stood still beside him watching Harry./was watching too and sweating all over his face so it shone like it was smeared thick with face cream.

ER He had *the* blue airplane.
OR He had blue/airplane.

ER The shallow basin of Salt Creek Wash became a gathering pool of darkness where a band of eight hundred sheep with their lambs were bedding down for the night on a small patch of meadow.
OR The shallow basin of Salt Creek Wash became a gathering pool of darkness where a band of eight hundred sheep *were*/with their lambs were bedding down for the night on a small patch of meadow.

2 *The miscue results in a structure which is syntactically acceptable only with the following portion of the sentence.* It would be possible to complete this segment and produce an acceptable grammatical structure.

ER He pulled the kitchen stepladder *out* into the hall.
OR He pulled the kitchen stepladder/*walked* into the hall.

ER Both of us *together* can open the door.
OR Both of us/*Tommy* can open the door.

ER "Is my little monkey here?" said the man.
OR "Is my little/the monkey here?" said the man.

3 *The miscue results in a structure which is syntactically acceptable only within the sentence.* The OR sentence is a completely acceptable structure. However, it does not fit within the structural restraints that are operating within the larger context of the material.

ER *Where* did you get your pretty hat?
OR Did you get your pretty new hat?

(The plot of the story revolves around a number of people commenting on a new hat which Mrs. Duck is unaware of wearing. The question must reflect the person's awareness of the hat.)

ER Every year they *give* a prize to the student with the most original outside project.
OR Every year they *gave* a prize to the student with the most original outside project.

(The plot involves the author's attempt to win the prize. The action must be continuing.)

4 *The miscue results in a structure which is syntactically acceptable within the total passage.* The OR sentence is a completely acceptable structure which fits within the structural restraints operating within the larger context of the material.

ER He *wanted* to see what was inside.
OR He *went* to see what was inside.

ER He was making an electric bell *as a surprise* for his mother.
OR He was making an electric bell *to surprise* his mother.

ER He started to go *quickly* across the room.
OR He started to go *quick* across the room.

Additional Notes: When a miscue is an omission, the word following (preceding) must be included in the reading for the miscue to be syntactically acceptable with prior portion of sentence (6.1),

ER Mrs. Duck looked *here* and there.
OR Mrs. Duck looked and/there.

ER The expression *was* in the eyes and around the mouth.
OR The expression in/the eyes and around the mouth.

or syntactically acceptable with following portion of sentence (6.2).

ER "He did not stop here," said Sue.
OR "He did/not here," said Sue.

ER "If it bothers you *to* think of it as baby sitting," my father said, . . .
OR "If it bothers/you think of it as baby sitting," my father said, . . .

When either the first or the last word of a sentence is involved in a miscue, the possible structural relationships to the rest of the sentence are limited to "total acceptability," (either 6.3 or 6.4)

ER *Then* one day Freddie made an interesting mixture.
OR One day Freddie made an interesting mixture.

ER From the strings she made beautiful *baskets*.
OR From the strings she made beautiful *blankets*.

ER *Where* did you get your pretty hat?
OR Did you get your pretty hat?

or to "total unacceptability" (6.0).

ER *A* policeman stared at them.
OR *I* policeman stared at them.

ER *His* eyes caught sight of a red jacket.
OR *He* eyes caught sight of a red jacket.

ER I'll be back *soon*.
OR I'll be back *so*.

7 SEMANTIC ACCEPTABILITY

The acceptability of the meaning involved in the OR sentence is the concern. Multiple miscues can occur within a sentence. The reader has the option of correcting them or of altering the material. When determining semantic acceptability, the entire sentence will be read with all uncorrected miscues intact. (An "entire sentence" will be defined as being a Minimal Terminable Unit.)

He was speaking slowly and trying to think the thing out while he talked.

The omission of *the* is unacceptable with any portion of the sentence and will be marked 7.0. Because of this first miscue the substitution of *we* for *he* will only be marked acceptable with following, 7.2.

The structural organization of a sentence forms the basis for semantic relationships. Meaning, as a language system, is dependent upon syntax. It is the order of items and the use of inflection that indicate the meaning relationships of the items. The syntactic order is separate from and can precede the meaning but the meaning can not exist without the order. Semantic acceptability can never be scored higher than syntactic acceptability.

She was a small yellow canary.

syntactic acceptability 6.4
semantic acceptability 7.0

0 *The miscue results in a structure which is completely semantically*
   unacceptable. The miscue disrupts the meaning of the sentence and does
   not have any possible semantic relationship with either prior or following
   portions of the sentence.

   E R One of the things he liked most was *cranberry* picking in the fall.
   OR One of the things he liked most was *$carberry* picking in the fall.

   E R Kitten Jones would not have changed her white *fur* coat for anything.
   OR Kitten Jones would not have changed her white *few* coat for anything.

   E R Billy liked to take part in the work of *his* tribe.
   OR Billy liked to take part in the work of tribe.

1 *The miscue results in a structure which is semantically acceptable only*
   with the prior portion of the sentence. It would be possible to complete this
   segment and produce an acceptable grammatical structure.

   E R I thought I would faint. I thought the refrigerator would explode. I
        knew *it* was Freddie's fault.

   OR I thought I would faint. I thought the refrigerator would explode. I
        knew *I/*was Freddie's fault.

   E R "You're just like your Uncle August—never *letting* well enough alone."
   OR "You're just like your Uncle August—never *lifting/*well enough alone."

   E R It helps me to remember the word definitions *if* I read them out loud.
   OR It helps me to remember the word definitions *I/*read them out loud.

2 *The miscue results in a structure which is semantically acceptable only*
   with the following portion of the sentence. It would be possible to complete
   this segment and produce an acceptable grammatical structure.

   E R His Uncle Maximilian was a real *chemist* with a company in
        Switzerland.
   OR His Uncle Maximilian was a real/*chemistry* with a company in
        Switzerland.

   E R At *once* Freddie set to work seriously.
   OR At */only* Freddie set to work seriously.

   E R Suddenly I jumped from the chair, a wonderful idea *implanted* in my
        brain.
   OR Suddenly I jumped from the chair, a wonderful idea/*implant* in my
        brain.

3 *The miscue results in a structure which is semantically acceptable only*
   within the sentence. The OR sentence is completely semantically accept-

able. However, it does not fit within the semantic restraints that are operating within the larger context of the material.

ER Danny had to hold up the wires for him.
OR Danny had to hold up the *telephone* wires for him.
(Telephone wires are not in the story, nor do they fit in.)

ER She taught him to know the kind of *roots* used by Winnebago Indians for many years.
OR She taught him to know the kind of *roofs* used by Winnebago Indians for many years. (They lived in tepees.)

4 *The miscue results in a structure which is semantically acceptable within the total passage.* The OR sentence is completely semantically acceptable and fits within the semantic restraints that are operating within the larger context of the material.

ER He *wanted* to see what was inside.
OR He *went* to see what was inside.

ER Freddie tried, with all his strength, but he couldn't open the *closet* door.
OR Freddie tried, with all his strength, but he couldn't open the *closed* door.

ER He started to go *quickly* across the room.
OR He started to go *quick* across the room.

ER "I've been waiting for *you."* *He* raised his eyes and looked at me.
OR "I've been waiting for *you,"* *he* raised his eyes and looked at me.

Additional Notes: As with Syntactic Acceptability, when the miscue is an omission, the word following (preceding) must be included in the reading for the miscue to be semantically acceptable with prior portion of sentence (7.1).

ER But he still thought *it* more fun to pretend to be a great scientist . . .
OR But he still thought more/fun to pretend to be a great scientist . . .

ER You haven't told me *what* the idea is yet.
OR You haven't told me the/idea is yet.

or semantically acceptable with following portion of sentence (7.2).

ER When 200 million Americans sign a Sunday New York Times ad opposed *to* the Vietnam War, the Pentagon will retreat.
OR When 200 million Americans sign a Sunday New York Times ad/opposed the Vietnam War, the Pentagon will retreat.

ER There two men were signaling to each other, and *one* was pointing to the clock.
OR There two men were signaling to each other,/and was pointing to the clock.

When either the first or the last word of a sentence is involved in a miscue, the possible semantic relationships to the rest of the sentence are limited to "total acceptability," (either 7.3 or 7.4)

ER *He* will make a good pet.
OR *We* will make a good pet.

ER He and the fawn would race together through the *forest.*
OR He and the fawn would race together through the *field.*

or to "total unacceptability" (7.0).

ER *All* of them were living in Switzerland.
OR *Any* of them were living in Switzerland.

ER She made her own paints from the roots that Billy gathered from the *swamps.*
OR She made her own paints from the roots that Billy gathered from the *stamps.*

8 TRANSFORMATION

A reader works with already generated and transformed grammatical structures. His miscues reflect his anticipation of the deep structure, surface structure and the meaning with which he is dealing. It is possible for a miscue to cause a change in either or both.

Syntactic changes which the reader institutes can occur at either the deep or surface structure level. In this sense, he recreates the generative process of the author and transforms the material.

0 *A grammatical transformation is not involved.* The syntactic structure of the sentence is unchanged.

a A change involving only surface-level morphophonemic rules.

ER an   ER can not
OR a   OR can't

b A change involving meaning only.

ER It *sounded* like a fire siren.
OR It *shouted* like a fire siren.

ER He *taped* the batteries end to end.
OR He *tapped* the batteries end to end.

c Changes occurring within the noun and noun modifier category.

1 Distinctions between masculine and feminine in nouns and titles.

ER Mr.   ER boy
OR Mrs.   OR girl

> ER John
> OR Joan
>
> ER aviator
> OR aviatrix

2 Substitutions of one noun type for another.

> ER The *surprise* is in my box. (common noun)
> OR The *five* is in my box. (word as word name)

3 Changes occurring between noun modifier fillers.

> ER ... during the *television* program. (noun adjunct)
> OR ... during the *televised* program. (verb derived noun)

> ER ... the ears of the *larger* dog. (comparative)
> OR ... the ears of the *large* dog.

4 Some changes between pronouns.

> ER he (she)
> OR it

When the noun referred to is an animal or object.

d An omission or insertion within a grammatical function.

> ER "Look at me," said *Yellow Bird.*
> OR "Look at me," said *Bird.*

Both *Yellow* and *Bird* are keyed as noun phrasal unit, so that the word omission does not cause the omission of the grammatical function.

e Movements of adverbs or particles within a sentence.

> ER Take your shoes *off.*
> OR Take *off* your shoes.

> ER He ran *happily.*
> OR *Happily* he ran.

f Variations not involved in the sentence structure.

> ER The words "*corrals*" and "boss" meant things to Peggy.
> OR The words "*corral*" and "boss" meant things to Peggy.

1 *A transformation occurs which involves a difference in deep structure between the ER and OR. In some instances both syntax and meaning are changed, in others, the syntax changes while the meaning is retained.*

a Differences in tense or number.

> ER As they approached the tent, the thin wail of coyotes reached *her* ears from upstream.
> OR As they approached the tent, the thin wail of coyotes reached *their* ears from upstream.

ER He saw *the* spring flowers.
OR He saw *a* spring flowers.

Determiner substitutions do not usually involve a transformation, but in this case, the determiner substitution causes a move from singular to plural.

b Omissions or insertions of a grammatical function.

ER All of them were living in Switzerland.
OR All of them were living in *about* Switzerland.

ER His father *usually* called him Tinker.
OR His father called him Tinker.

ER She put on a *bright* cotton dress.
OR She put on a cotton dress.

ER He was straining to get the *words* out.
OR He was straining to get out.

ER We have many goals for tomorrow.
OR We have *made* many goals for tomorrow.

c Changes in the relationship of phrases and/or clauses.

ER I'm going to give you an injection. Serum.
OR I'm going to give you an injection of serum.

ER It went in smooth as into cheese.
    (as if it were going into cheese)
OR It went in smooth as cheese.
    (as cheese is smooth)

ER Here, take one. (*you* take one)
OR Here's one. (one *for you*)

ER Typical, that's it, typical. (*that* as a pronoun)
OR Typical, that is, typical. (*that* as a clause marker)

ER On nights when the fires were burning, she often heard coyotes singing *a protest* from distant ridges.
OR On nights when the fires were burning, she often heard coyotes singing *to protest* from distant ridges.

ER He said to keep *quite* still.
OR He said to keep *quiet*, still.

ER I switched off the headlamps of the car so the beam wouldn't swing in through the window of the side bedroom and *wake* Harry Pope.
    (*The beam* wouldn't swing in and *the beam* wouldn't wake)

> OR I switched off the headlamps of the car so the beam wouldn't swing in through the window of the side bedroom and *woke* Harry Pope. (*I* switched off and *I woke*)

2 *A transformation occurs in which the deep structure of the ER and the OR remains the same while the surface structure of the OR is generated by a different set of compulsory rules.* The author and the reader have a different set of obligatory transformations in their grammars.

  a Regional or social dialect variations are involved.

> ER She tore *bunches* of fur from his back.
> OR She tore *bunch* of fur from his back.

> ER He *has* gone to the store.
> OR He gone to the store.

  b The author has produced a structure which is either unusual for the situation or not entirely correct.

> ER Billy knew that fawns *were* very shy.
> OR Billy knew that fawns *are* very shy.

> The shyness of fawns is a continuing situation and need not be past tense because of the verb *knew* in the sentence.

> ER Knew I mustn't move. (This is not a usual surface level deletion.)
> OR *I* knew I mustn't move.

  c Compulsory rule shifts have become involved due to a change in terms.

> ER After *school* one day Ted went for a walk in the park.
> OR After *the show* one day Ted went for a walk in the park.

3 *A transformation occurs in which the deep structure of the ER and the OR remains the same while the surface structure of the OR is generated by alternate available rules.* The reader has available, in his grammar, the transform rules for both ER and OR surface structures.

> ER This senseless, futile debate between *the* obstetrician and the mortician will end.
> OR This senseless, futile debate between obstetrician and the mortician will end.

> To be fully syntactically acceptable *the* before *mortician* would also need to be omitted.

> ER One of them tore chunks of fur and hide from her neck *while* the other slashed a hind foot.
> OR One of them tore chunks of fur and hide from her *neck. The* other slashed a hind foot.

ER   When Freddie told how he *had fixed* the clock Mrs. Miller said, "You're just like Uncle Charles."

OR   When Freddie told how he *fixed* the clock Mrs. Miller said, "You're just like Uncle Charles."

The variation in forms of the past tense does not alter the meaning.

ER   He started to go *quickly* across the room.
OR   He started to go *quick* across the room.

An alternate acceptable adverbial form.

ER   ... counting each step carefully in the dark so I wouldn't take an extra *one* which wasn't there ...

OR   ... counting each step carefully in the dark so I wouldn't take an extra *step* which wasn't there ...

Involves the same antecedent.

ER   The building of coyote fires was not new to her ...
OR   The building of *the* coyote fires was not new to her ...

ER   The herder patted Chip and gave an arm signal ...
OR   The herder patted Chip and gave *him* an arm signal ...

4   *The deep structure has been lost or garbled.* Sometimes the reader is completely unsuccessful in handling the grammatical structure produced by the author because it is new to him, or he fails either to recognize or anticipate it. He does not produce the structure used by the author and he fails to produce any recognizable portion of an alternate structure. (The coding of Phrase—15—and Clause—16—is optional when Transformation is coded "lost or garbled.")

a   The structure has been lost.

ER   "*A doctor.* Of course. That's it. I'll get Ganderbai."
OR   "Of course. That's its. I'll get Ganderbai."

ER   ... "I'm going to give you an injection. *Serum.* Just a prick but try not to move."

OR   ... "I'm going to give you an injection. Just a prick but try not to move."

b   The structure has been garbled. (Syntactic Acceptability has been coded "not acceptable"—6.0)

ER   What his mother called him *depended* on what he had done last.
OR   What his mother called him *$dipedee* on what he had done last.

Neither the use of an inflectional ending or of intonation made it possible to assign a grammatical function to this non-word.

ER *None* of the chemicals in his set was harmful.
OR *Known* of the chemicals in his set was harmful.

ER They were not likely to *explode.*
OR They were not likely to *employed.*

9 *There is some question of whether or not a transformation is involved in the miscue.* Sometimes there might be a doubt as to whether the change which has occurred falls within the parameters of the transformation category. This confusion can be due either to the OR containing a very limited portion of structure or to some confusion concerning the limits of the parameters themselves.

In such situations the Transformation category should be marked "doubtful" (8.9) and the miscue should be keyed, in the rest of the taxonomy categories, as if no transformation is involved.

9 & 10 SYNTACTIC AND SEMANTIC CHANGE

In two previous categories, the syntactic and semantic acceptability of the OR has been measured. The question now becomes one of evaluating how extensive a change the miscue has caused in both the structure and the meaning of the ER.

Like the Graphic Proximity and Phonemic Proximity categories, Syntactic Change and Semantic Change are scored using a zero through nine scale of increasing similarity. The points on the scales are intended to have equal weight across the two categories.

When a miscue produces a sentence which is syntactically acceptable (6.3 or 6.4), the degree of syntactic change between the ER and the OR is measured.

Because syntax can be examined with ever increasing finiteness, the following set of parameters is used for this category.

a In coding Syntactic Change, phrase structure is considered to consist of a surface level NP and VP so that changes involving adverbial phrases are treated as changes within the verb phrase and not as changes in phrase structure.

b The surface structure of a sentence is treated as being composed of independent, dependent and embedded clauses.

independent　　　*He ran home.*
　　　　　　　　The dog bit the man when he entered the cage.

dependent:　　　The girl screamed *when the cars hit.*
　　　　　　　　After the game ended, the team celebrated.

embedded:　　　The *yellow* bird ... (adjective)
　　　　　　　　His house ... (possessive pronominal)
　　　　　　　　He wanted *to buy* a toy. (infinitive)

c Conjunctions are not treated as a part of either the phrase or clause structure when connecting two independent units.

ER He ran and he jumped.   clause—no involvement
OR He ran. He jumped.   phrase—no involvement

ER It was blue and green.   phrase —substitution
OR It was blue-green.   clause—omission

ER He ran and then he sat.   clause—no involvement
OR He ran, then he sat.   phrase—no involvement

When reading the text sentence to determine Syntactic Change all uncorrected miscues made previous to the miscue being keyed must be read intact.

9 SYNTACTIC CHANGE

Blank   *This category is inappropriate.* The miscue involves either no or partial syntactic acceptability (Syntactic Acceptability "0," "1" or "2").

0 *The syntax of the OR and the ER are unrelated.* They retain no single common element of a particular phrase structure.

ER Where'd it bite you?
OR A bite?

1 *The syntax of the OR and the ER have a single element in common.*

2 *The syntax of the OR has a key element which retains the syntactic function of the ER.*

ER You do not have to stay home.
OR You may go and have fun.

Retention of the noun phrase.

3 *There is a major change in the syntax of the OR.*

ER "Sue," said the man. "He did have it."
OR Sue said. "The man, he did have it."

All of the phrases remain present but their basic relationships are altered.

ER He was lying there very still and tense *as though* he was holding onto himself hard because of sharp pain.
OR He was lying there very still and tense *as he thought* he was holding onto himself hard because of sharp pain.

Addition of a clause.

ER "Oh, I like it here."
OR "Go. I like it here."

Addition of a clause.

4 *There is a minor change in the syntax of the OR.*

ER When summer *ended, the* Whitemoons packed their belongings
   again.
OR The summer *ended. The* Whitemoons packed their belongings again.

Move from dependent to independent clause.

ER He was speaking more slowly than ever *now and* so softly I had to lean
   close to hear him.
OR He was speaking more slowly than ever *and now* so softly I had to lean
   close to hear him.

Change in dependency of adverb.

ER Soon he returned *with* two straight sticks.
OR Soon he returned two straight sticks.

Move from prepositional phrase to direct object.

ER "Well, he's home a lot, " *I said.*
OR "Well, he's home a lot."

Omission of the dialogue carrier.

ER He was wearing a pair of pajamas *with blue, brown* and white stripes.
OR He was wearing a pair of pajamas, *blue and brown, with* white stripes.

Move from adjectives embedded in prepositional phrase to subject complements.

5 *There is a major change within the structure of the phrase.* This includes the
   insertion, deletion or substitution within the phrase of any structure having
   more than one constituent.

ER I want you to save half your allowance *for it* each week.
OR I want you to save half your allowance each week.

Omission of a prepositional phrase.

ER He had a carriage.
OR He had a *horse-drawn* carriage.
   (that was drawn by a horse)

Insertion of an embedded clause.

ER I will tell it *all over* Green Hills.
OR I will tell it *all on* Green Hills.

With the substitution of one preposition for another (*over* for *on*), *all* moves from being a function word quantifier to the direct object. Yet the basic structural outlines of the sentence have not changed.

ER He is going *on* nine.
OR He is going *to be* nine.

A verb particle is replaced by an infinitive form.

ER "Then I will find work," said Ted.
OR "Then I will work," said Ted.

The direct object replaces the verb.

6 *There is a minor change within the structure of the phrase.* This includes the insertion, deletion or substitution of any single constituent within the phrase structure.

ER He did see the fires.
OR He did *not* see the fires.

Insertion of the negative.

ER She pounded the young trees into *long* strings.
OR She pounded the young trees into strings.

Omission of embedded adjective.

ER I leaned on the *baby* bed.
OR I leaned on the *baby's* bed.

Move from adjective to possessive noun modifier.

ER ...most of them came from *jungle rivers* where...
OR ...most of them came from *Jungle River* where...

Move from common to proper noun.

ER He raised his eyes and looked *at me*.
OR He raised his eyes and looked *now*.

Move from prepositional phrase to adverb.

ER I *could see* he was awake.
OR I *could have seen* he was awake.

Move from past tense to past perfect.

7 *There is a change in person, tense, number or gender of the OR.*

ER How he *wanted* to go back.
OR How he *wants* to go back.

ER Billy sang for all the *tribe*.
OR Billy sang for all the *tribes*.

E R *I* made a special mixture.
OR *He* made a special mixture.

E R *You* not in bed yet?
OR *You're* not in bed yet.

The move away from the question does not alter the relationship of the sentence to the rest of the text.

8 *There is a change in choice of function word or another minor shift in the OR.* This includes changes within subcategories of a function word and the omission or insertion of optional surface structure. No miscues which cause a change in either dependency or modification will be coded in this subcategory.

a Changes in choice of a function word.

   E R There was *a* dinosaur.
   OR There was *one* dinosaur.

   E R Young dissidents have been widely berated for lacking an alternative *to* the present system.
   OR Young dissidents have been widely berated for lacking an alternative *in* the present system.

   E R ... and the generation now in power will widen *into* a new national fault line.
   OR ... and the generation now in power will widen *to* a new national fault line.

b Omission or insertion of optional surface structure.

   E R He heard the rustling of leaves.
   OR He heard the rustling of *the* leaves.

   E R It is impossible to grow, change, mature or expand, ...
   OR It is impossible to grow, change *and* mature or expand, ...

   E R I saw *that* my mother was smiling broadly.
   OR I saw my mother was smiling broadly.

   E R Knew I mustn't move.
   OR *I* knew I mustn't move.

   E R "Quickly Timber, *but* take your shoes off."
   OR "Quickly Timber, *you* take your shoes off."

   E R I swear *it*.
   OR I swear.

9   *The syntax of the OR is unchanged from the syntax of the ER.* Only form
    class (noun, verb, adjective, adverb) substitutions will be marked here.
    Included are all null forms for tense or number which are dialect variations.

ER The windows were full of *puppies* and kittens.
OR The windows were full of *pets* and kittens.

ER What *queer* experiment was it this time?
OR What *queen* experiment was it this time?

ER What his mother called him *depended* on what he had done last.
OR What his mother called him *depend* on what he had done last.

10   SEMANTIC CHANGE

When a miscue produces a sentence which is semantically acceptable (7.3 or
7.4) the degree of semantic change between the ER and the OR is measured.

In reading the text sentence to determine Semantic Change all uncorrected
miscues made previous to the miscue being keyed must be read intact.

Blank   *This category is inappropriate.* The miscue involves either no or
partial semantic acceptability (Semantic Acceptability marked 0, 1 or 2).

0   *The OR is completely anomalous to the rest of the story.* A concept, action
    or relationship is introduced which is totally incongruous to the rest of the
    story.

ER The bulb began to *glow*.
OR The bulb began to *grow*.

The bulb is an electric light.

ER He came out of his *slump* and looked around.
OR He came out of his *slum* and looked around.

The reference was to how a TV producer was sitting.

ER She turned questioning eyes to the coughing herder and then to the
    sheep and the shadowy figure of *Chip* moving about the band.
OR She turned questioning eyes to the coughing herder and then to the
    sheep and the shadowy figure of *the chimp* moving about the band.

The story involves a sheep herder, two dogs, and a herd of sheep.

1   *There is a change or loss affecting the plot in basic sense or creating major
    anomalies.*

ER It was no less than an hour before *dawn*.
OR It was no less than an hour before *dark*.

The coyotes in the story become a danger to the sheep during the late hours
of the night.

ER *Just* like your Uncle Maximilian!
OR *I* like your Uncle Maximilian!

This line is repeated throughout the story as the mother compares her son to his uncles.

ER We're two days out from the *corrals* and a day late on the drive.
OR We're two days out from the *quarrel* and a day late on the drive.

The possibility of help hinges on their expected arrival at the corrals.

2   *There is a change or loss involving key aspects of the story or seriously interfering with subplots.*

ER "*Oh*, I like it here."
OR "*Go*. I like it here."

The character who is speaking likes her locale because of the other characters. She does not want them to leave.

ER This is the *last* day of Fair Week.
OR This is the *light* day of Fair Week.

This was the main character's only chance to earn money and see the fair.

ER Then her eyes caught a movement in the *sage* near the top of the knoll.
OR Then her eyes caught a movement in the *same* near the top of the knoll.

The plot hinges on the dog successfully picking up the cues of a coyote attack.

3   *There is a change or loss resulting in inconsistency concerning a major incident, major character or major sequence.*

ER Freddie tried with all his strength, but he couldn't open the closet door *either*.
OR Freddie tried with all his strength, but he couldn't open the closet door *enough*.

If the door had opened at all the sister would have had light and Freddie would not have had to construct a flashlight to keep her from being frightened until help came.

ER In one corner of the kitchen, *Freddie* was busy working on an experiment.
OR In one corner of the kitchen, *mother* was busy working on an experiment.

Mother, and the rest of the family, object to Freddie's experimenting.

ER "*Find* the toys!" said the man.
OR "The toys!" said the man.

The hunt for the missing toys is the main action of the story.

4 *There is a change or loss resulting in inconsistency concerning a minor incident, minor character or minor aspect of sequence.*

ER We have to buy *feed* for the *horse.*
OR We have to buy *rugs* for the *house.*

The main point is that the family must spend their money on things other than tickets to the fair.

ER Then it stopped moving and now it's lying there in the warmth.
OR Then it stopped moving and now it's *probably* lying there in the warmth.

There is no doubt in the character's mind that a snake is lying there.

5 *There is a change or loss of aspect which is significant but does not create inconsistencies within the story.*

ER He had been experimenting with his *chemistry* set.
OR He had been experimenting with his set.

This is the first mention of the chemistry set in the story and the omission limits information on a significant aspect.

6 *There is a change or loss of an unimportant detail of the story.*

ER One of the things he *liked* most was cranberry picking.
OR One of the things he *got* most was cranberry picking.

This is just one of a number of jobs which the boy in the story does for the tribe.

ER I want *you* to save half your allowance for it each week.
OR I want to save half your allowance for it each week.

There is a change in detail concerning whether the mother or the boy will be responsible for saving the money.

ER Next he placed the bulb so that it touched the cap on the *top* battery.
OR Next he placed the bulb so that it touched the cap on the battery.

There is a change in the number of batteries the boy uses in making his flashlight.

7 *There is a change in person, tense, number, comparative, etc. which is non-critical to the story.*

ER Andrew *had* made a very favorable impression.
OR Andrew made a very favorable impression.

ER "Where are you?" *he* shouted.
OR "Where are you?" *she* shouted.

8 *There is a slight change in connotation.*

ER Then he noticed *that this one's leg* was broken.
OR Then he noticed *that one leg* was broken.

ER Then they all *crowded* into the car.
OR Then they all *crawled* into the car.

ER Ganderbai took a piece of *red* rubber tubing from his bag and slid one end under and up and around Harry's bicep.
OR Ganderbai took a piece of rubber tubing from his bag and slid one end under and up and around Harry's bicep.

or, substitution of a similar name which doesn't confuse the cast.

ER Billy Whitemoon was a *Winnebago* Indian boy.
OR Billy Whitemoon was a *$Wonniebago* Indian boy.

ER I went across to the door of *Harry's* room, opened it quietly, and looked in.
OR I went across to the door of *Henry's* room, opened it quietly, and looked in.

9 *No change has occurred involving story meaning.*

ER They covered it* with deer *hides* to keep the family dry in rainy weather.
OR They covered it with deer *hide* to keep the family dry in rainy weather.

(* a summer house)

ER He heard the rustling of leaves.
OR He heard the rustling of *the* leaves.

ER *When* summer ended, *the* Whitemoons packed their belongings again.
OR *The* summer ended. *The* Whitemoons packed their belongings again.

ER "I've been waiting for you." *He* raised his eyes and looked at me.
OR "I've been waiting for you," *he* raised his eyes and looked at me.

11 INTONATION

Changes in intonation are involved in almost all miscues. This category attempts to register only those situations where the intonation change is part of the direct cause of the miscue and not only a result of other changes.

0 *Intonation is not involved in the miscue.* Within these miscues the intonation shifts which occur result from other changes which the reader has made.

ER "You *are* too little," said Father.
OR "You *is* too little," said Father.

ER Here is something *you can do.*
OR Here is something *to get down.*

ER Come, Peggy.
OR Come *on,* Peggy.

1 *An intonation shift within a word is involved.* The shift in intonation creates either a nonword or a different lexical item.

ER *"Philosophical!"* I yelled.
OR *"Philoso=phical!"* I yelled.

ER ...lingered over the high Arizona *desert,...*
OR ...lingered over the high Arizona *de=sert,...*

ER ...the tendon above one hind leg was *severed,...*
OR ...the tendon above one hind leg was *se=vered,...*

2 *An intonation shift is involved between words within one phrase structure of the sentence.* The shift does not cause changes which cross phrase structure boundaries.

ER ...came from *jungle rivers* where...
OR ...came from *Jungle River* where...

Jungle moves from an adjective position to a part of a proper name (noun phrase).

ER ...that grew *under water, snails,* and...
OR ...that grew *underwater snails,* and...

Snails moves from being the first in a list of items that grow under water to being a specifically modified kind of snail.

3 *Intonation is involved which is relative to the phrase or clause structure of the sentence.* The intonation shift causes changes which cross phrase and/or clause boundaries.

ER Tomorrow we must crown a Miss America who has buck teeth, *cash in Las Vegas,* abandon our calling cards and list everyone in Who's Who.
OR Tomorrow we must crown a Miss America who has buck teeth, *cash* in Las Vegas, abandon our calling cards and list everyone in Who's Who.

In the ER sentence *cash in* is a verb plus particle meaning "to turn in." The reader anticipated a noun meaning "money" plus a prepositional phrase.

ER ...a last look assured her that all was well *and* that her mate was patrolling the far side.
OR ...a last look assured her that all was well, that her mate was patrolling the far side.

ER The dogs' *uneasiness, growing* for the past few days, now became more acute.

OR The dogs' *ungreasy growl* for the past few days, now became more acute.

4 *A shift in terminal sentence intonation is involved.*

ER It was fun to go to *school. When* he wasn't in *school,* he skated with his friends.

OR It was fun to go to *school when* he wasn't in *school.* He skated with his friends.

ER And bring serum for a krait bite.

OR And bring serum for a krait bite?

ER Her muscles *tensed. As* she started *forward, Chip* wheeled to face the knoll.

OR Her muscles *tensed as* she started *forward. Chip* wheeled to face the knoll.

5 *The intonation change involves a substitution of a conjunction for terminal punctuation or the reverse.*

ER The boys fished *and* then they cooked their catch.

OR The boys fished. Then they cooked their catch.

ER She pounded the young trees into long strings. From the strings she made beautiful baskets.

OR She pounded the young trees into long strings *and* from the strings she made beautiful baskets.

6 *The intonation change involves direct quotes.*

ER "Tom," said mother.

OR Tom said, "Mother."

ER Mr. Miller sighed. "*Seriously, Tinker,* sometimes I wish you didn't want to be a scientist."

OR Mr. Miller sighed *seriously.* "*Tinker* sometimes I wish you didn't want to be a scientist."

LEVELS 12 THROUGH 16

Previous categories have registered the occurrence of any syntactic change. The following set of categories records these changes for both surface and deep structure in relation to the varying structural constituents.

Language constituents are interrelated so that a change within one can also mean a change in another. Where possible, these compulsory relationships are indicated.

In many ways, change at one structural level causes changes at all of the succeeding levels. For this reason, the categories in this section become increasingly selective of the phenomena which they record as they incorporate subsequent categories.

The kind and level of miscue can restrict the possible involvement of structural constituents. When a category is either not involved or restricted from involvement zero will be marked.

12 SUBMORPHEMIC

Sound differences between the ER and the OR are recorded. These differences are limited to one and two phoneme sequences and bound morphemes which are composed of a schwa plus a consonant.

0   *The submorphemic level is not involved.*

    a   There is a difference of a two phoneme sequence which is either co-terminus with the morpheme or within a three to four phoneme sequence.

ER an	ER of	ER the
OR ā	OR it	OR this
ER bigger	ER had	
OR better	OR made	

    b   The miscue is a word level substitution with a difference greater than a two phoneme sequence.

ER Maximilian	ER explode	ER cranberry
OR $Maxmil	OR employed	OR $canderberry

    c   The miscue involves a whole word omission/insertion, or a phrase level miscue.

ER It's very dark *in* here.
OR It's very dark here.

ER I can't get out.
OR I can't get *it* out.

ER He put it *aside.*
OR He put it *to the side.*

1. *There is a substitution of phonemes.* This can include a substitution between a one and two phoneme sequence.

ER bit	ER then	ER none
OR bat	OR when	OR known

ER weakened   ER hunger   ER rocky
OR widened   OR hungry   OR rocks

A one phoneme sequence can be co-terminus with the morpheme.

ER I
OR A

2   *There is an insertion of a phoneme(s).*

ER tanks   ER Tom   ER your
OR $tranks   OR Tommy   OR yours

ER a   ER high
OR the   OR higher

3   *There is an omission of a phoneme(s).*

ER tracks   ER quickly   ER feasted
OR tacks   OR quick   OR feast

ER midst   ER noses
OR mist   OR nose

4   *There is a reversal of phonemes.*

ER pilot   ER Spot   ER girl   ER split
OR polite   OR stop   OR grill   OR slipped

5   *There are multiple minor phonemic variations.* This involves the occurrence of more than one substitution, insertion, or omission of a one or two phoneme sequence within a longer morpheme.

ER dinosaur   ER Winnebago   ER experimenting
OR $dinc+oh staur   OR $Wonniebag   OR $espairamenteeng

13 BOUND & COMBINED MORPHEME LEVEL

Miscues involving bound or combined morphemes are marked first for the physical qualities of the miscue—substitution, insertion, omission, reversal—and then for the kind of morphemic involvement. The examples are presented from the perspective of the morphemic involvement.

Included here are all miscues involving inflectional, derivational or contractional morphemes.

Irregularly formed bound morphemes which involve spelling changes internal to the root word (come/came, woman/women, ox/oxen) are included within the category.

Also included are variant base forms which cause the use of bound morpheme allomorphs (breakfas, breakfases). (See Word and Free Morpheme categories also.)

00   *This category is not involved:*

   a   There is a word level substitution which does not involve bound or combined morphemes.

     ER when   ER and   ER cranberry
     OR then   OR had   OR $canberry

     ER backward   ER toward   ER tucked
     OR backwards   OR towards   OR stuck

   b   The miscue involves an irregularly formed bound morpheme which does not involve internal spelling changes.

     ER read   ER lead
     OR read   OR lead

   c   The miscue involves either the omission or insertion of a whole word or phrase.

     ER Billy smiled *shyly.* Then he began to sing.
     OR Billy smiled. Then he began to sing.

     ER All of them were living in Switzerland.
     OR All of them were living in *about* Switzerland.

   d   There is a change in phrase or sentence level intonation.

     ER It was fun to go to *school. When* he wasn't in *school, he* skated with his friends.
     OR It was fun to go to *school when* he wasn't in *school. He* skated with his friends.

_1   *The miscue involves an inflectional suffix.*

   11 substitution

     ER frightened   ER help   ER horse
     OR frighten*ing*   OR help*ed*   OR houses

     ER walk*ed*   ER girl   ER Freddie's
     OR want*ing*   OR girls   OR Teddie (dialect)

All miscues involving tense and number changes through inflectional endings will be treated as substitutions.

    Dialect related miscues involving a null form of the possessive will be treated as substitutions.

   21 insertion

     ER Freddie   ER small   ER high
     OR Freddie's   OR small*est*   OR high*er*

     ER hurt
     OR hunt*ing*

31 omission

ER quick*ly*	ER grow*ing*	ER cook*ing*
OR quick	OR growl	OR cook

41 reversal

ER coyote's walk
OR coyote walks

_2   *The miscue involves a noninflected form.* This is restricted to situations in which both the ER and OR are words which indicate inflection through internal spelling changes.

12 substitution

ER woman	ER men	ER come
OR women	OR woman	OR came

This subcategory will never involve insertions, omissions, or reversals.

_3   *The miscue involves a contractional suffix.*

13 substitution

ER you've	ER I'm
OR it's	OR I'll

23 insertion

ER you	ER could	ER I
OR you've	OR couldn't	OR I'*ll*

33 omission

ER could*n't*	ER he's
OR could	OR he

43 reversal

ER needn't have
OR needed hadn't

_4   *The miscue involves a derivational suffix.*

14 substitution

ER hope*fully*
OR hope*lessly*

24 insertion

ER Tom	ER hunger
OR Tommy (diminutive)	OR hungry

ER reassure
OR reassur*ance*

34 omission

> ER sunny *beach*   ER meaning*less*
> OR sun beach   OR meaning
>
> ER herd*er*
> OR herd

44 reversal

_5   *The miscue involves a prefix.*

15 substitution

> ER *ex*ternal   ER *pre*conception
> OR *in*ternal   OR $reconception
>
> ER *im*partial
> OR $*un*partial

25 insertion

> ER usual   ER regardless
> OR *un*usual   OR *ir*regardless
>
> ER *ur*gently
> OR *un*gently

35 omission

> ER *pre*determined   ER *de*scendant
> ER determined   OR $scendant

45 reversal

> ER *pre*determined requisition
> OR determined $*pre*requisition

_6   *The miscue crosses affix types.*

16 substitution

> ER televis*ed* program   ER use*less*
> OR televis*ion* program   OR *un*less
>
> ER need*n't*
> OR need*ed*

46 reversal

> ER small work*er*
> OR small*er* work

This subcategory will never involve omissions or insertions.

_7   *The miscue involves the base.* There is some confusion over what constitutes the root word.

    17 substitution

ER sheep (pl.)	ER women
OR sheeps	OR womens
ER drowned	
OR $drownded	

    This subcategory will never include insertions, omissions, or reversals.

Additional Notes: In some instances a single miscue involves two or more changes which fall with the Bound and Combined Morpheme category. In such instances submiscues are used and all of the changes noted.

ER institutionalizing	ER tight
OR institute	OR tightened

14 WORD AND FREE MORPHEME LEVEL

Free morphemes are oral meaning bearing units within the language which can function independently or in combination with other free or bound morphemes. Words are graphic representations of free morphemes, and free and bound morpheme combinations.

    Miscues involving words and/or free morphemes are marked first for the physical qualities of the miscue—substitution, insertion, omission, reversal—and then for the kind of morphemic involvement. The examples are presented from the perspective of the morphemic involvement.

00   *This category is not involved.*

    a The miscue involves either a misarticulation,

ER *sickly* whisper	ER soft-*soled* shoes
OR $*slicky* whisper	OR $soft-*sholed* shoes

    or, a morphophonemic variant of a word.

ER little	ER just	ER reassuring
OR $lit+tle	OR $jus	OR $resuring

    b The word involved in the miscue is not physically changed but its grammatical function and/or meaning is altered.

ER He went *in* the house. (preposition)
OR He went *in.* (proadverb)

ER He was a *criminal* lawyer. (noun adjunct)
OR He was a *criminal.* (noun)

c The miscue is at the phrase level.

ER You *do not have to stay home.*
OR You *may go and have fun.*

ER He is going *on* nine.
OR He is going *to be* nine.

ER I *haven't.*
OR I *have not.*

_ 1   *The ER and/or the OR involve a multiple morpheme word.*

11 substitution

ER He *looked* at the doll.
OR He *looks* at the doll.

ER She *thumped* the camera . . .
OR She *climbs* the camera . . .

ER It was *useless.*
OR It was *unless.*

ER They packed their *belongings.*
OR They packed their *belonging.*

ER Mr. Jones *finished* the pictures . . .
OR Mr. Jones *fishing* the pictures . . .

21 insertion

ER All of them were living in Switzerland.
OR All of them were living in *about* Switzerland.

ER I suspect that the gap between . . .
OR I suspect that the *generation* gap between . . .

ER We'll just have to build fires again.
OR We'll just have to build *bigger* fires again.

31 omission

ER He heard a little *moaning* cry.
OR He heard a little cry.

ER The chicken pecked *rapidly.*
OR The chicken pecked.

ER The *helpless* animal at her feet . . .
OR The animal at her feet . . .

40 reversal

Any reordering of already existing elements within the text will be treated as a word reversal. Word level reversals are not marked according to the number or kind of morphemes contained within the two words involved in the miscue.

ER *I can* do it.
OR *Can I* do it?

ER A *first look.*
OR A *look first.*

ER He was taking *the shoes off.*
OR He was taking *off the shoes.*

_2   The ER *and/or the OR involve a single morpheme word.*

12 substitution

ER The *train* was . . .
OR The *toy* was . . .

ER The *women* came. (irregularly formed plural)
OR The *woman* came.

ER He *came.* (irregularly formed past tense)
OR He *went.*

ER . . . to accept *a* future they want and . . .
OR . . . to accept *the* future they want and . . .

22 insertion

ER He heard the rustling of leaves.
OR He heard the rustling of *the* leaves.

ER The boy ran.
OR The *young* boy ran.

ER . . . we have many goals for tomorrow.
OR . . . we have *made* many goals for tomorrow.

32 omission

ER The owner of the store explained *that* the fish . . .
OR The owner of the store explained the fish . . .

ER He returned *with* two sticks.
OR He returned two sticks.

ER . . . wandered away from its mother, *and* she raced to it . . .
OR . . . wandered away from its mother, she raced to it . . .

_3   *The ER is a single morpheme word and the OR is a multiple morpheme*
      word.

    13 substitution

        ER How do I know he is *your* deer?
        OR How do I know he is *yours*, dear?

        ER He sang for all the *tribe.*
        OR He sang for all the *tribes.*

        ER Yet by *accident* he might discover something.
        OR Yet by *accidently* he might discover something.

        ER ... that maturity will *force* the young to stop fighting ...
        OR ... that maturity will *enforce* the young to stop fighting ...

This subcategory will never involve insertions, omissions or reversals.

_4   *The ER is a multiple morpheme word and the OR is a single morpheme*
      word.

    14 substitution

        ER One of the things he *liked* most was cranberry picking.
        OR One of the things he *got* most was cranberry picking.

        ER This *one's* leg was broken.
        OR This *one* leg was broken.

This subcategory will never involve insertions, omissions, or reversals.

_5   *The miscue involves a free morpheme within a longer word.*

    15 substitution

        ER They *crowded* into the car.
        OR They *crawled* into the car.

        ER He *looked.*
        OR He *jumped.*

        ER ... and *tinting* the bold face of Antelope Rim.
        OR ... and *tilting* the bold face of Antelope Rim.

        ER His hold *weakened.*
        OR His hold *widened.*

    25 insertion

        ER He was being quiet.
        OR He was be*coming* quiet.

    35 omission

        ER He was be*coming* quiet.
        OR He was being quiet.

_6 *The miscue involves one or both of the free morphemes in a compound or hyphenated word.*

16 substitution

E R He must smash his *shock*-proof gold watch, ...
OR He must smash his *stock*-proof gold watch, ...

E R ... when our *sputnik-obsessed* teachers began clobbering us with homework ...
OR ... when our *$sprutnik-observed* teachers began clobbering us with homework ...

E R ... to the *saddlebag* home of her five puppies, ...
OR ... to the *sandbag* home of her five puppies, ...

E R His mother was making a *headband*.
OR His mother was making a *handbag*.

26 insertion

E R ... on a small patch of meadow.
OR ... on a small patch of meadow*land*.

E R She scampered up the hill.
OR She scampered up the hill*side*.

36 omission

E R ... gave her attention to her left *forepaw* ...
OR ... gave her attention to her left paw ...

E R ... spilled the contents of a saddlebag *onto* the ground.
OR ... spilled the contents of a saddlebag *to* the ground.

E R The *airplane* landed safely.
OR The *plane* landed safely.

46 reversal

E R The anchor was in the *boathouse*.
OR The anchor was in the *houseboat*.

_7 *The OR is a nonword.*

E R Inside there was usually a *parrot* or a monkey.
OR Inside there was usually a *$partroot* or a monkey.

E R ... the rocky tip of *Badger* Mountain ...
OR ... the rocky tip of *$Bagger* Mountain ...

E R ... and send them to the *contest*.
OR ... and send them to the *$consate*.

This subcategory will never involve insertions, omissions or reversals.

_8   *The OR is a phonemic or morphophonemic dialect alternate of the ER.*

  ER She suddenly *wanted* a drink ...
  OR She suddenly *want* (past tense) a drink ...

  ER The water *spilled* all over the floor.
  OR The water *$spilleded* all over the floor.

  ER ... *laying* the book on the bed.
  OR ... *lying* the book on the bed.

  This subcategory will never involve insertions, omissions, or reversals.

15 PHRASE

Within this category, the surface structure of a sentence is treated as being composed of possible noun and verb phrases with the verb phrase consisting of possible verb and adverb phrases. Recognizable structural changes within any of these three phrases are recorded. Any of the three phrases can be represented by a single constituent.

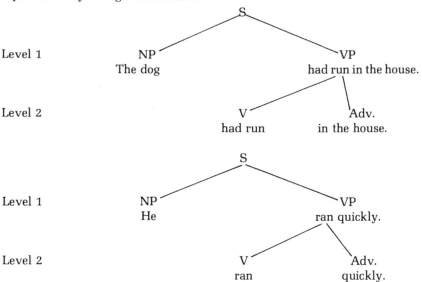

0   *This category is not involved.*

  a An OR word for which a grammatical function can not be assigned.

          to
  "You see," I said, "it helps ..."

  To could be either a verb marker or a preposition.

b A phonemic or word level substitution dialect miscue is involved in which there is no change of grammatical function.

ER He *went.*
OR He *goed.*

ER Penny and Sue Jones *liked* to wear pretty colored dresses.
OR Penny and Sue Jones *like* (past tense) to wear pretty colored dresses.

c A surface phrase represented by a single word in which the OR does not change the grammatical function regardless of the grammatical filler.

ER *Coyotes* run away.
OR *Wolves* run away.

ER *She* said.
OR *Susan* said.

ER He ran *home.*
OR He ran *rapidly.*

ER He went *in.*
OR He went *home.*

ER Give me two *pencils.*
OR Give me two *reds.*

d Shifts in number (singular ⟷ plural) or tense (present ⟷ past, etc.) which don't cause other structural changes in the phrase or within categories where no transformation has been marked (adj → noun adjunct, adjunct ⟶ verb derived adj).

ER I leaned on the baby bed.
OR I leaned on the baby bed*s.*

ER They impress my mind better that way.
OR They impress*ed* my mind better that way.

ER He was a *criminal* lawyer.
OR He was a *busy* lawyer.

1 *A substitution is involved at the phrase level.* This can involve a change in phrase structure or the substitution of one phrase structure for another.

ER The *yellow* dog ...
OR the dog ...

ER ... started *toward* the rimrock.
OR ... started *to work* the rimrock.

ER ... is quite a *businessman.*
OR ... is quite a *busy man.*

ER I haven't ...
OR I have not ...

ER I was not ...
OR I wasn't ...

ER The sight of his pet *frightened* Billy, for Lightfoot was off Winnebago land.
OR The sight of his pet *frightening* Billy, for Lightfoot was off Winnebago land.

The noun phrase changes from *The sight of his pet* to *The sight of his pet*
frightening Billy.

2   *An insertion is involved at the phrase level.* This must be the introduction of a phrase structure which was not present in the ER.

ER She was little more than ...
OR She was little, more than ...

ER Knew I mustn't move.
OR *I* knew I mustn't move.

ER "Quickly Timber, *but* take your shoes off."
OR "Quickly Timber, *you* take your shoes off."

3   *An omission is involved at the phrase level.* This must be the loss of a
phrase structure which was in the ER.

ER ... that grew under *water, snails,* and ...
OR ... that grew *underwater snails,* and ...

ER But *first* he wanted to buy a present for his mother.
OR But he wanted to buy a present for his mother.

First is a proadverb for the deep structure phrase *in the first instance.*

4   *A reversal is involved at the phrase level.* This must involve the movement from one clause to another of either a phrase or an element from a
phrase.

ER He was speaking more slowly than ever *now and* so softly I had to
lean close to hear him.
OR He was speaking more slowly than ever *and now* so softly I had to
lean close to hear him.

ER Mr. Miller sighed. "*Seriously,* Tinker, sometimes I wish you didn't
want to be a scientist."
OR Mr. Miller sighed *curiously.* "Sometimes I wish you didn't want to
be a scientist."

16 CLAUSE

The surface structure of a sentence can be composed of varying combinations of independent, dependent and embedded clauses. At the deep structure level, a clause is considered to be composed of a noun phrase and a verb phrase. At the surface level, a clause might retain both its noun and verb phrases or might be represented by any one or several of its constituents.

the *yellow* dog (surface structure)

Adjectives embedded within noun phrases represent deep structure clauses.

The dog. *The dog is yellow.* (deep structure)

The boy *walking down the street* is my brother. (surface structure)

The boy is walking down the street. The boy is my brother. (deep structure)

0   *The clause level is not involved in the miscue.*

a   The miscue involves phonemic, bound morpheme, free morpheme, word, or phrase level changes which do not cause changes in clausal relationships.

ER It was fully dark when the alert ears of the *larger* dog caught the sound of a sharp whistle.

OR It was fully dark when the alert ears of the *large* dog caught the sound of a sharp whistle.

ER I was only washing the doll *to* make it look like new.

OR I was only washing the doll *and* make it look like new.

ER We could have a contest and pick a baby out of all *the* babies in town.

OR We could have a contest and pick a baby out of all babies in town.

b   The miscue involves an OR word for which a grammatical function can not be found.

ER ... I said, "*It* helps me to remember the ..."

OR ... I said, "*to* helps me to remember the ..."

to could be either a verb marker or a preposition.

c   If either the ER or the OR does not progress as far as the verb, we do *not* mark the clause level.

ⓒ Then
Take it away.

ⓒ though
I could feel it through my pajamas, moving on my stomach.

1   *A substitution is involved at the clause level.* This involves surface level
     variations for the same deep structure, the substitution of one deep
     structure for another, as well as moves between active and passive,
     declarative and question, positive and negative.

     ER The book *which* you gave me was exciting.
     OR The book you gave me was exciting.

     ER Where did it bite you?
     OR A bite?

     ER ·This baby isn't typical.
     OR This baby isn't typical?

     ER I approached the gates ... (active)
     OR I was approached ... (passive)

2   *An insertion is involved at the clause level.* This can be a surface level
     word insertion which represents a deep level clause, or the insertion of a
     surface level clause.

     ER The flowers were for the party.
     OR The *yellow* flowers were for the party.

     ER ... quite a *businessman.*
     OR ... quite a *busy man.*

     ER I would like to win one *of* those.
     OR I would like to win one *if* those.

     ER Mr. *Vine* was excited when he saw the picture of the crow.
     OR Mr. *Vine's* was excited when he saw the picture of the crow.

3   *An omission is involved at the clause level.* This can be a surface level
     word omission which represents a deep level clause or, the omission of a
     surface level clause.

     ER As a matter of fact it wasn't *a* surprising thing for a krait to do.
     OR As a matter of fact it wasn't surprising , thing for a krait to do.

     The way to attach the final clause to the sentence is lost.

     ER Such wishful thinking arises from the preconception that maturity
         will force the young to stop fighting for a future they want and begin
         to accept a future they can get.
     OR Such wishful thinking arises from the preconception that maturity
         will force the young to stop fighting for a future . they want and
         begin to accept a future they can get.

     The way to attach the final clauses to the sentence is lost.

ER They took pictures of *their* mother wearing her party clothes.
OR They took pictures of mother wearing her party clothes.

ER The *frantic* bleating became less frequent.
OR The bleating became less frequent.

4 *A reversal is involved at the clause level.* It is a resequencing or reorganizing of existing elements without a change in clause dependency.

5 *Clause dependency is altered within the sentence.* Only one ER sentence should be involved in the miscue.

ER When I arrived he was there.
OR I arrived when he was there.

ER He was wearing a pair of pajamas with blue, brown and white stripes.
OR He was wearing a pair of pajamas, blue and brown with white stripes.

Blue and *brown* represent embedded clauses which move in dependency from stripes to *pajamas.*

ER I was only washing the doll *to* make it look like new.
OR I was only washing the doll *and* make it look like new.

The deep structure for the ER and OR remain the same—*I was washing the doll, I will make it look like new.*—the dependency changes.

ER "Our Kitten!" the Jones children said.
OR "Our Kitten Jones!" children said.

6 *Clause dependency is altered across sentences.* Two ER sentences should be involved in the miscue.

ER "Ganderbai's coming. He said for you to lie still."
OR "Ganderbai's coming," he said. for you to lie still."

ER But his hands were steady *and* I noticed that his eyes were watching.
OR But his hands were steady. I noticed that his eyes were watching.

ER As he was eating, Freddie decided to fix the clock.
OR He was eating. Freddie decided to fix the clock.

ER I found her with the camera. *I* thought she was just playing.
OR I found her with the camera *and* thought she was just playing.

17 GRAMMATICAL CATEGORY AND SURFACE STRUCTURE
OF OBSERVED RESPONSE

Researchers face a problem in dealing with the grammatical structure of language passages. Traditional, Latin based grammars are incomplete and inappropriate for describing English because they incorporate many misconceptions. Grammatical systems based on descriptive linguistics are better, but they fail to explore fully all aspects of grammar and are inadequate for dealing with language process. Generative transformational models are better suited to process, but do not fully explain surface structures, their relationships to deep structures, and the rules used for generating them.

For our research on reading miscues—unexpected oral responses to printed texts—a system is required that can be used to assign a grammatical function to each and every text word of a piece of prose. In our studies we are comparing the writer's surface structure with one regenerated by the reader.

Such a need immediately forces us to deal with phenomena beyond those which linguists have yet explored. At times it is necessary to make arbitrary distinctions in "grey areas" so that we can achieve consistency even though our system "leaks."

There are two reasons for lack of information about some aspects of English grammar:

a Modern insights have not been applied yet to many phenomena.
b Linguists have done little recent work that goes beyond sentences to connected discourse.

Our grammatical system has been organized by augmenting a descriptive grammar developed by Fries with the use of transformational analysis.

The system has five general categories—noun, verb, noun modifier, verb modifier, and function word. Two additional categories are used for words of indeterminate grammatical function and for contractions. Nouns, verbs, adjectives, and adverbs are additionally marked for filler and function aspects.

The canary lived in *space.*

category — noun
filler   — common noun
function — noun in prepositional phrase

Function words are marked by type (noun marker, verb marker, verb particle, etc.). And, contractions are marked according to the functions of their left and right components. As we have not yet found a consistent way of handling numerals and initials they are treated as place holders and coded zero.

F.B.I.   S.S.T.   H.E.W.
He lives at 942 Main Street.
Mary read Part *B.*

Blank *This category is not appropriate.* The miscue involves:

   a A phrase level miscue which cannot be broken into word level submiscues.

   b Any one of the following allologs:
contraction/full
full/contraction
contraction not represented in print
long and short forms, or syllable deletion/insertion
misarticulation

   c A phonemic level dialect miscue.

   d An inflectional dialect miscue which involves an alternate surface form for the ER grammatical structure.

     ER He walk(ed) home.

Walk is being keyed as dialect involved past tense form and so category 17 will be blank.

1__ **Noun Category.** Nouns are words that have concrete or abstract referents. They are things or ideas, entities which function as subjects, objects or in related ways.

Noun Filler

10_ *indeterminate*

11_ *common noun.* It is simplest to say that all nouns that aren't otherwise designated are common.

                11 7
"He's a pretty good brother," I said.

12_ *proper noun.* Included are all names of specific people or places.

  John   Chicago   Cherokee   Mary   England

Each of the words in two-word names are coded separately as proper nouns.

12_ 12_	12_ 12_	12_ 12_	12_ 12_
John Smith	Detroit River	Kansas City	Boston University

Where phrases have been turned into names or when the name has a direct semantic descriptive tied to the person or place "noun phrasal" unit is marked. (See 15_).

13_ *pronoun.* Included are any nominative, reflexive, or objective forms which take the place of a noun or phrase or clause acting as a noun in subsequent text occurrences.

everything, he, I, she, they, you, him, it, me, them
I want a red *one*.
This is mine.
We beat *ourselves*.
I want *some*.

14_   *verb derived noun*. These are nouns that are derived directly from a verb
in a deep structure clause. At the surface level the word looks like a
gerund or other verbal.

    |4|
The fighting was severe.
(Someone was fighting. That was severe.)
       |4|
Jogging can be invigorating.
(Someone is jogging. That can be invigorating.)

When more than the verb has been retained from the deep structure
clause then the word is coded as a verb.

   22|
Fighting the Vietcong is difficult.
(Someone is fighting the Vietcong. That is difficult.)

15_   *phrasal unit noun*. Phrases can be turned into names. The original grammatical relationships of the words in the phrase are lost and the phrase
operates as a unitary element in the deep structure. Two types of phrasal
unit are possible: a hyphenated word sequence which is inflected at the
end like a noun

    15—   15—
brother-in-law   dog-catcher

or, a phrase which has become a proper name.

15— 15— 15—   15— 15—   15— 15— 15—
New York City   Candy Man   Air Force One

Old Mill Road   Michigan State University

16_   *word as word name*. Any word may be used as a noun when it is the
name of the word.

       16¬   16¬
The words "corral" and "boss" meant something to the dog.
       162
He spelled "philosophical" correctly.

These word names must not be confused with words out of context.
(See 62_)

17_ *quantifier or ordinal as noun.* Quantifiers and ordinals may appear in noun positions when the noun they introduce has been deleted from the surface structure.

176   176
At last (the last time).   At first (the first time).

172
I want the third (thing).

171
Another (ship) was due any day.

171
Few (people) were available.

171
Three (something) of them came home.

18_ *noun modifier as noun.* Noun modifiers may sometimes be the remnants of deep structure noun phrases.

186
He flew off into the blue (sky).

182
You took mine. (my something)

182
She has a new convertible. (car)

181
He knew that his (something) was a serious case.

185
"Excuse me, mister (someone)," I said.

Noun Function

1_0 *indeterminate*

1_1 *subject.* Sentence subjects exist at two different levels: deep structure and surface structure levels. At either level, the relationship of the subject to the rest of the sentence is that of head noun in the noun phrase immediately dominated by S. The surface level manifestation of the subject may or may not be the same, then, as the deep structure subject. For instance:

a imperative transformations result in deleted subject, *you,*

   Get out! (*You* get out)

b passive transformations result in an objectified subject,

   Tom was hit by the ball. (The ball hit Tom)

c embedding transformations can result in a deleted subject or a subject that is replaced by a clause marker.

Findings of Research in Miscue Analysis

The boys, having chosen up sides, decided to play baseball. (The boys chose sides. The boys decided to play baseball.)

For our purposes, nouns are coded as *surface level subjects* when they are the head nouns of noun phrases immediately dominated by *S*. (Jacobson & Rosenbaum, *English Transformational Grammar*). Each sentence needs at least one subject but may have as many as there are deep structure verbs. Some clauses may not have surface subjects.

|5| |5|
The Detroit River is not wide.
|5| |5|
Kitten Jones was her pet.
|3| |3|
He knew that she would win.

Nouns may retain a subject function even though the verb is deleted from the surface structure.

|1| |1|
The moon is bigger than the biggest mountain. (is big)
|1| |1|
After the show (was over) the boys walked to Fifth Street.

There and *it* can occur as function words (rather than as verb modifier and pronoun, respectively). When these words occur as function words at the beginning of a NP, the deep structure subject of the sentence is coded as the subject.*

5(11)0 |1|
There is going to be a big show.

A big show is the subject in the deep structure and determines agreement of subject and verb at the surface level. *Show*, then, is coded as the subject of the sentence.

But in:

5(11)0 241
It is going to rain.

To rain, an infinitive verb form, is the deep structure subject, though not coded as subject. *It* is coded as a function word. *It* is not a pronoun since it represents no antecedent noun phrase.

Since the subject is in a particular relational position in the sentence, phrase and clause units can serve the subject function. These units are not coded as subject phrases. The words within them are coded according to their function within the embedded phrase or clause.

---

*Numbering systems for function words (5__), verbs (2__), etc. may be found further on in this section.—Ed.

221   112
Playing tennis is strenuous.
550 131   221
What he wanted was a drink.
530 241
To win was his ambition.

1–2   *direct object.* The direct object's relationship to the rest of the sentence can be described as that of the NP (excluding prepositional phrase) immediately dominated by the main verb in the verb phrase.

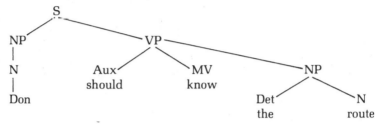

The direct object can be made the subject of a passive form of the sentence: *The route should be known by Don.* but can not have a preposition or phrase marker as an optional surface structure marker. *Don should know to the route.*

    In some surface structures the direct object can occur between the verb and the verb particle.

221   112 530
Don put the fire out.

An adverbial element is also part of the verb phrase but holds a different relationship to the rest of the sentence structure. It can not be made the subject of a passive sentence.

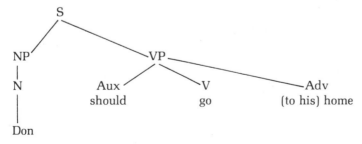

Cross references: transitive verbs (22–), verb particles (53–), indirect object (1–3), intransitive verb (23–).

1_3   *indirect object.* This function is the head noun in a noun phrase
immediately dominated by the verb phrase. It is distinguished from the
direct object by the feature + preposition. The preposition (usually *to*
or *for*) is absent from the surface structure when the noun is coded as
1_3:

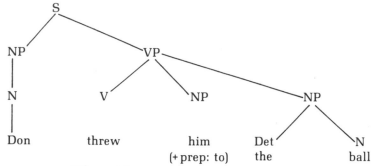

```
                      133      112
```
Don threw him the ball.
```
                      112      116
```
Don threw the ball to him.

A direct object may not always accompany an indirect object in the
surface structure. Verbs such as *pay, promise, tell, ask, allow, let* have
indirect objects with omitted direct objects:

```
          133
```
He paid him. (He paid something to him.)
```
          123
```
He asked Don. (He asked something of Don.)

1_4   *appositive.* This function involves the restatement of a noun for
purposes of identification. The noun in the appositive position follows
its noun equivalent in the surface structure.

```
          114
```
John, the barber, worked quickly.
```
              114
```
My mother, the telephone operator, cooks well.

The appositive is a surface structure manifestation of a deep structure
subject complement:

```
          117
```
John is the barber.

John worked quickly.

This function includes a deep structure predicate nominative that is transformed via embedding and reduction to a position following the head noun of a clause or phrase.

It is possible, then, to insert a dependent clause beginning with *who is* before the noun functioning as an appositive and retain an acceptable sentence structure:

John (who is) the barber, worked quickly.
My mother (who is) the telephone operator, cooks well.
We (who are) the boys will go in.

In children's speech, the appositive sometimes changes position:
|2| |34
Jim, he ran away. (he = Jim)

Rather than:
|3| |24
He, Jim, ran away.
    ||4 |3|
The men over there, they are coaches.
   ||4 |3|
Us boys, we are going.

Cross references: address (1_5), object complement (3_3), subject complement (3_3), subject complement (3_1).

Owen P. Thomas in *Transformational Grammar and the Teacher of English* (Holt, Rinehart & Winston, 1965) calls an appositive a noun modifier position (p. 95). We call it an equivalent form.

1_5   *address.* The noun in this function serves as an attention getter, director or organizer. It can occur in various positions in a sentence, and in fact is not part of the basic structure. It appears to be an optional element in dialogue.

|2_5
John, where is the hammer?
   |25
"Come, Peggy. Let's go."
   |25
"Here, Peggy, old girl," he said.
|25 |25
Jimmy! Jimmy!
   |25
Look, Sally, look.
||5
Boys, we will go in.

Nouns in the address function sometimes look like appositives if preceded or followed by a pronoun.

125   131
John, you are to stay here.
131   125
You, John, are to stay here.

1_6   *noun in prepositional phrase.* This function is that of object or head noun in a phrasal unit begun by function words called phrase markers (prepositions). Or, the noun may be in an adverbial phrase consisting of noun marker or adverbial noun modifier with the phrase marker deleted from the surface structure.

     411   560 560 510 116
He fell down out of the tree.

       560 156 156   156   560
The shallow basin of Salt Creek Wash became a gathering pool of dark-
116   560   116 560   116
ness where a band of eight hundred sheep with their lambs were bedding
530 560 116
down for night.

                                    560   116
She sniffed the cool air of the late spring drifting down the wash.

560 176
At first the flowers failed to bloom.

560 176
At last the war was ended.

          560 176
The call was returned at once.

        510   116
(On, During) That night the storm hit.

        382 116
(On, During) Last night he completed the task.

         372   116
(On, During) Tomorrow night...

        510 116
(On, During) One day... (Here, *one* is not a quantifier, but is comparable to *that* or *the*.)

        510 116
(On, During) Some day...

                              116
She had eaten mutton (during) many times.

Note: It is possible to have a compound phrase marker or a compound verb particle, but not a compound adverb. (Proadverb: See 41_, below.)

1_7 *subject complement.* This function might also be labeled predicate noun.
The noun follows a form of the verb *be* or *become*, *remain* or *stay* (special
cases of copulative verbs). Generally, the subject complement can be
regarded as an equivalent statement and can be interchanged with the
subject.

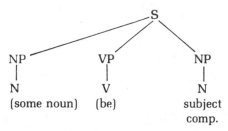

|3| ||7
He remained a blacksmith all his life.
|3| ||7
They would become easy prey to the coyotes.
|3| ||7
It was a house of fine architectural design.
|3| |27
He was Mr. Big in the industry.

Function word place holders must be distinguished from the subject of
the sentence in determining subject complements.

5|| 570 |7|
There was nothing more to eat.

Note: Forms of *be* can be substituted for *become*, *remain* and *stay* when
they are followed by a subject complement.

1_8 *object complement.* This function co-occurs with and is an equivalent
statement for the direct object. Transitive verbs such as *name*, *elect*,
appoint, *make* often are followed by object complements. The surface
structure is a result of embedding and deleting.

They appointed Fred.
Fred is President.
They appointed Fred President.

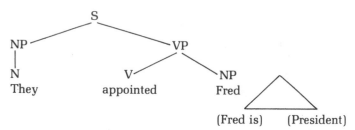

(Fred is)   (President)

The object complement can generally be preceded by *to be*.

122   118
They appointed Fred (to be) President.

122   118
They elected Don (to be) senator.

131   128
They named him (to be) Don.

Cross references: appositive (1_4), address (1_5), subject complement (1_7), transitive verb (22_), direct object (1_2).

1_9 *noun in a phrase of intensification.* The intensifier function qualifies or indicates degree with respect to adverbials and adjectives.

570   422
He is very happy.

570 560   116
He lives far down the river.

The two examples above are function word intensifiers. Nouns can serve a similar kind of function.

119 560 560   116   119 423
We're two days out from the corrals and a day late on the drive.

119 421
A coyote emerged from the edge of the sage not fifty feet away.

119   311
A star is many many times bigger than you are.

570 119   423
All night long she cried.

Cross references: intensifier (57_), adverb (42_).

2__ **Verb Category**

Verb Filler

20_ *indeterminate*

21_ "be" form. This includes forms of be used as the main verb in a sentence, but does not include forms of be used as (auxiliary) verb markers. Some sentences contain both uses of be.

520 211
He is being helpful.

211
Sally was the victor.

Cross reference: function word (5__).

22_ transitive verb. These verbs can be followed by one or two NP's. Generally, transitive verbs are characterized as (1) those head verbs whose VP's have in their surface structures NP's immediately dominated by the VP, (2) verbs which can undergo the passive transformation. However, this definition must be augmented by noting:

1 The direct object NP can be eliminated from the surface structure.

He pays (to) him (something).
He asks (of) him (something).
He promises (to) him (something).
He sold (to) him (a bill of goods).
He smokes (something).
He sings (something).
He plays (something).

2 Some transitive verbs can not undergo the passive transformation. Gleason calls these pseudotransitive, Owen Thomas calls them middle verbs.

It cost ten dollars.
The trip took two days.

Cross references: indirect object (1_3), direct object (1_2), verb markers (52_).

23_ intransitive verb. These verbs do not have a passive form and have adverbial or adjectival phrases in the VP rather than NP's functioning as direct and indirect objects.

231
He was working hard.

231
She sat very still in her chair.

The category includes verbs such as seem, remain, stay and become which can be replaced by a form of be.

231   211
He became frightened. He was frightened.

231
He remained at home. He was at home.
211

231
He seems talented. He is talented.
211

Some verb forms traditionally labeled gerunds are coded as verbs.

231 231
They sat talking on the fence.

231 231
He went fishing in the river.

231 231
He came running down the road.

231 231
He went hunting in the woods.

The sentences can be restated as:

They sat and (they) talked on the fence.
They went and (they) fished in the river.
He came (down the road) (and he was) running down the road.
He went (in the woods) (and he was) hunting in the woods.

Subject complements can be distinguished from verbs by attempting to insert an intensifier.

331
He was (very) interesting.

311
He was (very) capable.

331
They seemed (very) ashamed.

Cross references: verb marker (5_2, noun modifier (18_).

24_   *infinitive.* A sequence of the verb particle *to* + verb generally signals the presence of the infinitive form of the verb:

530 520 241
He wanted it to be done.

530 241
He wanted to do it.

In some sentences, the element *to* is omitted from the surface structure:

241
He had him come.   (He had him to come.)
                              530 241

241
Let him go.   (Let him to go.)

241
Let go of it.   ((You) let it to go.)

241
See Spot run.   (See Spot to run.)

An infinitive form represents a deep structure clause:

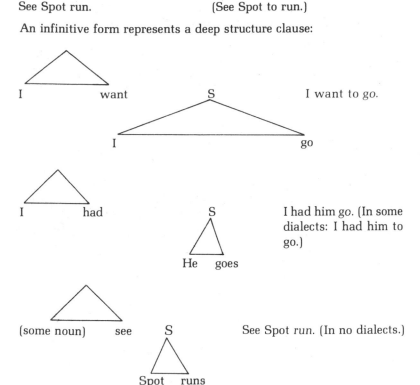

I   want   S   I want to go.

I   go

I   had   S   I had him go. (In some
                                                                  dialects: I had him to
                                                                  go.)
                                            He   goes

(some noun)   see   S   See Spot run. (In no dialects.)

                                            Spot   runs

Note: Martin Joos, *The English Verb: Form and Meanings* (University of Wisconsin, 1968), recognizes the infinitive only when it is preceded by the marker *to*; the other form—minus the marker—he calls a presentative. (p.16)

25_ *proverbs*. These verbs function much as do the elements traditionally identified as pronouns; i.e., they are an abbreviated surface structure representation of an entire phrase, in this case, the verb phrase. They are the first elements in the verb phrase.

Sam was going to buy candy.

251
John wished he could too.

The deep structure VP includes *buy candy*, but the VP is reduced to include only the modal in the surface structure.

A proverb may also be a verb of duration (see verb marker under function word) that is not followed by the main verb.

251   251
Stop, Dick, stop.

This is the surface representation of *Stop pushing the merry-go-round, Dick, stop pushing the merry-go-round.*

Verb Function

2_0 indeterminate

2_1 active

2_2 passive. Traditional grammar identifies the verb characteristic voice. In the active voice the deep structure and the surface structure subject are identical. In the passive voice the deep structure subject becomes the surface structure agent.

John kissed the girl. (active)
The girl was kissed by John. (passive)

The storm uprooted the tree. (active)
The tree was uprooted by the storm. (passive)

The passive transformation involves (1) the inversion of the first NP in a sentence with one of the other NP's immediately dominated by the VP, (2) the inclusion of *be* or *get* prior to the verb markers and/or main verb, and (3) the inclusion of *by* + NP, at the end of the clause.
  Passive verb forms can be identified in the surface structure by the presence of *be* or *get* as verb markers along with the agentive VP phrase begun with *by* + (some noun or noun phrase). Often the *by* or agentive phrase is missing from the surface structure.

The girl was kissed (by someone).
The girl got kissed (by someone).

Note: *Most* transitive verbs but *no* intransitive verbs function in the passive voice.

2_3 imperative. The imperative most often is incompletely characterized as the presence of the main verb at the beginning of a clause and the absence of a subject NP in the surface structure. Traditional grammar characterizes the imperative verb form as having as a deleted subject *you*, which is "understood." The tag question transformation lends validity to the idea that *you* is the subject.

223
Check the parking meter.

can be transformed to:

223
Check the parking meter, will you.
223
You will check the parking meter.
223
You check the parking meter.

The imperative is characterized by a syntactic context including (1) a second person pronoun for a subject which may or may not be in the surface structure, (2) *will* as the one and only auxiliary which is present in the surface structure when the pronoun subject is present, and (3) the present tense.

213
Be on time.
223
If you can, come at six.
223 530
Look at that car!

2_4 *subjunctive.* Conditional status is indicated by the subjunctive verb. It is marked by a dependent clause begun with *if* and the subjunctive verb forms *be* or *were.* The subjunctive is becoming archaic in speech though it is present in writing.

214
If he be king . . .
214
If I were you . . .
234
If Nixon were elected . . .

3__ **Noun Modifier Category**

Noun Modifier Filler

30_ *indeterminate*

31_ *adjective.* An adjective qualifies as a noun. The test for adjectives is:

111   311
The _____ is _____.

The new wagon arrived.   The lively kitten played with twine.
111   311   111   311
The wagon is new.   The kitten is lively.

Some adjectives can be easily confused with proper noun and noun
adjunct:

312
The oak trees are beautiful.

311
The trees are oak.

117
The trees are oaks.

187
The tree is an oak. (tree)

312
The Cherokee boy arrived.

311
He is Cherokee.

131   127
He is a Cherokee.

127
They are Cherokees.

312   127
The American boy arrived. The boys are Americans.

111   311
The boy is American.

127
The boy is an American.

311
The boys are American.

32_   *noun adjunct.* A noun adjunct is a noun functioning in an adjective
      position.

circus tent   *criminal* lawyer   *ice-cream* man   *fire* hydrant

A noun adjunct must fit one of the following tests.
1 It may be transformed to the noun in a prepositional phrase.

   the tent *for the circus*
   the lawyer *for criminals*
   the hydrant *for the fire department*

2 It may be the direct object of an embedded, deleted sentence.

   the man (the man sells ice-cream)
   the man (who sells ice-cream)
   the ice-cream man

3 It may be the subject complement of an embedded, deleted sentence.

the teacher (the teacher is a student)
the teacher (who is a student)
the student teacher

33_ *verb derived modifier.* This includes verbs which are placed in a modifying position prior to a noun.

332
The painted fence is new.
Running water is available.

The test for verb derived modifiers:

$$\text{The } \underset{\text{noun}}{\underline{\overset{1\_1}{}}} \text{ is } \underset{\text{verb}}{\underline{\overset{2\_\_}{}}}.$$

222
The fence is painted (by me).
231
The water is running.

34_ *possessive noun*

35_ *possessive pronoun.* These are nouns and pronouns of the following sort:

342
Mr. Green's car arrived.
352
His car was green.

Some pronouns have two possessive forms—one to use in embedded position and the other as subject complement or noun substitute.

Embedded:	352 Her car arrived.
Subject complement:	351 The car is hers.
Noun substitute:	181 Hers is new.

Note: Embedded possessives have a double function since they replace the noun marker when they are embedded.

351   352
The car is green.   The car is his.   His car is green.

We choose to classify possessives as noun modifiers only since handling both functions carries our analysis to another level of complexity.

36_ *titles.* Titles occur with proper nouns.

Mr., Mrs.
Grandfather
Grandmother
Uncle, Aunt   } + proper noun
Doctor
General
President
King, Queen

Some of these items may exist by themselves with no proper noun or
phrasal unit attached. If so, they are coded as proper nouns.

     12 _

The President of the United States
362 12 _
King George
   362   12 _
Grandfather Eastman

Cross references: nominal phrasal unit (15_), proper noun (12_).

37_ *adverbial.* Adverbs which are placed in a modifying position prior to a
noun. These modifiers qualify nouns with respect to time and place and
seem to be remnants of embedded adverbial phrases.

    372
tomorrow night . . .
(the night of tomorrow . . .)
    372
yesterday morning . . .
(the morning of yesterday . . .)
   37_
front yard . . .
(the yard in the front . . .)
37_
side lot . . .
(the lot at the side . . .)
37_
top floor . . .
(the floor at the top . . .)

Cross references: noun modifier (3__), ordinal number (38_),
adjective (31_).

38— *ordinal number.* This grouping indicates sequence.

    382   121
Next Monday is the parade.

      382 116
He went home last week.

    382 111
The third game was lost.

39— *phrasal unit.* This includes both hyphenated and unhyphenated noun phrasal units placed in a modifying position prior to a noun. The unit, not each word, is the modifier.

     392   392
the dining room table.

    392   392
an internal combustion engine

      392
a mother-in-law phobia

Noun Modifier Function

3—1 *subject complement.* This function might also be labeled predicate adjective. The noun modifier follows a form of *be* or of *become, remain, stay,* or *feel* for which some form of *be* can be substituted.

     371
He was late.

     311
He is young.

       311
He remained alert.
(He was alert.)

      311
He stays awake.
(He is awake.)

      311
They felt happy.
(They were happy.)

Sometimes a subject complement begins a sentence and is the only remaining element of a deep structure sentence:

   311
Desperate, he ducked into a dark passageway.

     311
(He was) desperate, (and) he ducked into a dark passageway.

3_2   *embedded.* Noun modifiers which precede the element modified are
surface structure representations of embedded clauses.

    312 312 11_
the new red wagon . . .
(the wagon is new)
(the wagon is red)
    382 392 392   11_
the first dog catcher truck . . .
(the truck is the first)
(the truck is for the dog catcher)
   312 362 12_
little Miss Muffet . . .
(Muffet is little)
(Muffet is a Miss)

3_3   *object complement.* In sentences such as *He painted the fence green.*, the
noun modifier, *green*, is the remains of an embedded clause. It modifies
the head noun in a noun phrase immediately dominated by the verb
phrase.

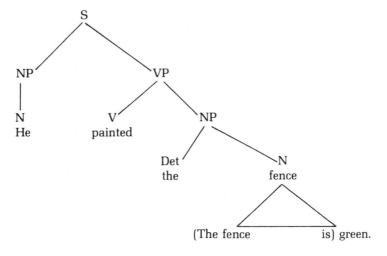

4__   **Verb Modifier**

Verb Modifier Filler

40_   *indeterminate*

41_   *proadverb.* A proadverb functions much as do proverbs and the
elements traditionally labeled pronouns. A proadverb stands for an

entire adverbial phrase which is not present in the surface structure. Proadverbs include: (1) the first element of a compound phrase marker; (2) the phrase marker without a following noun phrase.

$$411$$
He went back.
$$560\ 560$$
(He went back to someplace).
$$411$$
He ran out.
$$560\ 560$$
(He ran out of someplace).

A proadverb will be only the first of any sequence of phrase markers. Proadverbs can not exist in compound or consecutive sequences.

$$411$$
He fell down.
$$560\ 560\ 560$$
He fell down out of the tree.

Cross references: verb particle (53_), noun in adverbial phrase (1_6), adverb (42_), phrase marker (56_).

42_   adverb. Single words which qualify the head verb in the verb phrase with respect to time, place, manner or any "other" way and which are, themselves, immediately dominated by VP are coded as adverbs. They are frequently marked morphologically by the -ly suffix, but this is not true in all dialects.

$$422$$
. . . he tied the tubing tight with a knot.

43_   noun form. Nouns which are the remaining elements of a deep structure adverbial phrase are included here.

$$431$$
He went home.   He went $\left\{ \begin{array}{l} \text{back home.} \\ \text{to his home.} \end{array} \right.$

$$431$$
There is Dick. $\left. \begin{array}{l} \text{Over} \\ \text{Down} \end{array} \right\}$ there is Dick.

$$431$$
Come here.   Come $\left\{ \begin{array}{l} \text{over} \\ \text{in} \end{array} \right\}$ here.

433
He should be here (by) now.
433
That was (on) yesterday.

Cross references: noun in adverbial or other prepositional phrase (1_6), adverb (42_), proadverb (41_).

Verb Modifier Function

4_0   *indeterminate*

4_1   *place.* Verb modifiers will indicate where the verb operates.

431
He ate there.

Most frequently, adverbials of place are prepositional phrases. Where they are not, they frequently are proverbs with the preposition left in the surface structure and noun deleted.

411
He waited outside (the door).

Or nouns as verb modifiers with prepositions deleted.

431   431
He went (to) home.   He went (to) there.

4_2   *manner.* Verb modifiers will indicate how the verb operates.

422
He ran rapidly.

4_3   *time.* Verb modifiers will indicate when (or for how long) the verb operates.

423
Please come now.

Adverbials of time will often be prepositional phrases or transformed phrases that result in nouns remaining after preposition deletions.

433   433
He came (on) yesterday.   (On) Monday he went home.

433
It lasted (for) weeks.

4_4   *reason.* Adverbials of reason add reason to the verb's operation. They are generally prepositional phrases.

424
He did it purposely.

4_5   *other.* A small collection including *too, also,* etc.

Note: All words in prepositional phrases are separately coded regardless of the function of the whole phrase.

$$126$$
I'm going on next Monday.

When only the preposition is deleted the coding remains the same.

$$126$$
I'm going next Monday.

But when only the noun remains, then it is coded as a verb modifier.

$$433$$
I'm going Monday.

5__ **Function Word Category** *

Function Word Filler

50_   *indeterminate*

51_   *noun marker.* Words which signal the presence of nouns and which have little concrete or abstract meaning are noun markers.

One day . . .
Some day . . .

That, this, these, those, the, followed by a noun are noun markers.

Noun markers—with the exception of the and a—can also function as pronouns.

Cross references: pronoun (13_), quantifier (5(10)_).

52_   *verb marker.* These include auxiliary verbs in the verb phrase. The modals, have and be can be verb markers when the main verb is included in the surface structure.

$$520 \quad 520$$
He should have come.

$$520$$
He is coming.

Do is also a verb marker when the main verb is present in the surface structure.

$$520$$
He did arrive late.

---

   * In the 5_ (Function Word) Category, the third element, designating function, becomes redundant and is represented by an underline (_) in the list, by (0) over examples.—Ed.

520
Did he get home?

Verb markers can occur in multiple sequences:

    520   520
He should have been here.
   520 520 530 520 530 240
Jane is going to have to go to Paris.
   520 520 630 241
Tom will have to mow the lawn.

There are verb markers which seem to indicate duration of time: keep +
on, go + on, went + on, stop, continue.

   520 530
He went on walking.
  520
He kept (on) walking.

Other examples which might be noted.

  520
He ought to do it.
  520
He must do it.
  520
He has to do it.

Going is often used as a tense marker. In speech, *going* is the future tense
marker more often than is *will* or *shall*.

  520
I'm going to go.
 520
I will go.
(I shall go).

Get and its alternate forms can also be verb markers.

  520
He got going.
  520
She gets started early.

They are particularly common as passive markers.

  520
He got hit by the ball.
  520
She gets kissed often (by men).

Cross references: verbs, transitive (22_) and intransitive (23_).

53_ *verb particle.* Verb particles are words that can look like prepositions or adverbs but which are essential to the full meaning of the verb. For example, in the sentence *He turned off the light.* The separable element *off* is essential to the meaning of the verb *turn.* If *off* is left out of the sentence, the meaning is significantly changed: *He turned the light.*

There is a sequence of tests which can be used to judge verb particles.

Semantic

1   A synonym seems to be a possible equivalent for the two-word verbal.

He *turned* the lights *off.*
(He extinguished the lights.)

2   The particle seems to go with the main verb and, in fact, seems essential to its meaning.

Syntactic

1   Are the verb and following element separable?

He *turned off* the lights.
He *turned* the lights *off.*

He *put up* his bike.
He *put* his bike *up.*

Note: When a pronoun is present, a noun needs to be substituted:

He put it up.
*He put up it (the bike).

2   If the particle and main verb are not separable, can the sentence be transformed into a *semantically similar* and *acceptable* "how" or "where" question *without* the use of the particle? For example:

particle
needed
{
The car (ran into   ) the store.
        (hit, struck)

What did the car run into?
Answer: the store.
}

prepositional
phrase not
necessary to
form question
{
The boy (ran into) the store.
        (entered)

Where did the boy run?
Answer: into the store.
}

3 Can the main verb and particle be transformed into a passive sentence?

He was watching for the police.
(The police were being watched for by him.)

But the same words can have a different deep structure.

He was watching for the police.
(The police asked him to watch something.)

No passive possible.

4 Does the main verb have a latinate prefix which duplicates the meaning of the separate element?

He departed from . . .   He contracted with . . .
He entered into . . .   She dispensed with . . .

Notice that the syntactic question has been whether the NP dominated by the VP is the object of the verb (including particle) or the object of a preposition.

Problems arise in both the semantic and syntactic realms when one attempts to identify a category of separable verbs exclusive of large numbers of exceptions and special cases.

The to marking infinitive verb forms is coded as a verb particle.

     530 241
Tom will have to mow the lawn.
     530 241
"I was only washing the doll to make it look like new," Freddie explained.

54 _ *question marker.* Question patterns are generally indicated in two ways: (1) the inversion of auxiliary + tense and the noun phrase; (2) the inclusion of one of a group of question words at the beginning of the sentence. These question words include: *what, when, which, why, where, how.*

  540
Which chair is ready to ship?
  540
How do you play chess?

But notice that when a question is embedded in a larger structure and functions as a dependent clause, the question marker function is superseded by the clause marker function (see below).

    550
Do you know which chair is ready to ship?

550
Does anyone know how you turn on the air conditioner?
550
(In some dialects this would be: Anybody know how do you turn on the air conditioner?)
550
Do you know why he is leaving the company?

55 _ *clause marker.* Clause markers begin dependent clauses and join them to the independent clauses.

550 510 III 2II 3II
He knew that the car was new.

550
The news that the plane was late wasn't startling.

550
The play which John wrote was performed.

550
Ted is bigger than John. (is big)

550
He ran as fast as he could.

550
After the show (was over), the boys went to the drive-in.

In the last three examples above, the verb phrase of the relative clause is incomplete or absent. The last two examples above show that words traditionally labeled prepositions can also be clause markers. In the last example, the verb phrase is missing completely from the surface structure.

56 _ *phrase marker.* These are words which introduce an adverbial or other prepositional phrase. These may occur in a series.

560
His home is *by the expressway.*

560   560
The hat *on his head* fell *over his eyes.*

560
Sam ran *down the road.*

560 560 560
Ted fell *down out of the tree.* (In some dialects: Ted fell *down out the tree.*)

560 560
I'm going *over to* Judy's.

Cross references: proadverb (41_), verb particle (53_), adverb (42_), adverb (42_), adverb particle (5(12)_), clause marker (55_).

57_ *intensifier.* Intensifiers indicate amount or degree with respect to *adjectives* and *adverbs.* Adjectives and adverbs are *intensified*; noun forms are *quantified.* They can modify either single words or phrases.

570 420
Very well.

570 423
Just then, he arrived.

570   311
He is indeed clever.

570   331
He was very tired.

570   422
The doctor moved very quickly.

570 560 186 560 136
Put it right on top of this.

The bottle was {
570 311
almost full.

570
half

570
quite

570
barely
}

John was {
570   311
hardly happy.

570
completely
}

570   } 560 510   116
Precisely { at that moment, he arrived.
570
Right

Intensifiers may occur in two word sequences.

570 570 423
All too soon it was time to go.

570 570 311
A ladybug is very, very small.

Cross references: noun in intensification (1_9), quantifiers (5(10)_).

58_ *conjunction.* Words which conjoin clauses or phrases or elements within clauses or phrases are conjunctions. Only parallel and equal elements may be conjoined.

580
John and Sue arrived.

580   580
He wanted neither red nor white.

580
The dish is broken, therefore, she'll buy another.

580 580
He knew what to do and so he began.

59_ *negative.* Both *no* and *not* are included in this category. When *not* occurs in a contraction, it is coded as part of the contraction (see contractions).

510_ *quantifier.* Nouns are quantified, adjectives and adverbs are intensified.

5⟨10⟩0
What fun this is.
5⟨10⟩0
Few people came.
5⟨10⟩0 510 119 311
The water is half a foot deep.
5⟨10⟩0 119 371
They are three days late.

Negative quantifiers include:

He is
5⟨10⟩0
scarcely an athlete.
590 5⟨10⟩0
not exactly
5⟨10⟩0
hardly

511_ *other.* This category contains special instances of *it* and *there.*

5⟨11⟩0
It is raining.
5⟨11⟩0
There is a good restaurant in the Union.

Here is included when its "place" reference is diminished from a specific *in this place* to a general, idiomatic usage.

5⟨11⟩0
Here you are.
5⟨11⟩0
Here is my idea.
5⟨11⟩0
Now see here.

Yes is included in this category. Actually *yes* is a special case. It is included here to avoid creating a special category for one word.

512_ *adverb particle.* These elements may look like prepositions but do not mark the beginning of a phrase; rather, they are pattern completers which add little to meaning.

425 5⟨12⟩0
He is better off.
423 5⟨12⟩0
We'll discuss it later on.
423 5⟨12⟩0
Earlier on they'd discussed it.
425 5⟨12⟩0
Right on!

6__ Indeterminate Category

Indeterminate Filler

60_ *indeterminate*

61_ *interjection*

    Hell!   Oh!   Well!   Indeed!   Gracious!   Damn! (in the nominal
    sense of *damnation*)

62_ *words out of syntactic context.* When an isolated word or a list of words
occurs inside quotation marks, then the word is coded as lacking its
usual syntactic contexts. Included, too, are full mailing addresses and
signs.

       620
    "Philosophical," he said.
    620   620   620
    "Savage: wild, not tamed."
    620   620   620   620
    "Sinewy: stringy, strong or powerful."
    620 620 620
    Mr. J. Johns
    000 620 620
    224 Park Street
    620 620 620 620
    New York, New York

Note: Numbers and alphabetic initials are not coded, since they involve
another system and do not elicit any single, correct, expected response.

       116   000
He lives in apartment 3A.
       116   000
He ran toward number 749.

63_ *defies classification/ambiguous.* This category is used in the rare case
that some tentative assignment to another category can not be made.

64_ *greetings.* This category includes all *one*-word greetings and *two*-word
greetings such as *good morning.* Greetings such as *How do you do?* are
treated literally.

7__ Contraction Category. This category allows us to code both parts of
either an ER or OR contraction.

Left Part of Contraction

71_ *pronoun.* All words coded as pronouns which appear as left parts of
contractions.

711
He's coming.
712
That's mine.

72_ *verb marker.* All words coded as verb markers which appear as left parts of contractions. *Be, have* and *do* forms are differentiated from their verb marker counterparts.

724
He isn't coming.
729
They don't see us.

73_ *be forms.* All *be* forms in copula position. Note that *be* forms also appear as right parts of contractions.

734
He isn't here.
734
They aren't happy.

74_ *let.* This verb as a contraction appears only with the pronoun *us.*

745
Let's go.

75_ *question marker/clause marker.* All words which are normally coded question or clause markers.

752
What's his name?
751
How've you been?
751
Where're we going?
751
The house that's falling down.
751
That's the boy who's crying?

76_ *it/there/here.* These three words are coded here, when they would normally be coded *511–other* under function word if they appeared separately.

762
Here's a job for you.
761
It's raining.
761
There'll be a hot time tonight.

77 _ *adverb.* Words such as *here* and *there* used as adverbs.

772
Here's mine.

772
There's the man.

78 _ *noun.* All words (other than pronouns) coded as nouns.

781
Tom's leaving.

781
Mary'll come too.

782
Bob's happy now.

79 _ *transitive verb* (have). Forms of *have* may appear as transitive verbs in left parts. Rarely, they also appear in right parts (see 7 _ 3).

794
He hasn't any money.

794
They haven't any food.

Note: Avoid confusing *has* forms used as verb markers.

724
He hasn't left yet.

Right Part of Contraction. A smaller number of possibilities may be right parts of contractions. One example is given with each possible left part. Obviously many combinations are not possible in English.

7 _ 1 *verb marker.* All words normally coded verb markers which occur as right parts.

711
He's coming.

761
It's raining.

781
Mary's got it.

751
He is the one who'll try.

7 _ 2 *be forms.* In copula position as right part.

712
It's here.

752
Who's home?

7̄7̄2̄
Here's the place.
7̄8̄2̄
Mary's home now.

7_3 *have* (transitive verb). Rarely, forms of *have* may occur in American English as right parts.

7̄1̄3̄
They've a new car.

7_4 *negative*. Always appears as *n't*.
7̄2̄4̄
They aren't coming.

7̄3̄4̄
They aren't here.

7̄4̄4̄
They haven't any.

7_5 *pronoun(us)*. Some pronouns appear to be contracted, such as *him* and *them*, but are not written as contractions. They are not normally counted as miscues.

7̄9̄5̄
Let's go.

Additional Notes:

Idioms. Idioms are treated literally, e.g.:

2̄2̄1̄ 5̄1̄0̄ 1̄1̄2̄ 5̄6̄0̄ 5̄1̄0̄ 1̄1̄6̄
She's had a heck of a time.

This procedure is followed despite the probability that idioms exist as single lexical entries in deep structure.

Partial Sentences. Syntactic structures preceding and following the sentence fragment are reviewed, and grammatical functions assigned in accordance with prior and subsequent occurrences, e.g.:

4̄2̄1̄
I want to go outside.
4̄2̄1̄
Outside! It's too cold out there.

18 OBSERVED RESPONSE IN VISUAL PERIPHERY

The possibility exists that any substitution or insertion miscue which a reader makes has been partially cued by an item in the reader's visual peripheral field—that as the reader scans the text, what he reads can be influenced by text items in the periphery of his vision.

This category is limited to word level substitution and insertion miscues and to consideration of the five text lines immediately surrounding the miscue.

Mother looked at Freddie.
She said, "You are too little
to help Father and Jack.   } near } extended
You are not too little to help me.
Here is something you can do."

Blank   *This category is inappropriate.* An omission, nonword substitution, or phrase level miscue is involved.

0   *The visual periphery are not involved in the miscue.* The OR item can not be found within the surrounding five lines of text.

Mother looked at Freddie.
She said, "You are too little
  work
to help Father and Jack.
You are not too little to help me.
Here is something you can do."

1   *The OR can be found in the near visual periphery.* The OR can be found in the text within the three lines surrounding the miscue.

Mother looked at Freddie.
She said, "You are too little
      said
to help Father and Jack.   } near
You are not too little to help me.
Here is something you can do."

2   *The OR can be found in the extended visual periphery.* The OR can be found in the text within the second line before or after the line containing the miscue.

Mother looked at Freddie.
She said "You are too little
     Mother   } extended
to help Father and Jack.
You are not too little to help me.
Here is something you can do."

9   *It is doubtful whether the visual periphery were involved in the miscue.* The OR can be found within the visual periphery but there is an unusual amount of intervening space caused either by paragraphing or the use of double columns of print.

Developing a Comprehension Rating

Editor's Note: The data basis for miscue analysis is an audio tape recording of a student's oral reading and retelling of a story. After a short conversation to put the student at ease, the researcher asks the student to read an entire story aloud without assistance or interference from the researcher, and, after finishing the story, to close the book and retell the researcher as much of the story as can be remembered. After the student relates as much as he or she can, the researcher asks further questions which are designed to elicit all possible remembered information, but these questions do not refer to anything the student has not already mentioned. If, for example, the student does not mention a character, the researcher can ask, "Was there anyone else in the story?" but may not ask, "Who was _____?"

Guide Questions to Aid Story Retelling

1 Now, would you tell me everything you remember about the story you just read?
(Do not interrupt or interject any questions until the child has completed this retelling. Keep in mind the Story Comprehension form. Then, ask any of the following kinds of questions to elicit responses in areas the child either failed to cover or was ambiguous about.)

2 Can you think of anything else that happened? (events)

3 Who else was in the story? (character recall) Tell me about them.

4 What happened that's funny, exciting or sad in the story? (subtleties)

5 What do you think the story was telling you? (theme)

6 Where did the story take place? (setting)

7 Tell me more about (key character). (character development)

8 Tell me why (key event) happened. (plot)

Additional Instructions

1 If the child seems to grope for words or stops, the researcher may pick up a question or comment from the child's final statement (#1 above) to encourage further response.

2 Inserting questions such as "What happened next?", "How did that happen?", etc. may also encourage further response.

3 If the child's response has left it unclear whether or not he knows the plot, etc., then additional specific questions are in order. The unique organization of some stories might necessitate preparing such questions prior to the taping.

4 When using any of the suggestions provided above, no specific information may be used in a question if the child has not already provided that information.

5 Always check the reader's comprehension of any unusual key words from the text.

Story Outline
A content outline should be developed for each piece of reading material, with one hundred points being distributed across the items within each of the categories.

Character recall (list characters)	15
Character development (modifying statements)	15
Theme	20
Plot	20
Events (list occurrences)	30

Information Outline

Major concept(s)	30
Generalization(s)	30
Specific points or examples	40

The reader's retelling is compared to the outline and points are deducted from the total of one hundred for missing or confused information.

Appendix B: The Oral Reading Miscue Studies

Allen, Paul David. *A psycholinguistic analysis of the substitution miscues of selected oral readers in grades two, four, and six and the relationship of these miscues to the reading process: A descriptive study.* (Doctoral dissertation, Wayne State University) Ann Arbor, Mich.: University Microfilms, 1970. No. 70-03414.

Burke, Carolyn L. *A psycholinguistic description of grammatical restructurings in the oral reading of a selected group of middle school children.* (Doctoral dissertation, Wayne State University) Ann Arbor, Mich.: University Microfilms, 1970. No. 70-03416.

Carlson, Kenneth L. *A psycholinguistic description of selected fourth grade children reading a variety of contextual material.* (Doctoral dissertation, Wayne State University) Ann Arbor, Mich.: University Microfilms, 1971. No. 71-17243.

Coomber, James E. *A psycholinguistic analysis of oral reading errors made by good, average, and poor readers.* (Doctoral dissertation, The University of Wisconsin) Ann Arbor, Mich.: University Microfilms, 1972. No. 72-18972.

Davey, Beth. *A psycholinguistic investigation of cognitive styles and oral reading strategies in achieving and under-achieving fourth grade boys.* (Doctoral dissertation, Case Western Reserve University) Ann Arbor, Mich.: University Microfilms, 1972. No. 72-06282.

DeLawter, Jayne Anne. Oral reading errors of second grade children exposed to two different reading approaches. Unpublished doctoral dissertation, Teachers College, Columbia University, 1970.

Dunkeld, Colin G. *The validity of the informal reading inventory for the designation of instructional reading levels: A study of the relationships between children's gains in reading achievement and the difficulty of instructional materials.* (Doctoral dissertation, University of Illinois) Ann Arbor, Mich.: University Microfilms, 1970. No. 71-14733.

Goodman, Kenneth S. *Study of children's behavior while reading orally.* (USOE Final Report, Project No. S425, Contract No. OE-6-10-136) Washington, D. C., U. S. Department of Health, Education, and Welfare, March, 1968.

Goodman, Kenneth S., & Burke, Carolyn L. *A study of oral reading miscues that result in grammatical retransformations.* (USOE Final Report, Project No. 7-E-219, Contract No. OEG-0-8-070219-2806 [010]) Washington, D. C., U. S. Department of Health, Education, and Welfare, June, 1969.

Goodman, Kenneth S., & Burke, Carolyn L. *Theoretically based studies of patterns of miscues in oral reading performance.* (USOE Project No. 90375, Grant No. OEG-0-9-320375-4269) Washington, D. C., U. S.

Department of Health, Education, and Welfare, March, 1973.

Goodman, Yetta M. *A psycholinguistic description of observed oral reading phenomena in selected young beginning readers.* (Doctoral dissertation, Wayne State University) Ann Arbor, Mich.: University Microfilms, 1968. No. 68-09961.

Goodman, Yetta M. *Longitudinal study of children's oral reading behavior.* (USOE Final Report, Project No. 9-E-062, Grant No. OEG-5-9-325062-0046) Washington, D. C., U. S. Department of Health, Education, and Welfare, September, 1971.

Gutknecht, Bruce A. *A psycholinguistic analysis of the oral reading behavior of selected children identified as perceptually handicapped.* (Doctoral dissertation, Wayne State University) Ann Arbor, Mich.: University Microfilms, 1972. No. 72-14563.

Jensen, Louise J. *A pyscholinguistic analysis of the oral reading behavior of selected proficient, average, and weak readers reading the same material.* (Doctoral dissertation, Michigan State University) Ann Arbor, Mich.: University Microfilms, 1973. No. 73-05408.

Martellock, Helen A. *A psycholinguistic description of the oral and written language of a selected group of middle school children.* (Doctoral dissertation, Wayne State University) Ann Arbor, Mich.: University Microfilms, 1972. No. 72-14598.

Menosky, Dorothy M. *A psycholinguistic analysis of oral reading miscues generated during the reading of varying portions of text by selected readers from grades two, four, six and eight.* (Doctoral dissertation, Wayne State University) Ann Arbor, Mich.: University Microfilms, 1972. No. 72-14600.

Moir, Leo H. *A linguistic analysis of certain stylistic elements of selected works of literature for children and their relationship to readability.* (Doctoral dissertation, Wayne State University) Ann Arbor, Mich.: University Microfilms, 1970. No. 70-03433.

Page, William D. *A psycholinguistic description of patterns of miscues generated by a proficient reader in second grade, an average reader in fourth grade, and an average reader in sixth grade encountering ten basal reader selections ranging from pre-primer to sixth grade.* (Doctoral dissertation, Wayne State University) Ann Arbor, Mich.: University Microfilms, 1971. No. 71-17298.

Romatowski, Jane A. *A psycholinguistic description of miscues generated by selected bilingual subjects during the oral reading of instructional reading material as presented in Polish readers and in English basal readers.* (Doctoral dissertation, Wayne State University) Ann Arbor, Mich.: University Microfilms, 1973. No. 73-12586.

Rousch, Peter D. *A psycho-linguistic investigation into the relationship between prior conceptual knowledge, oral reading miscues, silent* reading, and post-reading performance. (Doctoral dissertation, Wayne State University) Ann Arbor, Mich.: University Microfilms, 1973. No. 73-12588.

Sims, Rudine. *A psycholinguistic description of miscues generated by selected young readers during the oral reading of text material in black dialect and standard English.* (Doctoral dissertation, Wayne State University) Ann Arbor, Mich.: University Microfilms, 1972. No. 72-28487.

Steinruck, Yvonne S. *The effects of instruction in miscue analysis on teachers' perceptions of the reading process and on their instruction in reading.* (Doctoral dissertation, University of Toledo) Ann Arbor, Mich.: University Microfilms, 1976. No. 76-08365.

Thornton, Mervin F. *A psycholinguistic description of purposive oral reading and its effect on comprehension for subjects with different reading backgrounds.* (Doctoral dissertation, Wayne State University) Ann Arbor, Mich.: University Microfilms, 1973. No. 73-31787.

Watson, Dorothy J. *A psycholinguistic description of the oral reading miscues generated by selected readers prior to and following exposure to a saturated book program.* (Doctoral dissertation, Wayne State University) Ann Arbor, Mich.: University Microfilms, 1973. No. 73-31791.

Appendix C: Bibliography of Related Readings

Allen, P. D. Cue systems available during the reading process: A psycholinguistic viewpoint. *Elementary School Journal*, 1972, **72**, 258-264. (a)

Allen, P. D. What teachers of reading should know about the writing system. In R. Hodges & E. H. Rudorf (Eds.), *Language and learning to read: What teachers should know about language.* Boston: Houghton Mifflin, 1972. (b)

Beebe, M. J. *Case studies of grade level effects on children's miscues and reading comprehension.* Paper presented for the annual meeting of the Canadian Society for the Study of Education, Edmonton, Alberta, June 1975.

Buck, C. Miscues of non-native speakers of English. In K. S. Goodman (Ed.), *Miscue analysis: Applications to reading instruction.* Urbana, Ill.: ERIC Clearinghouse on Reading and Communication Skills and National Council of Teachers of English, 1973.

Burke, C. L. The language process: Systems or systematic? In R. Hodges & E. H. Rudorf (Eds.), *Language and learning to read: What teachers should know about language.* Boston: Houghton Mifflin, 1972.

Burke, C. L. Preparing elementary teachers to teach reading. In K. S. Goodman (Ed.), *Miscue analysis: Applications to reading instruction*. Urbana, Ill.: ERIC/RCS, NCTE, 1973.

Burke, C. L. Oral reading analysis: A view of the reading process. In W. D. Page (Ed.), *Help for the reading teacher: New directions in research*. Urbana, Ill.: National Conference on Research in English, ERIC/RCS, National Institute of Education, 1975.

Burke, C. L. & Goodman, K. S. When a child reads: A psycholinguistic analysis. *Elementary English*, 1970, **47**, 121-129.

Carlson, K. S. A different look at reading in the content areas. In W. D. Page (Ed.), *Help for the reading teacher: New directions in research*. Urbana, Ill.: National Conference on Research in English, ERIC/RCS, National Institute of Education, 1975.

DeLawter, J. A. The module and the miscue. In K. S. Goodman (Ed.), *Miscue analysis: Applications to reading instruction*. Urbana, Ill.: ERIC/RCS, NCTE, 1973.

DeLawter, J. A. The relationship of beginning reading instruction and miscue patterns. In W. D. Page (Ed.), *Help for the reading teacher: New directions in research*. Urbana, Ill.: National Conference on Research in English, ERIC/RCS, National Institute of Education, 1975.

Gates, V. Organizing a seventh grade reading class based on psycholinguistic insights. In K. S. Goodman (Ed.), *Miscue analysis: Applications to reading instruction*. Urbana, Ill.: ERIC/RCS, NCTE, 1973.

Goodman, K. S. The linguistics of reading. *Elementary School Journal*, 1964, **64**(7), 355-361.

Goodman, K. S. Dialect barriers to reading comprehension. *Elementary English*, 1965, **42**, 853-860.

Goodman, K. S. A linguistic study of cues and miscues in reading. *Elementary English*, 1965, **42**, 639-643. (b)

Goodman, K. S. Reading: A psycholinguistic guessing game. *Journal of the Reading Specialist*, 1967, **4**, 126-135.

Goodman, K. S. The psycholinguistic nature of the reading process. In K. S. Goodman (Ed.), *The psycholinguistic nature of the reading process*. Detroit: Wayne State Press, 1968.

Goodman, K. S. Linguistics in a relevant curriculum. *Education*, 1969, **89**, 303-306.

Goodman, K. S. A psycholinguistic approach to reading: Implications for the mentally retarded. *Australian Journal on the Education of Backward Children*, 1969, **16**, 85-90.

Goodman, K. S. Words and morphemes in reading. In K. S. Goodman & J. Fleming, *Psycholinguistics and the teaching of reading*. Newark, Del.: International Reading Association, 1969.

Goodman, K. S. Behind the eye: What happens in reading. In K. S. Goodman & O. Niles (Eds.), *Reading: Process and program*. Urbana, Ill.: NCTE, 1970.

Goodman, K. S. Comprehension-centered reading. *Claremont Reading Confer-ence Yearbook*, 1970, **34**, 125-135.

Goodman, K. S. Dialect rejection and reading: A response. *Reading Research Quarterly*, 1970, **5**, 600-603.

Goodman, K. S. Review of reading tests and reviews. *American Educational Research Journal,* 1971, **8**(1), 169-171.

Goodman, K. S. The search called reading. In H. M. Robinson (Ed.), *Coordinating reading instruction.* Glenview, Ill.: Scott, Foresman, 1971.

Goodman, K. S. Oral language miscues. *Viewpoints,* 1972, **48**(1), 13-28.

Goodman, K. S. Orthography in a theory of reading instruction. *Elementary English,* 1972, **49**, 1254-1261.

Goodman, K. S. Reading: The key is in children's language. *Reading Teacher,* 1972, **25**, 505-508.

Goodman, K. S. The reading process: Theory and practice. In R. Hodges & E. H. Rudorf (Eds.), *Language and learning to read: What teachers should know about language.* Boston: Houghton Mifflin, 1972.

Goodman, K. S. Analysis of oral reading miscues: Applied psycholinguistics. *Reading Research Quarterly*, 1969, **5**, 9-30, and in F. Smith (Ed.), *Psycholinguistics and reading.* New York: Holt, Rinehart & Winston, 1973.

Goodman, K. S. (Ed.), *Miscue analysis: Applications to reading instruction.* Urbana, Ill.: ERIC/RCS, NCTE, 1973.

Goodman, K. S. Miscues: Windows on the reading process. In K. S. Goodman (Ed.), *Miscue analysis: Applications to reading instruction.* Urbana, Ill.: ERIC/RCS, NCTE, 1973.

Goodman, K. S. Psycholinguistic universals in the reading process. In F. Smith (Ed.), *Psycholinguistics and reading.* New York: Holt, Rinehart & Winston, 1973.

Goodman, K. S. Influences of the visual peripheral field in reading. *Research in the Teaching of English,* 1975, **9**, 210-222.

Goodman, K. S. & Burke, C. L. *Study of children's behavior while reading orally.* (Final Report, Project No. S 425, Contract No. OE-6-10-136) Washington, D. C.: United States Department of Health, Education, and Welfare, Office of Education, March 1968.

Goodman, K. S., & Burke, C. L. *Theoretically based studies of patterns of miscues in oral reading performance.* (Final Report, Project No. 9-0375, Grant No. OEG-0-9-320375-4269) Washington, D. C.: U. S. Department of Health, Education, and Welfare, Office of Education, Bureau of Research, April, 1973.

Goodman, K. S. & Fleming, J. *Psycholinguistics and the teaching of reading.* Newark, Del.: IRA, 1969.

Goodman, K. S. & Menosky, D. Unlocking the program . . . two viewpoints. *Instructor,* 1971, **80**, 44-46.

Goodman, K. S., Olsen, H., Colvin, C., & Vanderlinde, L. *Choosing materials to teach reading*. Detroit: Wayne State Press, 1966.

Goodman, Y. M. Using children's reading miscues for new teaching strategies. *Reading Teacher*, 1970, **23**, 455-459.

Goodman, Y. M. *Longitudinal study of children's oral reading behavior*. (Final Report, Project No. 9-E-062, Grant No. OEG-5-9-325062-0046) Washington, D. C.: U. S. Department of Health, Education, and Welfare, Office of Education, Bureau of Research, September 1971.

Goodman, Y. M. Qualitative reading miscue analysis for teacher training. In R. Hodges & E. H. Rudorf (Eds.), *Language and learning to read: What teachers should know about language*. Boston: Houghton Mifflin, 1972. (a)

Goodman, Y. M. Reading diagnosis—qualitative or quantitative? *Reading Teacher*, 1972, **26**, 32-37. (b)

Goodman, Y. M. Miscue analysis for in-service reading teachers. In K. S. Goodman (Ed.), *Miscue analysis: Applications to reading instruction*. Urbana, Ill.: ERIC/RCS, NCTE, 1973.

Goodman, Y. M. Reading strategy lessons: Expanding reading effectiveness. In W. D. Page (Ed.), *Help for the reading teacher: New directions in research*. Urbana, Ill.: National Conference on Research in English, ERIC/RCS, National Institute of Education, 1975.

Goodman, Y. M. & Burke, C. L. *Reading miscue inventory: Procedure for diagnosis and evaluation*. New York: Macmillan, 1972.

Goodman, Y. M. & Goodman, K. S. *Linguistics and the teaching of reading: An annotated bibliography*. Newark, Del.: IRA, 1967.

Hittleman, D. R. Seeking a psycholinguistic definition of readability. *Reading Teacher*, 1973, **26**, 783-789.

Hodges, R. E. The psychological bases of spelling. *Elementary English*, 1965, **42**, 629-635.

Hodges, R. E. & Rudorf, E. H. (Eds.), *Language and learning to read: What teachers should know about language*. Boston: Houghton Mifflin, 1972.

Hoffner, D. R. *A psycholinguistic analysis of oral reading miscues by junior college students*. Thesis abstract, Rutgers University, 1974.

Ludwig, J. B. & Stalker, J. C. Miscue analysis and the training of junior and senior high school English teachers. In K. S. Goodman (Ed.), *Miscue analysis: Applications to reading instruction*. Urbana, Ill.: ERIC/RCS, NCTE, 1973.

Moe, A. J. Using the child's oral language in beginning reading instruction. *Reading Horizons*, 1975, **16**, 32-35.

Nieratka, E. Using miscue analysis to advise content area teachers. In K. S. Goodman (Ed.), *Miscue analysis: Applications to reading instruction*. Urbana, Ill.: ERIC/RCS, NCTE, 1973.

Nieratka, S. Miscue analysis in a special education resource room. In K. S. Goodman (Ed.), *Miscue analysis: Applications to reading instruction.* Urbana, Ill.: ERIC/RCS, NCTE, 1973.

Page, W. D. Environmental context: Key to a broader spectrum on the word recognition scene. *Michigan Reading Journal,* 1970, **4,** 17-20.

Page, W. D. A linguistic appraisal of isolated word recognition testing. *Michigan Reading Journal,* 1971, **5**(2), 28-35.

Page, W. D. Clinical uses of miscue research. In K. S. Goodman (Ed.), *Miscue analysis: Applications to reading instruction.* Urbana, Ill.: ERIC/RCS, NCTE, 1973. (a)

Page, W. D. Inquiry into an unknown word. *School Review,* 1973, **83**(3), 461-477. (b)

Page, W. D. Observing oral reading: A language-bound process. *Illinois Reading Council Journal,* 1973, **1**(1), 17-18. (c)

Page, W. D. Are we beginning to understand oral reading? *Reading World,* 1974, **13**(3), 161-170. (a)

Page, W. D. The author and the reader in writing and reading. *Research in the Teaching of English,* 1974, **8,** 170-183. (b)

Page, W. D. The reading process: Its evaluation through miscues. *Educating Children: Early and Middle Years,* 1975, **20**(2), 17-21.

Page, W. D. Pseudocues, supercues, and comprehension. *Reading World,* May 1976. In press.

Page, W. D. The post-oral reading cloze test: New link between oral reading and comprehension. *Journal of Reading Behavior.* Winter 1976. In press.

Page, W. D. & Barr, R. C. Use of informal reading inventories. In W. D. Page (Ed.), *Help for the reading teacher: New directions in research.* Urbana, Ill.: National Conference on Research in English, ERIC/RCS, National Institute of Education, 1975.

Page, W. D. & Carlson, K. L. The process of observing oral reading scores. *Reading Horizons,* 1975, **16,** 147-150.

Sherman, B. W. (Consultant). *Psycholinguistic approach to reading* (PAR). (Final Report, Project No. 37-67991-14-0314. Bureau of Program Planning and Development, Title III ESEA, Division of Instruction, Department of Education). Cajon Valley Union School District, El Cajon, California, June 1973.

Sims, R. Miscue analysis—emphasis on comprehension. *Journal of the New England Reading Association.* In press.

Singer, H. & Ruddell, R. (Eds.). *Theoretical models and processes in reading.* Newark, Del.: IRA, 1970.

Smith, E. B., Goodman, K. S., & Meredith, R., *Language and thinking in school* (2nd ed.). New York: Holt, Rinehart & Winston, 1976.

Smith, F. *Understanding reading: A psycholinguistic analysis of reading.* New York: Holt, Rinehart & Winston, 1971.

Smith, F. The learner and his language. In R. Hodges & E. H. Rudorf (Eds.), *Language and learning to read: What teachers should know about language.* Boston: Houghton Mifflin, 1972.

Smith, F. (Ed.). *Psycholinguistics and reading.* New York: Holt, Rinehart & Winston, 1973.

Smith, F. & Goodman, K. S. On the psycholinguistic method of teaching reading. *Elementary School Journal,* 1971, **71**, 177-181.

Smith, F. & Goodman, K. S. On the psycholinguistic method of teaching reading. In F. Smith (Ed.), *Psycholinguistics and reading.* New York: Holt, Rinehart & Winston, 1973.

Smith, F. & Holmes, D. L. The independence of letter, word, and meaning identification in reading. *Reading Research Quarterly,* 1971, **6**, 394-415.

Smith, L. A. & Lindberg, M. Building instructional materials. In K. S. Goodman (Ed.), *Miscue analysis: Applications to reading instruction.* Urbana, Ill.: ERIC/RCS, NCTE, 1973.

Thorndike, E. L. Reading as reasoning: A study of mistakes in paragraph reading. *Reading Research Quarterly,* 1971, **6**, 425-434.

Tortelli, J. P. Help for the ineffective reader! In D. Umstattd (Ed.), *Michigan Reading Journal,* **9**(3). Saginaw, Mich.: Michigan Reading Association, Fall 1975.

Tortelli, J. P. Simplified psycholinguistic diagnosis. *Reading Teacher,* 1976, **29**, 637-639.

Watson, D. J. Helping the reader: From miscue analysis to strategy lessons. In K. S. Goodman (Ed.), *Miscue analysis: Applications to reading instruction.* Urbana, Ill.: ERIC/RCS, NCTE, 1973.

Watson, D. J. Strategies for reading comprehension. In D. Waterman and V. Gibbs (Eds.), *Oral language and reading.* Proceedings of the 1973 Third Annual Reading Conference. Terre Haute, Ind.: Indiana State University, 1973, pp. 5-15.

Weber, R. A linguistic analysis of first-grade reading errors. *Reading Research Quarterly,* 1970, **3**, 427-451.

Weber, R. The study of oral reading errors: A survey of the literature. *Reading Research Quarterly,* 1968, **4**, 96-119.